Uniquely Canadian

Donald Allan Gillmore

UNUSUAL COPYRIGHT

Canadian Unity Symbol - Front Cover:
Please note that this symbol is trademarked.

Uniquely Canadian

Pocketbook
ISBN   978-0-9918903-1-6

Hardcover 6-Volume Set
ISBN   978-0-9918903-0-9
Applies to Volumes I to VI inclusive. Individual volumes
    not sold separately.

Author: Donald Allan Gillmore

Graphic Artist: Valentina Gillmore

Typesetting: Donald Allan Gillmore

Communications: William Bolton, Kitchener, Ontario, Canada

Photographer: Michael Bedford, Ottawa, Ontario, Canada

Purchased Graphics: Heraldry Canada www.vector-images.com; Map of Canada www.mapresources.ca

Publisher: True People Endeavours Inc., Victoria, British Columbia, Canada

Printer: Red & Blue Color Printing Co., Ltd., New Taipei City, Taiwan.

Web address: www.firstincanada.ca

Uniquely Canadian was printed using environmentally friendly, soya-based inks.

WHAT'S INSIDE!

WELCOME TO CANADA!

Dear Reader:

This pocketbook contains a selection of the shorter stories most but not all of which are included in the full blown, 6-volume, hardcover series of *Uniquely Canadian*. Any stories unable to fit into the final format of the hardcover series are included here. This abridged version contains over 1,000 firsts or distinctive Canadian people and events covering 28 different categories.

Aboriginal Peoples	*Music*
Animals/Wildlife	*Pastimes/Amusements*
Business	*People*
Communication	*Politics*
Education	*Publishing*
Environment	*Religion*
Film	*Science*
Food/Agriculture	*Sports-Individual*
Geography	*Sports-Team*
History	*Structures*
Industry/Commerce	*Transportation-Air*
Legal	*Transportation-Land*
Medicine	*Transportation-Sea*
Military	*Visual Arts*

WELCOME TO CANADA!

The full, hardcover version is **more than 12 times as extensive** as this pocketbook and contains numerous additional advantages. Most stories are generally far more in-depth and there is a list of sub-categories used.

All the stories are separated chronologically by time into 17 chapters, divided into different, convenient time periods. I also have included background and other interesting information before the first chapter covering a range of national interests: National Coat of Arms, Flag, and Map; Definitions; Floral and Animal Emblems; Provincial/Territorial Flags and Coats of Arms; Population, Land, and Water statistics; plus English and French versions of our National Anthem.

The entire **6 volumes** are printed in **full colour** with interesting, creative graphics making it very visually attractive and easy to use.

The headers and footers include outlines of the federal and all the provincial and territorial legislative/parliament buildings, and wildlife commonly found in Canada.

Detailed **icons** representing each of the categories begin each story. This makes it effortless to scan each page when looking for stories in one particular category, particularly when so many stories cover more than one category.

Each "**first**" is highlighted in bold text. You can simply scan each page reading the title of each story, stopping to read the full story when you are interested while leaving the remainder of the book to read later.

I provided **both Imperial and metric measurements** as not all readers will necessarily be totally conversant in the more recent metric equivalents.

WELCOME TO CANADA!

I also included **birth and death (where applicable) dates plus place of birth** of people in this book whenever possible along with provinces, territories, states, and countries for each location.

Some stories are enclosed in a special box as I was unable to identify a date associated with them or the stories do not necessarily include a first but are of general interest.

There is a very extensive ***Bibliography*** containing more than 1,700 different sources. The contents of this pocketbook were researched from these same sources but obviously the list is too extensive to include in this smaller pocketbook.

The remarkably detailed ***Index***, some 22% of each volume, makes it easy for any reader to locate one or more stories on most any word search.

A convenient **silk bookmark** in each volume makes it very easy to mark where you last stopped reading.

Regrettably, I was forced to use more indirect verbs in my writing than desirable, for which I apologize, in an attempt not to plagiarise the writing of any other previous writer. All in all, I have made every effort to make this book as accurate, comprehensive, and original yet reader-friendly as possible.

This version is the perfect reading companion on the bus or plane, while lounging on the deck or beach, or any time you simply want to while away the time in a more fascinating way. It is both entertaining and educational.

I hope that you enjoy reading these fascinating stories as much as I did researching and writing them.

Enjoy!

Donald A. Gillmore

Accurately describing our indigenous peoples can be a difficult exercise in terminology. Various groups have their own particular preferences. The Royal Commission on **Aboriginal Peoples** defines Aboriginal as the three indigenous peoples recognized Constitutionally— First Nations (or Indians as stated in our Constitution), Métis, and Inuit. Each group has its own unique historical background, languages, cultural practices, spiritual beliefs, and political goals. The Assembly of First Nations prefers to use the term First Nations rather than Indians although there are many Indian nations which have not changed their preference. The Métis are descendants of early fur traders and Indian women. Inuit (the singular being Inuk) is the preferred term generally throughout Canada for Eskimo. Their national organization is called Inuit Tapirisat. The preferred term in Canada's Central Arctic is Inuinnaq with Inuit being more popular in the eastern Canadian Arctic and in government documents.

290 billion B.C.: Nova Scotia was the home of the Protoclepsydrobs and Archerpeton, the **1ˢᵗ reptiles in the world**.

2.6 - 1.1 billion B.C.: Ontario's University of Toronto geochemist Dr. Barbara Sherwood Lollar (b. 1963) of Jersey City, New Jersey, USA, and colleagues from McMaster University in Hamilton, Ontario, plus Manchester University and Lancaster University in the U.K., conducted research in May 2013 on boreholes 2.4 km *(1.5 mi.)* underground at Timmins Mine in Northeastern Ontario. They discovered the

oldest free-flowing water on earth. It is rich in dissolved gases hydrogen, methane, helium, neon, argon, and xenon. This ancient pocket of water appears never to have mixed with surface water, trapped for billions of years totally isolated inside the earth's crust. Microbes in this water, if found through further testing, would survive on chemicals created through interaction with surrounding radioactive rock instead of exposure to sunlight. This discovery raises questions pertaining to the potential for life on other planets like Mars.

The **east coast of Canada is considerably closer to London, England, than to our own West Coast**. St. John's, Newfoundland, to London is 3744.4 km *(2,326.7 mi.)*; St. John's to Victoria, British Columbia is 5078 km *(3,155.3 mi.)* as the goose flies and 7207 km *(4,778.2 mi.)* by road.

The dry belt and Peace River areas of British Columbia, Whiteshell Provincial Park in Manitoba, and the granite rocks along Mellon Creek near Kaladar, Ontario, all have the **most northerly growing cactus in the world**. It is **Canada's smallest cactus**, the little prickly pear, which grows singly or in colonies up to 1 m *(3.3 ft.)* across. The easily detached pads are 2 cm ⇨ 4 cm *(0.79 in.* ⇨ *1.57 in.)* long and 1 cm ⇨ 2 cm *(0.39 in.* ⇨ *0.79 in.))* wide while the small 1 cm ⇨ 2 cm *(0.39 in.* ⇨ *0.79 in.)* long spines are savagely barbed.

_23,000 B.C. – 8,000 B.C._: Anthropologists believe that ancestors of our Aboriginal peoples migrated from Asia across a land bridge crossing the Bering Sea. In so doing, Yukon of today became the **1ˢᵗ area in Canada to be settled by people**. Of Yukon's average population in 2011 of 33,897 residents, which fluctuates considerably, 20.1% are Aboriginal. Its capital city of Whitehorse is home to 75% of Yukon's total population. John Bell, a trader with the Hudson's Bay Company in 1846, was the **1ˢᵗ to use the name Yukon**. The word was derived from the Loucheux Indian word Yuchoo meaning "the greatest river".

> Canada is the **coldest country in the world** having an average annual temperature of only -5.6°C *(22°F)* and 50% of the country is covered in permafrost. Yet, the Arctic receives less snowfall than the rest of Canada and would be a desert if it were not for the cold temperatures. An average annual temperature of -19.4°C *(-3°F)* makes Eureka on Ellesmere Island, Nunavut, home to **Canada's coldest weather station**.

_8,000 B.C._: The Canadian Shield, also called the Precambrian Shield or Laurentian Plateau, covers an area of 10 515.4 km² *(4,060 mi.²)* in Eastern and Central Canada, three percent of Alberta, and a small portion of the northern United States. It covers half of Canada's total area. Glacier-scattered peaks eroded to an average height of 609.6 m *(2,000 ft.)* surround the Canadian Shield. This vast wilderness was known only to the Montagnais Indians for centuries and has been protected as a provincial park, known as Parc des Laurentides, since 1895. These happen to be the **oldest mountains on earth**.

4,000 B.C.: **Copper was 1ˢᵗ mined and manufactured into implements in Canada** at several locations around this time.

There are **55 indigenous languages** spoken in Canada, some of which are in danger of disappearing.

2,500 B.C.: Near Red Bank, New Brunswick, is the Augustine Mound, an elaborate burial site which is the **earliest known native earthen work construction in North America**.

1,000 B.C.: The Vikings built some interesting stone chamber boxes about 0.3 m *(1 ft.)* high to attract eider ducks. These **most northerly birdhouses in Canada** were discovered on Norman Lockyer Island inside the Arctic Circle. They are so far north that even Inuit haven't lived there for centuries!

According to native lore, a Canadian Iroquois named Iotiapatonom, "the lost one", paddled east from Canada in a dugout canoe. What is so interesting is that he did so many years before Christopher Columbus (1451-1506) of Genoa, Italy, sailed west from Europe in 1492. Thus, Iotiapatonom became the **1ˢᵗ North American to discover Europe**! He landed first in Portugal where he settled for the remainder of his life prospering so well that he had no interest in returning to North America.

636: The **tallest trees in Canada** grow in Cathedral Grove in Macmillan Provincial Park on the western slope of Vancouver Island, British Columbia. The **oldest known tree** in Canada is a Douglas fir dating from the year 636, which was felled and is on display in Duncan, British Columbia. Another Douglas fir still growing on the southern slope of Waterloo Mountain, also in Duncan, is **Canada's oldest living tree**. Although the Douglas fir often attains heights in the range of 84 m *(275 ft.)* with a circumference at the base of 9.1 m *(30 ft.)*, we had one which towered 127.1 m *(417 ft.)* with the first branch growing at almost 61 m *(200 ft.)* from its base.

Strathcona Provincial Park is within hiking distance of Port Alberni, British Columbia, and is 2020.2 km² *(780 mi.²)* in area. It is the oldest provincial park (1911) in British Columbia. In the park is Mount Golden Hind 2200 m *(7,218 ft.)*, the highest mountain on Vancouver Island, British Columbia, and Della Falls in the southern part of the park. Its triple cascade dropping 439.8 m *(1,443 ft.)* makes Della Falls the **highest waterfall in North America**. However, as the status of the major waterfalls around the world is based both on height of the fall and the volume of water flow, Della Falls is not regarded as a major waterfall.

1000: **Canada's 1ˢᵗ industrial undertaking** was smelting and casting of iron. Today, steel manufacturing is one of our country's few major industries largely owned by Canadians. Archaeological evidence at L'Anse aux Meadows, Newfoundland, reveals that the Vikings living there worked the **1ˢᵗ smelting of ore in producing iron in North America**. The original furnace was set up in a sod hut, and a large stone found nearby is believed to have been used as an anvil for the **1ˢᵗ hammering of iron in North America** after it was removed from the furnace. Indications are that only about 3 kg *(6.6 lb.)* of iron could be produced in each firing of this furnace. Greater production did not come until 1730 at Trois-Rivières, Lower Canada (Quebec).

1400: The Vineland Map dated 1400, if authentic, is the **oldest known map showing a part of Canada**. Between 1510-1520, navigator and cartographer Juan de la Cosa (1460-1509) of Santoña, Spain, drew a map of the world based on the cartographic record of John Cabot (1450-1499) of Genoa, Italy. Around 1547, the Harleian Map was the **1st map to use the name "Canada"**.

> Lake Wollaston in Saskatchewan flows north into the Mackenzie River basin. It also flows east into Hudson Bay. It has an area of 2681 km² *(1,035.1 mi.²)* making it the **largest lake in the world to drain naturally in two directions**.

1541: Jacques Cartier (1491-1557) of St. Malo, France, began construction of Charlesbourg-Royale at the mouth of the Cap-Rouge River on the western tip of Cape Diamond on his third trip to Canada. This was the **1st French settlement in North America** and the **1st French fort in Canada**. Cap-Rouge, Lower Canada, (Quebec) was abandoned the following year due to Indian attacks and bad weather.

1572: An anonymous Basque fisherman at Chateau Bay in Labrador purchased four scallops on September 7th. This was **Canada's 1st recorded business transaction**.

1604: On February 8th, the **1st chartered company in Canada**, the de Monts Trading Company, was formed.

Some of its members included some familiar names—Pierre du Gua, Sieur de Monts (1558-1628) of Saintonge, France, François Gravé, Sieur du Pont (c. 1554-c. 1629), and Samuel de Champlain (1567-1635) of Heirs Brouage, France.

The **oomiak** or umiak is a boat made of walrus or bearded seal skins traditionally rowed by Inuit women. It has a flat bottom and narrow bow and stern, and is usually 9.1 to 12.2 m *(30 to 40 ft.)* long, 1.4 m *(4.5 ft.)* wide, and 91.4 cm *(3 ft.)* deep. The oomiak is used for carrying freight and passengers.

1604: Of the 25 graves uncovered on St. Croix Island in the **oldest European cemetery in North America**, Burial No. 10 included a skull showing a unique cut making it the **1st skeletal evidence in North America of an early autopsy**.

1605: Expert hewers and dovetailers of logs were often hired by the North West Company to prepare building logs of a standard size and quality. The main structural timbers for building military posts in Canada were shipped here from England, all ready to assemble. The **1st prefabricated building arrived in Canada** this year and was unloaded in Nova Scotia.

1606: Use of Canada's lakes and rivers for travelling was so practical that road development was negligible prior to the 19th century. Samuel de Champlain (1567-1635) of Heirs Brouage, France, constructed the **1st graded road in Canada**, a 16-km *(9.9-mi.)* military road from Port Royal, Nova Scotia, to Digby Cape.

_1609:_ Poet Marc Lescarbot (1570-1641) of Vervins, France, wrote _Les Muses de la Nouvelle France_, the **1ˢᵗ French poetry in North America**. It was published in Paris, France, in 1609.

_1611:_ On July 20ᵗʰ, Samuel de Champlain (c. 1570-1635) of Heirs Brouage, France, **exported the 1ˢᵗ cargo of timber from Canada**.

_1613:_ The Indians of New France called oxen "the moose from France" since horses were not used here until 1647. Louis Hébert's (c. 1575-1627) son-in-law, Guillaume Couillard-Lespinay (c. 1591-1663), became in 1628 the **1ˢᵗ person in Canada to use a plow**, pulled naturally by oxen. Guillaume already had earned the distinction in 1613 of being **Canada's 1ˢᵗ permanent settler**.

_1617:_ Devoted nuns in early Canada generally provided nursing care for the sick and wounded, but the **1ˢᵗ Canadian nurse** was neither a nun nor a professional. Marie Hubou (d. 1694) was the widow of the French apothecary Louis Hébert (c. 1575-1627) of Paris, France, who came to Quebec City, Lower Canada, (Quebec) in 1617. She cared for the sick recommended to her care by the Jesuit Fathers. Mary and her family were **Canada's 1ˢᵗ resident European family**.

_1620:_ Hélène de Champlain, the wife of Samuel de Champlain (1567-1635) of Heirs Brouage, France, brought the **1ˢᵗ mirror to Canada**, wearing it around her neck as a pendant. The local Indians idolized her, as when each saw his image reflected in the mirror, he believed that it was his picture she carried close to her heart.

_1621:_ It seems that we Canadians have long desired to keep track of our new-born children! Canada is the **only**

country in the world with a continuous series of birth records for more than three centuries. The **1st registration of births, deaths, and marriages** on a regular and systematic basis was introduced in Lower Canada (Quebec), but unfortunately excluded the Indian population. Compulsory registration began in Europe in Sweden, only in 1686.

Various nationalities around the world have their own specific toast when celebrating. The English say "Cheers!" The Swedes say "Skol!" Germans say "Prosit!" The French say, "Salut!". Not to be left out, we also have our own **native Canadian toast**—"Chimo!" The word is pronounced either "chee-mo" or "chy-mo" and means "Cheers!" when used in a toast. The word originates from both First Nations and Inuit dialects and literally means "Greetings!"

1621: The Canadian beaver (*Castor canadensis*) was the early staple of the fur trade and has served many respected and industrious duties over the centuries. The **1st recorded heraldic use of our famous beaver** was on a coat of arms as directed by Sir William Alexander Stirling (1567-1640) of Menstrie Castle in Clackmannanshire, near Stirling, Scotland, who was granted title to Nova Scotia in 1621 by King James VI of Scotland (1566-1625) born in Edinburgh, Scotland, becoming King James I of England in 1603. William became the 1st Earl of Stirling. Forty years later, Louis de Baude Frontenac (1622-1698) of Paris, France, suggested that the beaver should be included on the coat of arms of New France. The Kebeca Liberata medal minted in 1690 to celebrate Louis' defence of Lower Canada (Quebec) marked the **1ˢᵗ French Canadian use of the beaver as a visual emblem**. In 1851, Sir Sandford Fleming (1827-1915) of Kirkcaldy, Fife, Scotland, used our beaver in his design of the **1ˢᵗ Canadian postage stamp**. And since 1936, the obverse of our five-cent piece has shown a detailed specimen. The **Canadian beaver 1ˢᵗ attained official status as an emblem of Canada**, receiving royal assent on March 24, 1975, of an *Act to Provide for the Recognition of the Beaver as a Symbol of the Sovereignty of Canada.*

That bird on the obverse of our dollar coin, which we affectionately refer to as our Loonie, is the loon. It just happens to be the **oldest bird in Canada**, with a bone structure very similar to that of its prehistoric ancestors. The loon is a very fast diver and swimmer living in the lakes of the north woods of Canada.

1621: While digging in the former Colony of Avalon, Newfoundland, archaeologist Aaron Miller unearthed at Ferryland in 2004 what is believed to be the **1ˢᵗ coin ever struck specifically for use in Canada**. The initials D.K. are engraved on it, likely referring to David Kirke (1597-1654) of Dieppe, Normandy, France, governor of Newfoundland at that time. David ran a tavern and was licensed by the king to make his own money. He used his unique coins as change in his tavern and likely only redeemable there as well. The little currency there in those days came from Europe and was scarce at best. A similar scenario played out in 1815 when Sir Isaac Coffin (1759-1839) of Boston, Massachusetts, USA, was granted the Îles-de-la-Madeleine this year as a reward for public service. Sir Isaac issued the **1ˢᵗ Magdalene penny in the world**, for use specifically on the island.

1623: The best known Récollet lay brother, missionary, and historian brought to Canada was Gabriel Sagard-Théodat of France, his religious name being Théodat. Father Gabriel worked diligently with the Huron people writing *Le Grand Voyage du pays des Hurons.* This work was invaluable to Europeans working in Canada at that time. He also wrote the **1st phrasebook in the world of the Huron language**.

1645: The **1st bell in Canada** appears to have arrived in Lower Canada (Quebec) around 1645 according to the Jesuit Relations, vol. 27, p101: "On the 25th November 1645 a larger bell was placed in the parish church, instead of the small one which was there." However, the **1st bells of Canadian origin** were three cast in 1664 in Quebec City, Lower Canada, then blessed and installed in a parish church there.

> Each time Aboriginal peoples crossed the Echimamish, they left offerings in tribute to this unique Canadian location. You see, there is a pond on a height of land in northern Manitoba known as "**the-river-that-flows-both-ways**". This pond flows east into the Hayes River and also flows west into the Nelson River. As a result, portaging between the two rivers was easy.

1647: Charles Huault de Montmagny (c. 1583-c. 1653), the governor of New France (Quebec), a Jesuit Superior and the governor of Montreal, Lower Canada (Quebec), established the Council of New France on March 27th of this year. This was the **1st constitutional body in Canadian history**.

1648: Jacques Boisson opened **Canada's 1st tavern** on September 19, 1648, in Quebec City, Lower Canada (Quebec).

Such establishments excluded women, though, until the early 1970s. Business doubled shortly thereafter at brasseries like Le Manoir in Point Claire, Quebec, after opening to the fair sex. Jacque's licence was granted on condition that he sell no liquor while religious services were being held. The **1st inn in Canada for English speaking travellers** did not open until April 8, 1751. William Pigott of Halifax, Nova Scotia was the innkeeper.

_1649:_ In July, Mme Tessier of Montreal, Lower Canada (Quebec), gave birth to the **1st twins born in Canada**. Unfortunately, they both died within five days of their birth.

_1650:_ From the burial ground at Ship Cove, Conception Bay, Newfoundland, comes the **1st and oldest inscription in Canada**, that of John Dawes who died in the year 1650.

_1650:_ On September 1st, Jesuit Father Gabriel Dreuillettes (1610-1681) travelled to Boston, Massachusetts, USA, in the capacity of the governor's ambassador. His mission was to negotiate a trade pact and to assist in establishing an alliance against the Iroquois. This was the **1st official Canadian envoy to a foreign country**.

> **More dinosaur bones have been found in Canada than in any other country** in the entire world.

_1654:_ Lady Sara Kirke came from England to Newfoundland with her husband, Sir David Kirke (1597-1654) of Dieppe, Normandy, France. She managed the Pool Plantation at Ferryland, Newfoundland, and in so doing became the **1st woman to operate a large business in British**

North America. She owned more stages and cod liver oil vats, and employed more fisherman and fish processors, than any other planter in English Canada.

1654: At the ripe old age of 11 years, 5 months, Marguerite Sedilot (1643-1710), the **youngest bride in Canadian records**, married Jean Aubuchon, of Trois-Rivières, Lower Canada (Quebec). However, the ceremony was not validated until Marguerite's twelfth birthday!

1657: An eggshell, no doubt part of some poor Jesuit's last meal before the Iroquois attacked at Sainte-Marie Among the Hurons near Midland, Upper Canada (Ontario), is the **oldest breakfast leftovers ever found in Canada**.

1663: On February 5th, the Great Quebec Earthquake became the **1st officially recorded major disaster in Canada, natural or manmade**, accounting for the loss of many lives. The quake was of a magnitude of 7.0 and occurred at 5:30 p.m. on February 5th at Longitude 47.6 N, Latitude 70.1 W.

1665: In 1665, Monseigneur François-Xavier de Laval de Montigny (1623-1708) instituted the celebration of the Holy Family for the second Sunday after Epiphany, although from 1685, it was held on the third Sunday after Pentecost. He called upon the second Canadian to be ordained priest, Charles-Amador Martin (1648-1711), to write the music for this celebration as Charles was also a singer and an accomplished musician. He wrote a piece of plain-chant which became the **1st musical composition in Canada which has been preserved**.

1679: Talk about a very old, pungent, round cheese, this one is still available today. The Aubertin family has been passing down the secret recipe for **Canada's 1st cheese**, Fromage Île d'Orléans, for over three hundred years. (Available only in Quebec City, Lower Canada [Quebec], and on nearby Île d'Orléans you say? Pity!)

<u>1685</u>: Long before the creation of the Royal Canadian Mint, most trade amongst early inhabitants was by barter. It was perfectly legal to purchase goods in exchange for wheat, moose skins, and various other pelts including beaver and even wildcat. In fact, you could buy a wonderful blanket for only eight wildcat skins! Coinage was minted and shipped to Canada but it always seemed to disappear or get returned to France by the soldiers who were not hunters and had to use the coins to pay for their board and lodging. The Intendant, Jacques de Meulles (d. 1703) of France then inaugurated his most imaginative and ingenious device—playing card money—the **1st paper money in Canada**. Jacques would cut a pack of playing cards into quarters, stamp them with the word "bon" meaning "good", sign them, seal them on the back, then authorize them as legal tender promising to redeem them for the annual supply of coinage when it arrived from France. This no doubt upset the local card players accustomed to using their decks to play their favourite card game called "maw" where the lucky cards to turn up were, Tiddy, Gleek, Tup-tup and Towser!

<u>1686</u>: The town of Grand Falls/Grand-Sault was founded this year in New Brunswick. It is the **1st and only town in Canada with an officially bilingual name**. Its population in 2011 was 5,706 residents.

<u>1689</u>: The house of the Longueuil family, a high-ranking family in Montreal, Lower Canada (Quebec), was fitted with the **1st glass windows in Canada**.

1700s: A one-of-a-kind relic discovered in storage in Britain was returned to its original home in Canada. It is the **world's oldest canoe**, now on display at the Canadian Canoe Museum in Peterborough, Ontario.

1708: The Royal Newfoundland Regiment, the **oldest militia in North America**, formed at St. John's, Newfoundland.

> The Rocky Mountains are the northern segment of a large mountain system extending in Canada 1200 km *(745.7 mi.)* from the American borders of British Columbia and Alberta to the Liard River Basin. They include magnificent mountain forms, commonly higher than 3050 m *(10,006.6 ft.)*. The **tallest peak of the Canadian Rockies** is Mount Robson rising 3919 m *(12,972 ft.)* above sea level in Jasper National Park, Alberta.

1709: For anyone interested in writing folk songs for a living, the approach taken by trapper Jean Cadieux (1670-1709) of Montreal, Lower Canada (Quebec), is not highly recommended. He was mortally wounded during an Iroquois attack but did live long enough to dig his own grave on the bank of the Ottawa River, then use his own blood to write his lament on birch bark. "Petite Rocher" ("Little Rock") is considered to be the **1ˢᵗ folk song written about an incident that took place in early Canada**.

1710: British troops led by Francis Nicholson (1655-1728) of York, England, captured Fort Anne in 1710. Reverend John Harrison held the **1ˢᵗ Church of England service in Canada** on September 2, 1710, on the old fort grounds at Annapolis Royal. The **1ˢᵗ Protestant orphanage in Canada** was started at St. Paul's in 1754 and the **1ˢᵗ Sunday School in Canada** was conducted there in 1783. St. Paul's also has the **only English church register in Canada maintained under the old Julian calendar.**

> The **1ˢᵗ and only site in the country called "Canada"** is Canada Bay, a natural harbour on the eastern shore of northern Newfoundland.

1717: The Ursuline Convent in Quebec City, Quebec, contains the **longest-burning lamp in Canada**, a flame which has never been extinguished since this year.

1719: The spectacular displays of the **Northern lights or Aurora Borealis were documented for the 1ˢᵗ time in North America** on December 11, 1719.

1727: The **1ˢᵗ timber business in Canada** started in Quebec City, Lower Canada (Quebec), on October 30ᵗʰ. **Canada's 1ˢᵗ export of wood to France** began shortly thereafter.

1731: Richard Norton was chief from 1731 to 1741 at Fort Prince of Wales, Manitoba, the **1ˢᵗ stone fort in the Arctic.**

1731: Pierre Gaultier de Varennes, Sieur de la Vérendrye (1685-1749) of Trois-Rivières, Lower Canada (Québec), had the distinction of being the **1ˢᵗ native born explorer of Canada.** On setting out from Montreal, Lower Canada, this year, his dream was to find an overland route to the Pacific Ocean, a rather difficult accomplishment considering that he never did cross the Rocky Mountains! But Pierre did become the **1ˢᵗ white** man to explore **Western Canada systematically** and his name is certainly a major element in Canada's history. In 1939, he was the **1**st **white man to discover the Saskatchewan River.**

_1734:_ The present-day Highway 138 passes through some of the oldest and best preserved villages in Quebec at Batiscan following much the same route as **Canada's 1**st **highway**, known as Chemin Du Roy or The King's Road. This highway hugs the north shore of the St. Lawrence River and originally linked the seigniorial of New France's most thickly populated area with Montreal, Lower Canada (Quebec), and Quebec City, Lower Canada. There were sixteen rivers and streams that had to be traversed by ferry or primitive bridge. It could take five days and up to thirty changes of horses and carriage to travel from one city to the other, a distance of about 241.4 km _(150 mi.)_. Even without oil changes, we drive this route much more quickly today although from 1736, horsemen covered the same distance in 30 hours carrying the mail.

_1736:_ The incredible rise and fall of the tide in the Bay of Fundy was a major advantage for the French artisans who constructed the **1**st **dry dock in North America** at Lower Jemseg, New Brunswick.

_1738:_ The Roman Catholic Church certainly had some strange controls in place in early Canada. Young 20-year old Esther Brandeau (born c. 1718 of Saint-Esprit, France, had to disguise herself as a ship's boy not only to sneak into Canada but also throughout almost a year living with the Récollet monks at Lower Canada (Quebec). Women were allowed to come to Canada, but non-Catholic immigrants were unacceptable. Esther became the **1**st **person of Jewish decent to set**

foot in Canada. Refusing to convert to Catholicism, she was immediately deported back to Bordeaux by Intendant Gilles Hocquart (1694-1783) of Mortagne-au-Perche, France, once her true sex and religious beliefs were identified.

1740: The body of Derrick Van Laan (d. 1740), a whaler who died on the shore of Frobisher Bay and was entombed along with identification, was perfectly preserved when discovered by an expedition in 1902. His tomb was resealed and his body, one would assume, still well refrigerated making it **Canada's longest-preserved body**.

1747: The Reverend Jean Dolbeau (1586-1652) of Anjou, France, a Récollet priest, established a mission to the Indians at Tadoussac, Lower Canada (Quebec), in 1615. In 1641, Jesuits took over the mission and constructed a brick and stone church. This was replaced by a wooden chapel in 1747, the **oldest surviving chapel in North America**. The bell from the first chapel now hangs in the 15.2-m *(50-ft.)* tower of the wooden chapel.

At some five times the size of Prince Edward Island, Great Bear Lake in the Northwest Territories is the **largest lake entirely within Canada's boundaries**. It covers 7.6% of the total area of Canada, an expanse of 31 328 km² *(12,095.8 mi.²)*. This freshwater lake is also the fourth largest lake on the North American continent.

1749: Canadian men are not likely to hesitate in bragging that the **1ˢᵗ miniskirt was a Canadian invention**, originating some two and a half centuries ago. Historians of fashion and costume note the journal of Pehr Kalm (1715-1779) of Finland, professor of botany at Uppsala University, made during his 1749 visit to Canada. On July 25th he wrote, "Every day but Sunday, they (Canadian women) wear a little neat jacket and a short skirt which hardly reaches halfway down the leg and sometimes not that far." So, Canadian women have been turning men's heads in the name of science for a long time now, a trend which certainly spread worldwide in the 20th century.

> The Cowichan Indians of southern Vancouver Island, British Columbia, knit a uniquely designed grey sweater from unbleached wool. It was originally black and white in colour although now is sometimes multi-coloured. The **Cowichan sweater** contains many symbolic designs and is a highly treasured garment.

1750: The Halifax Seaport Farmers' Market in Halifax, Nova Scotia, is located in the Keith's Brewery Building. Visitors can purchase a wide range of high quality seasonal fresh fruit, vegetables, herbs, plants, baked goods, wines, and meats plus innovative crafts and decorations from over one hundred vendors every Saturday of the year. Talented musicians also entertain throughout the old stone courtyards in this refurbished 19th century brewery. It also just happens to be the **oldest farmers' market in North America**!

1750: Spain and her colonies issued eight reales coins this year, the **1st dollars used in Canada**. They used the £sd system for accounting, pronounced and sometimes written LSD, the popular name for currencies used in the United

Kingdom and most of its Empire and colonies before they converted to decimal currencies. "£sd" stands for "pounds, shillings, and pence". The term originated from the Latin "librae, solidi, denarii" where there were 12 d (12 pence) in a shilling and 20s (20 shillings), or 240 d, in a pound. This currency system was based on fractions rather than decimals. While countries independent from Britain, like the USA, abandoned the £sd system quickly, it remained the monetary system of most of the British Commonwealth countries, except for Canada, for much of the 20th century. Different ratings were used in the different British colonies and because they used the £sd accounting system, they had to set a value for the Spanish dollar in £sd. The 1st **Halifax currency rating** was introduced c. 1750 and became the most commonly used system in the northern colonies valuing the Spanish dollar at 5 shillings. Under the London rating, the silver in the coin was equal to 4 shillings 6 pence. United Empire Loyalists who settled in Ontario after the American War of Independence (American Revolutionary War [1775-1893]) brought the York rating of 1 Spanish dollar equal to 8 shillings. This rating was named after New York and was outlawed officially in 1796 in favour of the Halifax rating although it continued in used well into the 19th century. In 1817, the Bank of Montreal issued notes denominated in £sd dollars. The Atlantic colonies preferred the £sd system linked to Britain than to the U.S. Few coins were issued because British authorities were unwilling to allow their colonies to mint their own coins. Some bank tokens were issued in denominations of 1/2 and 1 penny while some dollar banknotes bore the picture of the Spanish dollar coin(s) to which they were equal. The £sd and dollar system also quickly replaced the livre in the

French speaking parts of Canada following the conquest by Britain. Some French language banknotes called the dollar the piaster. Some bank tokens also were issued in 1 and 2 sous denominations which were equal to 1/2 and 1 penny. And thus evolved the world of currency in our country!

1750: Many of the canoes used by fur traders in the early days of Canada were very large, capable of carrying a crew of up to 12 people plus as much as 2400 kg *(5,291.1 lb.)* of cargo. In fact, the fur trade became so profitable that the French established the **world's 1st known canoe factory** at Trois-Rivières, Lower Canada (Québec), to handle the demand.

1752: The **1st regular saltwater ferry service in North America** began across the harbour to service the growing communities of Halifax and Dartmouth, Nova Scotia. Under a three-year charter, John Connor (1728-1757) charged either 3 pence or sixpence a trip (reports vary) on the two boats he operated regularly between sunrise and sunset. He made only one round trip on Sundays to enable Dartmouth citizens to attend church services in Halifax. His original boats essentially were rowboats with a single sail which also transported baggage at no additional charge.

> The Canadian Indian legend, the Algonquian "Great Rabbit", was the prototype for **B'rer Rabbit, one of the world's favourite children's characters**.

1753: Some 1,500 foreign Protestants, recruited from southern and central Germany, supported Britain in her struggle for domination of North America settling in Lunenburg, Nova Scotia, **Canada's 1st German**

community. It was named in honour of King George II, Duke of Braunschweig-Lunenburg (1683-1760) of Hanover, Germany, who had become King of England in 1727. Lured by the promise of free land, they each were allocated town lots, garden lots east of the town side, plus 0.12-km² and 1.2-km² *(30-acre and 300-acre)* farm lots in the remote areas.

1757: Winter conditions at the fort known as "The House of Peace" at Fort Niagara, Upper Canada (Ontario), were rather strenuous on the French troops living there. However, one energetic and imaginative soldier managed to write a play called *The Old Man Duped*. This was the **1ˢᵗ play staged in Canada**, performed by the members of the garrison dressed in home-made costumes.

1759: St. Andrew's Church in Quebec City, Lower Canada (Quebec), was built in 1810. It contains a beautifully hand-carved wooden pulpit, magnificent stained glass windows, and a spiral staircase leading to the choir loft which was formerly the governor's gallery. Even the original organ, dated 1843, and the original baptismal font remain in use there today. The men of the Fraser Highlanders marched through the streets to the beautiful sound of bagpipes on their way to services at the Old Jesuit College beginning in 1759, until St. Andrew's was built. Thus, St. Andrew's Church became home to the **1ˢᵗ congregation of Scottish origin in Canada**.

1759: So, when not fighting, what did bored Scottish soldiers do to pass the time while serving with General James Murray (1721-1794) of Ballencrieff, East Lothian, Scotland, and Major General James Wolfe (1727-1759) of Westerham, Kent, England, on the St. Charles and St. Lawrence Rivers from 1759 to 1763? Well, they introduced the **1ˢᵗ curling game**

played in Canada. This informal sport in this country at that time instigated the use of gun carriage hubs as curling stones.

1761: James Rivington (c. 1724-1802) of London, England, was a member of a well-known family of London booksellers. He established the **1ˢᵗ English language bookstore in British North America**. He first advertised his stock of books for sale in the May 14, 1761 issue of the *Halifax Gazette*.

1762: Joseph Frederick Wallet DesBarres (1721-1824) of Basel, Switzerland, was sent by the British Government to complete a hydrographic survey of the east coast of North America toward the end of the 18ᵗʰ century. He remained in Canada, founded Sydney, Nova Scotia, and became the first lieutenant governor of Cape Breton Island, Nova Scotia. His work was the **1ˢᵗ systematic undersea mapping study in the world** during which he charted the depth of water and the nature of Canadian coastlines.

1765: On May 17ᵗʰ, Irish troops serving in the British Army at Quebec City, Lower Canada (Quebec), celebrated the **1ˢᵗ St. Patrick's Day in Canada**.

1765: The town of Windsor, Nova Scotia, was settled by the French Acadians in 1684. In 1765, it held the **1ˢᵗ agricultural fair in North America** still operating to this day.

1768: Montreal, Lower Canada (Quebec), became home to the **1ˢᵗ Hebrew congregation** and **1ˢᵗ permanent Synagogue in Canada,** at the Portuguese Synagogue, thirty years after the deportation of Esther Brandeau (born c. 1718) of Bordeaux, France. It became the Shearith Israel Spanish and Portuguese Synagogue around 1838. In this synagogue are a number of ornate silver and velvet vessels containing examples of the Torah, most recently from Iraq. There also is one from England being more than 500 years old, and others on which the *Five Books of Moses* are inscribed.

> Long before the voyages of Christopher Columbus (1451-1506) of Genoa, Italy, John Cabot (1450-1499) of Genoa, and Jacques Cartier (1491-1557) of St. Malo, France, Norsemen and Basque fisherman plied the Grand Banks of Newfoundland. In fact, our Native peoples hunted and fished the lands and waters of Canada for thousands of years making fishing **Canada's oldest continuing industry**.

_1775:_ During the American Revolutionary War (1775-1783), the first American army was raised to fight the British forces. Two American employed privateers attacked the settlement of Charlottetown, Prince Edward Island, making this the **1ˢᵗ ever American military intrusion of foreign land**. There were enough *Canadiens* who volunteered to aid the cause that a separate battalion was formed for them. The U.S. Continental Congress appointed Roman Catholic Reverend Eustache Chartier de Lotbinière in 1776 as the **1ˢᵗ U.S. Army Chaplain** and ratified the appointment on August 12ᵗʰ to meet the needs of these French Canadian volunteers.

_1778:_ Prior to exploration into Western Canada, Europeans had to splice two trees together in order to construct masts for their tall ships. However, when Captain James Cook (1728-1779) of Marton, England, discovered Douglas fir trees in Nootka Sound, British Columbia, unlike anything ever seen before by a European, he ordered his sailors to replace the rotting masts of his ships with ones cut from these wonderful trees. This was the 1ˢᵗ **time a single tree had ever been used for an entire mast**.

Approximately 7.6 percent or 753 686.5 km² *(291,000 mi.²)* of Canada's total territory is comprised of lakes and rivers, or about one fifth of the world's fresh water. As such, Canada has **more usable fresh water than any other country in the world**.

1781: The 1ˢᵗ **legal lottery in Canada** was passed by the House of Assembly as a means of defraying the cost of £1500 needed to erect a proper school building. It was held in Halifax, Nova Scotia, in September 1781. The first batch of 5,000 tickets sold at 20 shillings each and raised half the desired goal, with prizes totalling £4250 and the biggest set at £2000.

1783: Ever heard of Digby Chicken? Well, Admiral Robert Digby (1732-1815) of Ireland was commander of *HMS Atlanta*, one of the ships that conveyed the United Empire Loyalist founders of the town of Digby, Nova Scotia, to the shores of this new land. Both the town and this interesting tiny smoked and salted herring were named after the good Admiral. **Digby Chicks** are what Maritimers call "fillets of these wee fish", named by impoverished early Digby settlers who served them once to replace chicken for Christmas dinner.

1783: The 1ˢᵗ **settlement for free black people in North America** was established when more than 1,500 black Loyalists moved to Birchtown, Nova Scotia. These were some of the 7,000 Loyalists who landed at Parr Town (Saint

John), New Brunswick, this year on the **1st ships bearing Loyalists to Canada**.

_1785_: **North America's last recorded Great Auk *(Penguinus impennis)*** was sighted this year on Funk Island, Newfoundland.

The Algonquian Indians refer to a rude shelter, hut, or lean-to as a **wickiup**. Originally, it was a brush or mat-covered shelter although the word now also refers to most any such structure including a conical leather lodge, a wigwam, or a tepee.

_1785_: Fredericton High School in Fredericton, New Brunswick, is the **oldest English high school in Canada** and the **largest high school in the British Commonwealth with more than 3,000 students**.

_1786_: King George III (1738-1820) of Hampshire, England, presented the **1st firefighting vehicle in Canada**, leather hose and all, to the residents of Shelburne, Nova Scotia, this year. It certainly is an interesting vehicle, however, as its fixed front wheels require it to be dragged around corners!

_1786_: Prince William, who later became King William IV (1765-1837) of London, England, came ashore on the East Coast of Newfoundland. He then visited the British naval installation at Halifax, Nova Scotia, on two different occasions. On October 5th, Prince William was the **1st member of the British Royal Family to set foot in Canada**.

_1786_: John Molson (1763-1836) of Lincolnshire, England, founded the Molson Brewery of Montreal, Lower Canada

(Quebec), this year. It is the **oldest continuously operating brewery in North America**. It also manufactures **North America's oldest beer brand**. The company repurchased one hundred percent of the Molson brands in the United States in 2001 and holds 50.1% interest in Molson USA. One of the world's fastest growing beer markets is in Brazil where Molson purchased Bavaria in 2000 and acquired the Kaiser brand in 2002. Molson is now the second largest brewer in Brazil and the fifteenth largest in the world.

_1788:_ The forerunner of Nova Scotia's King's College was the **1st residential boys' school in Canada**, built in Windsor, Nova Scotia, a year before the opening of King's College itself.

_1788:_ Captain John Meares (c. 1756-1809) was formerly a lieutenant in the British Navy. He arrived with two ships and ninety men at Nootka, Vancouver Island in British Columbia. He obtained a grant of land from the chief of the nearby Indian village and constructed a two-storey house, the first house of its kind built in British Columbia. He also completed the _North-West America_ on September 29th, the **1st ship built on the Pacific Coast of Canada**.

_1789:_ Horses once ran on a track on the Plains of Abraham, now Battlefield Park, in Quebec City, Lower Canada (Quebec), site of the Quebec Turf Club which is the **oldest riding association in Canada**.

_1789:_ The establishment of King's College in Windsor, Nova Scotia, included the creation of the **1st academic library in Canada**. University libraries were included in many colleges and universities founded throughout Canada since that time. Yet academic collections remained relatively small until the mid-20th century. Only then did they respond to the increased pressures in the field of higher education, particularly from the research sector, to expand their library resources dramatically.

_1789:_ One of the strangest situations in our country involves a bed of low-grade coal which has been smouldering at Fort Norman in the Northwest Territories since before 1789 making it **Canada's longest-burning fire**.

_1790:_ The Kings County Museum at Hampton, New Brunswick, contains the **oldest sunglasses in Canada**, dating from this year, and believe it or not, they're adjustable!

_1792:_ Another short-lived Canadian magazine which also lived for a mere three years was published by Samuel Neilson and Thomas Gilmore in Quebec City, Lower Canada (Quebec). However, being written half in English and half in French made _Le Magasin de Québec_ **Canada's 1ˢᵗ bilingual magazine**. This was our first attempt at using the printed word to help bring our two historic cultures together better. This also was the **1ˢᵗ periodical review in Canada**, issued for the first time on August 1ˢᵗ.

_1792:_ Until now, paper money in North America was considered virtually worthless. Nonetheless, the Canada Banking Company began circulating the **1ˢᵗ Canadian Bank Note** on August 10ᵗʰ valued at "five chelins". The only currency with real value, as far as the settlers were concerned, was still those hard coins you can really sink your teeth into, as it were.

_1797:_ The Law Society of Upper Canada was founded this year in what is now the province of Ontario making it **Canada's oldest legal association**.

1800: St. George's Round Church in Halifax, Nova Scotia, was the **1ˢᵗ Byzantine-style church built in British North America**. A national reconstruction campaign is currently under way to restore the damage from a tragic fire in 1994 which destroyed most of the wooden structure.

> There is an interesting clam off Canada's West Coast waters whose name originates from Nisqually from which it was taken into Chinook Jargon, the old trading language of southern British Columbia. The Gooeyduck is the **largest burrowing bivalve in the world** and its burrowing habit caused the Nisqually tribe to call it go-duk or "dig-deep".

1802: The Most Reverend Edmund Burke (1753-1820) of Maryborough, Portlaoighise, Ireland, founded Saint Mary's University, the **1ˢᵗ English Catholic institution of higher learning in Canada**. It became a lay university with an independent board of governors in 1970 and has developed well known undergraduate and graduate programmes for almost 8,000 full and part-time students as of 2011. Saint Mary's is known for its specialization in forensic science, environmental studies, Atlantic Canada studies, Irish studies, international development studies, Asian studies, and criminology. It is also the **1ˢᵗ university in the world to make education accessible to students with disabilities using voice-activated computer technology to deliver classroom lectures**.

1803: Queen Elizabeth II (b. 1926) of London, England, and Prince Philip (b. 1921) of Corfu, Greece, officially opened the site of Old Fort William, the **world's largest**

fur-trading post, to the public on July 3, 1973. It is located 14.5 km *(9 mi.)* upriver from its original site near the mouth of the Kaministiquia River near Thunder Bay, Ontario. A total of 42 buildings were reconstructed on the 0.1-km² *(25-acre)* site. The fort includes the naval stores building, smithy, cooperage, gunsmith's workshop, canoe sheds, and the Council House, where partners and traders met at the end of each trapping season in the Great Rendezvous from 1803 to 1821.

The Mudpuppy *(Necturus maculosus)* spends its entire life in the larval stage. Its average length when mature is 203 mm to 330 mm *(8 in. to 13 in.)* although one specimen on record measured 483 mm *(19 in.)* long. The Mudpuppy is **Canada's largest native salamander**.

1803: Niagara Falls' reputation as the honeymoon capital of Canada had a very early start when Jerome Bonaparte (1784-1860) of Ajaccio, Corsica, brother of Napoleon Bonaparte (1769-1821) of Ajaccio, married Elizabeth Patterson (1785-1879) of Baltimore, Maryland, USA. They decided to begin their life of wedded bliss with a honeymoon here becoming the **1ˢᵗ famous Niagara Falls honeymooners**. Seems the lack of bliss led to a lack of marriage in just two short years after which their marriage was annulled. No idea what ever happened to Elizabeth, but Jerome eventually moved to Germany where he became the King of Westphalia. He later moved again to become Marshal of France.

1805: The little village of St. Andrews, near Lachute, Lower Canada (Quebec), was chosen by a group of New England immigrant entrepreneurs as the most suitable site on which to construct the **1st Canadian paper mill**. Water from nearby rivers or streams was essential to provide the water power necessary to run machinery and to use in the paper-making processes. A hand method was implemented to convert rags into wrapping and printing paper which served the growing markets of merchants and publishers both locally and in Montreal, Lower Canada. Later, the Montreal stationer James Brown took over operation of this mill.

1806: Pierre Bédard (1762-1829) of Charlesbourg, Lower Canada (Quebec), was a lawyer and member of the Assembly of Lower Canada for Northumberland. He and the Parti Canadien established the nationalist newspaper *Le Canadien* on November 22nd. This was the **1st French-language newspaper in Canada**. It's purpose was to counter the attacks of the *Quebec Mercury* and to promote greater power and control of political patronage by French Canadians.

A **Montreal canoe** is a large freight canoe measuring approximately 14 m *(46 ft.)* long, 1.8 m *(6 ft.)* wide in midships, and 76.2 cm *(2.5 ft.)* deep. It was used particularly during the fur trade of early Canada to carry 3.6 to 4.5 metric tonnes *(4 to 5 tons)* of cargo from Montreal, Lower Canada (Quebec), to Grand Portage, Minnesota, USA. It took eight men to paddle a Montreal canoe.

1807: King's College was established in Windsor, Nova Scotia, in 1789 and received its royal charter in 1802. Roger Viets (1738-1811) of Simsbury, Connecticut, USA, and William Hill graduated from King's College in 1807 becoming **Canada's**

1st two university students. Roger moved on to become rector of the Anglican Church in Digby, Nova Scotia. William later became a Nova Scotia Supreme Court Justice.

_1808:_ Names from various Indian tribes on Canada's West Coast became the **1st names in the world for several common salmon** known to us today. **Coho** came about in 1808 while **sockeye** evolved in 1869 from the Coast Salish words for red fish, suk-kegh, a species of Pacific salmon. Qualla, meaning "striped", is a Salish Indian word describing the **dog salmon** (1884). Tyee (1912) is a Nootka Indian word meaning "chief, big", referring to a very large dog salmon (1907). And **chinook** comes from the name of a group of native Indians once living on the Pacific Coast.

_1809:_ Edward Jordan had seized a vessel that was previously his property. Convicted in **Canada's 1st piracy trial**, he was hanged on November 23rd. Then, his body was tarred, chained, and hung on a gibbet at the entrance to Halifax Harbour in Nova Scotia.

_1809:_ For those of you interested in the life of rural Ontario before Confederation, Black Creek Pioneer Village in North York, Ontario, is the place to visit. Included amongst the nearly forty restored and furnished buildings are a school, grist mill, fire hall, general store, church, flour mill, inn, and shops operated by a harness-maker, blacksmith, weaver, and shoemaker. They are all located around five original buildings erected on the site by Ernest Daniel Stong (1887-1958) of Toronto, Upper Canada (Ontario), as early as 1816. An extensive collection of wood carvings, along with the **largest collection of 19th-century toys in Canada**, are housed in a huge cantilever barn erected in 1809 as the Dalziel Barn Museum.

Gaspé is very proud of its history, considering Jacques Cartier (1491-1557) of St. Malo, France, landed there in 1534. The city also has the **only wooden cathedral in North America**.

_1814:_ A flurry of shipbuilding was generated by the War of 1812. The Kingston Navy Dockyard launched the _St. Lawrence_ on October 10th. This 3-deck warship had 102 guns, was larger than the _Victory_ commanded by Admiral Lord Horatio Nelson (1758-1805) of Burnham Thorpe, Norfolk, England, and was the **largest wooden ship in the world ever built on fresh water**.

Northern Canada was the origin of the **1st moose milk in the world**, a homebrew of rum and milk. Although recipes vary, one version contains emulsified fiddleheads and clam juice, liberally diluted with cheap wine. Fiddleheads are the spring-fresh fronds of the ostrich fern, an edible delicacy boiled and buttered before they unravel in the sun.

_1816:_ Frederick Hund lived in Quebec City, Lower Canada (Quebec), where he became the **1st piano maker in Canada**. Most such artisans came originally from Great Britain and Germany. Thomas D. Hood was another successful piano maker followed by four others in Toronto, Upper Canada (Ontario), ten in Montreal, Lower Canada, and three in Quebec City by 1851. Although there were several other successful piano manufacturers at this time, including Theodore August Heintzman (1817-1899) of Berlin, Mason &

Risch, established in 1871 in Toronto, R.S. Williams (1834-1906) of London, Upper Canada, and Lesage, only Heintzman and Lesage pianos were manufactured in Canada by 1980.

1817: Thomas Douglas (1771-1820) of St. Mary's Isle, Scotland, Fifth Earl of Selkirk, founded the **1st Red River Settlement**, known today as the city of Winnipeg, Manitoba. On July 18th, Lord Selkirk made the **1st treaty with local Ojibwa and Swampy Cree people on behalf of King George III** (1738-1820) of London, England.

1819: Sir William Edward Parry (1790-1855) of Bath, England, anchored off Melville Island in the Northwest Territories on September 26th. He was the **1st explorer to winter in the Arctic by choice**. All others to that time had done so only because they were stranded by the ice and had to wait until spring for it to break up.

1819: On Melville Island, Northwest Territories, explorer Sir William Edward Parry (1790-1855) of Bath, England, appropriately entitled the work he wrote, **Canada's most northerly operetta**, *The Northwest Passage*. At this time, Melville Island was 1609.3 km *(1,000 mi.)* further north than the most northerly trading post in the country.

1820: Horseman's Fort, the south gate of the early Halifax, Nova Scotia palisade, is the site of St. Mary's Basilica, one of the oldest stone edifices in Canada. It has the **tallest polished granite spire**, 57.6 m *(189 ft.)*, **in the world**. It also contains three important tablets: one is in memory of the Reverend Pierre Maillard (c. 1710-1762) of Chartres, France, a missionary to the Mi'kmaq Indians of Nova Scotia; one is in memory of the first Roman Catholic bishop of Halifax, the Most Reverend Edmund Burke (1753-1820) of Marysborough, Queen's County, Ireland, who planned the basilica and placed the cornerstone; and the third is of Sir John Sparrow David Thompson (1845-1894) of Halifax, a parishioner who became prime minister in 1892.

1821: Canadian Stanley Schwarts just happens to own the **only existing ticket to the funeral of Napoleon Bonaparte** (1769-1821) of Ajaccio, Corsica! It is part of the **largest collection of Napoleonic relics in Canada**.

1823: Uninhabited Seal Island, Nova Scotia, situated 24.1 km *(15 mi.)* west of Cape Sable Island near the entrance to the Bay of Fundy, proved disastrous to shipwrecked sailors who perished in the bitter cold Atlantic winds after reaching the island. Mary Crowell Hichens and her husband moved to the island and established the **1st lifesaving station in Canada** after which no more lives were lost there. In 1831, the provinces of Nova Scotia and New Brunswick jointly built a lighthouse at the southern end of the island and Richard Hichens became the island's first lighthouse keeper.

1823: You can tour a recreation of an Ontario rural community of the mid-1800s by touring Doon Pioneer Village in Doon, Upper Canada (Ontario), south of Kitchener, Upper Canada. Among its treasures is a Bible that belonged to Benjamin Eby (1785-1853) of Hammer Creek, Pennsylvania, USA, **Canada's 1st Mennonite bishop**. The Bible contains fraktur art—the decorative birds, flowers, and scrolls used by the Pennsylvania Dutch.

1823: The Royal Engineers spent £695 constructing the **1st railway in Canada**. This double-track balanced incline railway was used during the construction of Quebec's citadel in Quebec City, Lower Canada (Quebec). It

transported stone from a wharf on the St. Lawrence River
152.4 m *(500 ft.)* to the top of the escarpment. Two cable
cars were powered initially by a horse gin which later was
upgraded to a stationary steam engine. It pulled one car up
loaded with building material while the other came down
empty. It remained operational into the 1830s.

_1825_: The University of New Brunswick in Fredericton,
although the second university built in this country in 1785,
still holds other national records. Of the many historic
buildings on both campuses in Saint John and Fredericton
both in New Brunswick, the Old Arts Building (1825-1828)
in Fredericton is the **oldest university building still in
use in Canada today.** It is known as Sir Howard Douglas
Hall, named after Lieutenant Governor Sir Howard Douglas
(1776-1843) of Gosport, England, who opened King's College
(University of New Brunswick) and this building officially on
January 1st.

_1827_: Did you know that the **1st known trades union
in Canada** was formed by printers in Quebec City, Lower
Canada (Quebec), this year on September 23rd? Unlike the
goals of most current trades unions, this one concentrated
more on acting as a mutual aid society to care for the sick
and on providing its members with social and recreational
opportunities than on regulating wages.

_1827_: The Green family of Hamilton, Upper Canada
(Ontario), made the **1st matches in Canada** in 1827 in
a tiny cottage at Main and Ferguson although they likely
were not the type with which we are familiar today. Later, a
major Canadian producer of wood and paper products with
widespread lumbering interests, the E.B. Eddy Company
was established at Hull, Lower Canada (Quebec) in 1851 by

Ezra Butler Eddy (1827-1906) of Bristol, England. He was the inventor of the **1ˢᵗ friction matches in the world** and was still producing matches in blocks by the old hand system during the company's first few years in operation. Its product was merchandised over the years under several names including "Telegraph", which ignited quickly, "Parlour" which did not smell up the parlour, and "Eddy Matches" in honour of the founder. One special Eddy product is in the Mrazik Collection in Quebec City, Quebec, which includes the **only remaining Canadian Allumettes Frontenac matchbox label**. The E.B. Eddy Company later became the **world's largest mass producer of wooden matches** and was responsible for **introducing the 1ˢᵗ book match into Canada** in 1928.

> The Saskatchewan Museum of Natural History in Regina, Saskatchewan, has the **world's longest frieze**. It displays more than 300 figures of mammals, fish, and birds. It runs along three walls of the museum for a distance of almost 140.2 m *(460 ft.)*.

1829: The original meaning of the term *black ice*, way back in 1829, referred to new ice on bodies of water, which appeared dark because of its clearness and solidity. Today, this unique term describes a winter hazard resultant from a thin, clear layer of ice frozen on black roadways. The **origin of the term *black ice***, as we know it today, was courtesy of our friendly folks in British Columbia!

1830: **Canada's largest public reference library** is the Metropolitan Toronto Reference Library (MTRL). Historically, it originated in 1830 when the Toronto

Mechanic's Institute was founded, operated as the Toronto Public Library system for 85 years, then came into its current form in 1967. The Metro Toronto Library Board operates the MTRL consisting of: some 1.5 million volumes of monographs and bound periodicals; 2.5 million films, tapes, microfilms, maps, fine art, ephemera, and miscellaneous materials; plus 360 000 linear m *(1,081,102.4 ft.)* of manuscript materials. Ninety-nine percent of its collections are non-circulating and are at the undergraduate university level.

> The rare satyrid butterfly is rare in more ways than one. This butterfly is considered **Canada's most peculiar species range**. It is seen only east of Manitoba's Riding Mountain National Park in even-numbered years—but only west of the park in odd-numbered years!

1831: This is the year when James MacFarlane of Kingston, Upper Canada (Ontario), **published the 1ˢᵗ Canadian cookbook**. It was called *The Cook Not Mad* and was published in Kingston. Then, in 1840, two truly Canadian cookbooks were published, one in English and one in French. Quebec City, Lower Canada (Quebec), was home to the French-language *La cuisinière canadienne* (later called *La nouvelle cuisinière canadienne*). Grimsby published the English language book, *The Frugal Housewife's Manual*, by "A.B." However, in 1877 (reprinted in 1970), the most comprehensive early cookbook of Canadian cuisine, *The Canadian Home Cook Book*, was compiled by "Ladies of Toronto and Chief Cities and Towns in Canada" making it the **1ˢᵗ significant Canadian culinary guide**.

1833: A few of Canada's early newspapers published two or three times a week although most were weeklies. The *Montreal Daily Advertiser* was the **1ˢᵗ daily newspaper in British North America**, but it had a short life, going bankrupt within a year.

1835: The Toronto Cricket Club competed on August 15ᵗʰ against the Guelph Cricket Club. Guelph, Upper Canada (Ontario), won by 10 wickets in what was recorded as being the **1ˢᵗ known cricket match in Canada**. In 1845, Montreal, Lower Canada (Quebec), hosted the **1ˢᵗ international cricket match held in Canada**.

> For many years, the Saguenay River, **North America's only navigable fjord**, was an important fur trade route providing the only access to the white pine forests of the Lac Saint-Jean region of Lower Canada (Quebec).

1836: Born John Corby near London, England, this architect and watercolourist changed his name to John George Howard (1803-1890) before immigrating to York (Toronto), Upper Canada (Ontario), in 1832. From 1833 to 1856, John held the position of drawing master at Upper Canada College. He applied his architectural talents in a wide variety of styles, all related to the forms current in Late Georgian and Regency England, in designing numerous churches and Classical buildings throughout the area. He even designed, in 1846, one of the most advanced buildings of its day in North America, the lunatic asylum at 999 Queen Street West in Toronto, later demolished in 1976. Colborne Lodge forms the centre-piece of High Park on the country estate he gave to the City of Toronto. It was John's original home here which is considered the **1ˢᵗ picturesque Italianate villa in North America**.

Icebergs float by Newfoundland generally from May to August. They weigh an average of 508 032 metric tonnes *(500,000 tons)*, some measuring as much as 10 160 640 metric tonnes *(10 million tons)*. Only one-seventh of the total size of an iceberg generally appears above the surface of the water which is why they are such a dangerous hazard to ships. Most icebergs that pass by Newfoundland, considered the **non-polar iceberg capital of the world**, likely originate near Greenland and take two to three years to make their southward journey. Approximately 75% of the earth's fresh water is contained in icebergs.

<u>1836</u>: The city of Halifax, Nova Scotia, possesses an old-world charm enhanced by its many heritage buildings, quiet tree-lined streets, and imposing freestone and granite homes. Adding to this charm are the Halifax Public Gardens opened by the Nova Scotia Horticultural Society which date from this year. They were the **1ˢᵗ formal Victorian Gardens in North America**. The city purchased the original 2.02 hectares *(5 acres)* in 1874 and merged them with a nearby civic garden expanding the area to 6.47 hectares *(16 acres)*.

<u>1836</u>: Sandra and William MacKay donated a very unique book from the estate of Robert MacKay in 1979 to St. Francis Xavier University in Antigonish, Nova Scotia. It is entitled

Companach an oganaich: no an comhairliche taitneach (Youth — Conduct of Life). It was the **1ˢᵗ Gaelic book ever published in North America**.

1838: Two boys, William Lowe and James Conn, were killed instantly in an explosion in the General Mining Association Store Pit #2 in Pictou County, Nova Scotia, after announcing that their safety lamps indicated a heavy build-up of gas 9.1 m *(30 ft.)* into the shaft. Since this **1ˢᵗ major coal mine disaster in Canada**, some sixty million metric tonnes *(55 million tons)* of coal have been mined at the expense of more than 600 miners who have died in various mining accidents. The Hillcrest Explosion of 1914 in Alberta killed 189 miners, the **worst coal mine disaster ever in Canada**.

1839: If any of the following sporting activities interest you— running and standing high leaps, putting light and heavy stones, 91.4 m and 365.8 m *(100-yd. and 400-yd.)* foot races, running and standing hop-step-and-leap, hammer throws, steeplechase, or sack races—then you would have enjoyed the **1ˢᵗ track and field meet held in Canada**. It took place in the Toronto Athletic Games at Caer Howell Grounds near Toronto, Upper Canada (Ontario), on September 11ᵗʰ.

1839: James Elliott and Alexander McAvity living in New Brunswick conceived an idea for a diver to take his own supply of air down in the water to breathe while diving. Divers until now had to rely on someone on shore or on a boat to hand-pump air into a hose which was attached to the top of a diving helmet worn by the diver. This naturally restricted movement for a diver very much. After considerable experimentation, James and Alexander finally succeeded in building a copper tank which would contain air. On March 4ᵗʰ, they patented

41

the 1ˢᵗ **Scuba (Self-Contained Underwater Breathing Apparatus) tank in the world.** Today's scuba tanks are made of steel. Sophisticated regulators are used to control the flow of air into a mask worn by the diver. Scuba tanks are used worldwide today by tourists, explorers, scientists, police, recreational divers, contractors, and rescue people to name but a few, giving them total freedom to swim independently of anyone on the surface helping them to breathe under water.

_1839:_ The Book Room in Halifax, Nova Scotia, was **Canada's 1ˢᵗ bookstore**, which regrettably had to close in 2008.

Try wrapping your lips around some of these record-making tongue twisters! The **longest single-word place name in Canada** is a body of water in northern Manitoba called Pekwachnamaykoskwaskwaypinwanik Lake. A close second in this contest is derived from either Ojibwa or Cree meaning "Stone at the bottom of the river and the water is running over"— Kapeekwanapeekeepakeecheewonk Rapids in the Sasaginningak River, also in Manitoba. Not to be outdone, **Canada's longest legitimate combination place name** is the village of Coeur-Très-Pur-de-la-Bienheureuse-Vierge-Marie-de-Plaisance in Quebec meaning "Very-Pure-Heart-of-the-Blessed-Virgin-Mary-of-Plaissance".

_1839:_ Along the Bay of Fundy near Saint John, New Brunswick, this year, the **1ˢᵗ commercially canned food in Canada** was salmon, tinned by Tristrim Holliday.

_1840:_ William Cunnabel became the **1ˢᵗ printer in Canada to apply steam power to his all-metal Washington press** which he imported from the United States. With it, he published the first penny paper in Nova Scotia and the _Gospel of St. John_ translated into the Mi'kmaq language.

_1840:_ The **1ˢᵗ hot air balloon rose in the skies of Canada** from Barrack Square in Saint John, New Brunswick, back in 1840. It carried Professor Louis Anselm Lauriat (1785-1857) of Guadeloupe aboard the _Star of the East._ The cost for selected seat tickets was four shillings. Then, on July 31ˢᵗ of 1879, Richard Cowan, Charles Grimley, and Charles Page manned the **1ˢᵗ flight in Canada in a hydrogen balloon**, in Montreal, Lower Canada (Quebec).

One day, James Smith (c. 1800-1866) of St. Armand, Canada East (Quebec), received a very special formula from a journeyman who stopped at his newly opened restaurant. It was for a unique throat soother or cough drop which James began manufacturing. After his death, his two sons, William (1830-1913) and Andrew (1836-1895) moved to Poughkeepsie, New York, USA, and continued the business under the name **Smith Brothers**. They added engravings of themselves to the packaging as a trademark of this now worldwide renowned product.

_1841:_ An _Act of Union_ was passed in 1840, becoming effective on February 10, 1841. This _Act_ created the **1ˢᵗ Canadian parliament**. It united Upper Canada and Lower Canada as one political and geographical entity under one central government with an equal number of elected members representing both colonies in parliament. Thereafter, Upper Canada became known as Canada West while Lower Canada became Canada East, both represented by the central government in Kingston, Canada West (Ontario). Canada's capital moved to Kingston (1841-1843), to Montreal, Canada East (Quebec), in 1844, and then alternatively every four years between Toronto, Canada West, and Quebec City (1849-1865), Canada East. **Ottawa, Canada West, became Canada's permanent national capital for the 1ˢᵗ time** on December 31, 1857, on the choosing of Queen Victoria (1819-1901) of London, England. Charles Poulette Thomson, Lord Sydenham (1799-1841) of London, England, was appointed the **1ˢᵗ Governor General of United Canada.**

Major rivers and lakes draining northward to the Arctic Ocean dominate the landscape of the boreal forest region covering the northern half of the province of Alberta. Agriculture is truly feasible, essentially from a soil and climatic perspective, primarily in the parkland-like Peace River Region of the Northwest Territories. This is the **most northerly grain growing area in the world.**

1841: On December 1ˢᵗ, Alexander Davidson of the Niagara district, Canada West (Ontario), wrote *The Canadian Spelling Book*, published by Henry Roswell, Toronto, Canada West, which was granted the **1ˢᵗ copyright in Canada.**

1842: Louis Daguerre (1787-1851) of Paris, France, developed the art of photography in 1839 with his daguerreotype process. It involved producing an image on a silver-covered copper plate through long exposure to strong sunlight. To his studio, the **1ˢᵗ photographic studio in British North America,** Halifax, Nova Scotia portrait painter William Valentine (1798-1849) of Whitehaven, England, brought this popular new art in 1842 becoming the **1ˢᵗ permanent daguerreotypist in the British North American colonies.** He also produced the **1ˢᵗ known photograph in Canada.** Around the same time, John Clow, working with William, opened the **1ˢᵗ portrait studio in Canada** in Saint John, New Brunswick.

_1844:_ Originally established by Henry Yeoman Mott (1797-1866), John P. Mott & Co. of Dartmouth, Nova Scotia, under the direction of son John Mott, **produced the 1ˢᵗ chocolates in Canada.** This pioneer chocolate maker imported inexpensive sugar from the West Indies and operated successfully until the death of the company's last partner in 1920.

_1844:_ Canadian Joseph Medlicott Scriven (1819-1886) of Seapatrick, Northern Ireland, endured a difficult, and at times tragic, life. While still living in Ireland as a young man, his bride-to-be drowned in a stream just a few hours before the wedding ceremony. She had been thrown from her horse while out riding that day. He moved to Canada this year and fell in love with a girl who caught a chill after being immersed during a Baptist baptismal ceremony, ultimately resulting in her death. His faith surviving these great personal tragedies, it was in his house at Bewdley, Canada West (Ontario), where Joseph **penned one of the most famous hymns ever written,** the well-known hymn "What a Friend We Have in Jesus".

_1845:_ Saint John is New Brunswick's largest city and has **more people of Irish heritage per capita than any**

other place in North America. Some 30,000 Irish immigrants arrived between 1845 and 1847, the result of the Great Potato Famine of the mid-19th century. Irish Roman Catholics were the largest ethnic group in Saint John by 1850 and comprised 55% of the city's population by 1871. They founded the **1st St. Patrick's Society in Canada** in 1819.

_1845:_ **Canada's 1st department store** was Henry Morgan & Company founded this year on St. James Street in Montreal, Canada East (Quebec), by Henry Morgan (1819-1893) of Saline, Fife, Scotland. The company always prided itself on its high quality of its goods, and its customers were always willing to pay for that higher quality. It launched its mail order business around 1891 and also relocated to much more elegant, impressive, and spacious accommodation on Sainte Catherine Street that same year. Henry was the **1st to market using window displays** which he changed frequently to entice passers-by. The company remained a private family business until the Hudson's Bay Company bought it in 1960.

_1845:_ The Kingston General Hospital was built before Confederation and is the **oldest public hospital in Canada still in operation with most of its buildings intact**. On July 13, 1997, the Historic Sites and Monuments Board of Canada officially recognized this hospital as a site of national historic and architectural significance. Subsequent additions have enabled the Kingston General to evolve into the centre of scientific medicine it is today.

_1846:_ The Toronto, Hamilton, Niagara, and St. Catharines Electro-Magnetic Telegraph Company made history on December 19th when it used its line between Toronto and Queenston, both in Canada West (Ontario), to link the Mayor of Toronto with his counterpart in Hamilton, Canada West, to transmit **Canada's 1st electric telegram**. The origin of the word is Greek meaning "writing at a distance" which is exactly what newspaper correspondents in particular were most anxious to do using this incredible new means of instantaneous, long-range communication. This business, established on October 22nd, was also the **1st telegraph company in Canada**. The larger Montreal Telegraph Company bought the successful but limited Toronto, Hamilton and Niagara company in 1852.

> The **Canada jay**, *Perisoreus Canadensis*, is common throughout the forests of Canada and is a grey, crestless jay. It has been known by at least 30 different recorded names. It normally remains in Canada but will fly south briefly if forced to do so by very severe weather. It does not migrate regularly.

1847: In Halifax, Nova Scotia, Andrew Downs (1811-1892) of New Brunswick, New Jersey, USA, established the **1st zoo in North America north of Mexico**. It began as a 2-hectare *(5-acre)* retreat for Maritime wildlife. Yet, within 15 years, it expanded to 40.5 hectares *(100 acres)* to include a museum, aquarium, and greenhouse, plus native and exotic fauna. The zoo survived for 21 years.

1848: Bytown College was established this year in Ottawa, Canada West (Ontario). It attained university status in 1866 and its name changed to the University of Ottawa/Université d'Ottawa. It is the **1st bilingual university in Canada** and the **largest bilingual university in North America**. A wide range of support services and nine faculties, including specialty programmes such as criminology, international development, and translation, serve a total of 37,922 students as of the 2009 enrollment; 26,304 English-speaking (69.4%) and 11,618 (30.6%) French-speaking with females comprising 60.8% and males 39.2% of the total student body.

_1849:_ John Henry Walker (1831-1899) of Ireland created _Punch in Canada_ as a biweekly publication in Montreal, Canada East (Quebec), modelled after the British humour magazine _Punch_. This was the 1st **instance of cartooning in Canada**.

_c. 1850:_ Scholar, banker, teacher, and amateur mechanic, Father Belcourt (1803-1870) was born in La Baie du Febvre, Canada East (Quebec), a St. Lawrence river town between Montreal and Quebec City, both in Canada East. After his ordination, he worked among the Indians and Métis of the West for some 17 years during which time he compiled the 1st **Chippewa grammar book and dictionary in the world**. He even christened Louis Riel (1844-1885) of the Red River Settlement, Manitoba. He later moved to Shediac, New Brunswick, and Rustico, Prince Edward Island, living in the Maritimes for the remainder of his life.

_1850:_ For a membership subscription of just 10 shillings, you could use the 1st **prepared outdoor commercial skating rink in Canada**, built this year by a skating group in Montreal, Canada East (Quebec).

_1850:_ During the search for the Arctic expedition of Sir John Franklin (1786-1847) of Spilsby, Lincolnshire, England, leaflets were dropped by unmanned balloon over northern Canada, the 1st **record in the world of the transmission of messages by air**.

1850: The first McCausland family member of Robert McCausland Ltd. in Toronto, Canada West (Ontario), was trained in Ireland. The company was founded this year and was the **1st continuing stained glass studio in North America**. It produces traditional windows and has created two-thirds of all this country's stained glass. Having survived five generations in our country, it is also the **longest, continuously owned family company in Canada**.

1851: A native of Shelby County, Kentucky, USA, Henry Walton Bibb (1815-1854) escaped from slavery to Cincinnati, Ohio, USA, in 1837 but was recaptured when he returned to Kentucky for his wife. He escaped once again and moved to Detroit, Michigan, USA, where he became a noted lecturer for the anti-slavery movement. After the United States passed the *Fugitive Slave Act* in 1850, Henry moved to Canada. Founding *The Voice of the Fugitive* in Windsor, Canada West (Ontario), in 1851, Henry became the **1st black person to publish a newspaper in Canada**. His work included a close connection with the Refugee Home Society helping settle refugees in Sandwich Township, Illinois, USA. This also was the **1st African American newspaper published in Canada**.

1851: The old three-storey convent of the Grey Nuns in Winnipeg, Manitoba, houses the St. Boniface Museum. It was built between 1845 and 1851 and is the oldest building in Winnipeg. It also is the **largest oak log structure in North America**. The building has served many purposes since its construction. Over the years, it was the first hospital in the Canadian west. It also was used as a school, boarding school, and hospice for the sick and the poor. The Museum depicts how the French and Métis people of the early Red River Colony lived from day to day.

1851: Did you know that the word "prehistoric" originated in Canada? Well, it refers to any time before written historical records, essentially before 6,000 B.C., an arbitrary and now former date for the invention of writing. It appeared in the title of his book *Prehistoric Annals of Scotland*. It was Sir Daniel Wilson (1816-1892) of Edinburgh, Scotland, while professor of history and English at the University of Toronto in Canada West (Ontario), who **1**st **coined the word "prehistoric"**.

1851: Mathematician, astronomer, natural scientist, and educator William Brydone Jack (1817-1886) of Trailflatt, Scotland, was a professor at the University of New Brunswick (UNB) in Fredericton, New Brunswick, from 1840 to 1885 and president from 1861 to 1885. Now named the Brydone Jack Observatory, the **1**st **and oldest astronomical observatory still standing in Canada** was built by William on this campus in 1851 where the editorial offices of the literary magazine, *The Fiddlehead*, are also housed. This was the **1**st **university observatory in Canada**, which is now a museum. William delivered the **1**st **public lectures in astronomy in Canada** this same year at Fredericton. Thanks to his work at this observatory, Fredericton became the **1**st **location in Canada to have its longitude determined accurately**.

1852: Regular rail service from Montreal, Canada East (Quebec), via Caughnawaga, Canada East, opposite Lachine, Canada East, to the international boundary near the village of Hemmingford, Canada East, and on to Plattsburg, New York, USA, was inaugurated on September 20th by the Montreal and New York Railroad. This railroad was newly formed by the amalgamation of the Montreal and Lachine Railroad with the Lake St. Louis and Province Railway. It initially conveyed its passengers across the St. Lawrence River by boats. However, a few months later, the car ferry steamboat *Iroquois*, capable of carrying a locomotive and three cars, commenced running between Lachine and Caughnawaga. It was the **1st car ferry to operate in Canada**.

1852: The Inn, St. Andrews' first hotel, made St. Andrews, New Brunswick, **Canada's 1st seaside resort town**. It was home to the manager of the New Brunswick & Canada Railway but was later purchased by the Canadian Pacific Railway.

William C. Heubner of Toronto, Canada West (Ontario), developed the **1st system of using photomechanical plate-making equipment in lithography in the world** in the plant of Stone Limited. It later was merged into the firm of Rolph-Clark-Stone, Limited. William developed a process of printing the design directly onto a lithographic plate. Unfortunately, he never patented his process of photolithography, but the process itself was very successful.

1853: Tacony, a trotter, was the **1st Canadian-bred world champion harness racing horse**. There exist numerous top breeders across our country today including Armbro Farms of Brampton, Ontario, and Gunnholme Vu Farm of Lloydminster, Alberta.

1854: An odometer is a device that measures distance driven by a vehicle on land. In 1854, Samuel McKeen of Nova Scotia attached an odometer he designed to the side of a carriage. It measured the miles with the turning of the wheels and was the **1ˢᵗ version of the odometer in Canada**.

_1854:_ Three British army officers raced on the St. Lawrence River from Montreal to Quebec City, both in Canada East (Quebec), this year, the **1ˢᵗ recorded ice skating race in Canada**. This new sport soon became a popular winter event.

_1854:_ Royal Navy officer and explorer Robert McClure (1807-1873) of Wexford, Ireland, was a veteran of the search expedition for English explorer Sir John Franklin (1786-1847) of Spilsby, Lincolnshire, England, in 1848. From 1850 to 1854, Robert navigated an Arctic waterway linking the Atlantic and Pacific Oceans. In so doing, he completed the **1ˢᵗ crossing of the Northwest Passage from west to east**.

_1855:_ Linking Canada and the USA, the Niagara Suspension Bridge opened on March 8ᵗʰ. The first train crossed the bridge the following day. It was constructed by engineer John Augustus Roebling, born Johann August Röbling (1806-1869) of Mühlhausen, German Kingdom of Prussia, and was the **1ˢᵗ wire cable suspension bridge in the world to carry trains**.

_1855:_ Over the entire prairie region of Canada, an area in excess of 1 761 191.9 km² _(680,000 mi²)_, Father Albert Lacombe (1827-1916) of Saint-Sulpice, Canada East (Quebec), maintained control over the **largest Roman Catholic parish in the world**.

_1855:_ The **1ˢᵗ _Reciprocity Treaty_ between Canada and the United States** took effect on May 16, 1855. It permitted

American fishermen to fish within a 4.8-km *(3-mi.)* limit of Canada, to land anywhere to salt their fish, and to sail freely in the St. Lawrence River. The United States, in return, agreed to admit a wide range of Canadian products duty free, or tax free, into their country.

1855: A rowing crew from Saint John, New Brunswick, defeated an American crew at Boston, Massachusetts, USA, winning the 9.7-km *(6-mi.)* race and $600 in *Neptune.* This was the 1ˢᵗ **international rowing competition for Canadians**. The same crew brought home $2,000 in September by defeating another Boston crew over a 24.1-km *(15-mi.)* race.

1855: Between 1855 and 1859, Canada issued stamps showing both local currency and pound sterling values. These were the 1ˢᵗ **stamps in the world with values expressed in two currencies**.

1856: Centuries ago, long before European contact, the old Indian game of baggataway was played as a ritual honouring fallen warriors or the sick. A single match would be played by hundreds of ceremoniously-dressed participants on a field with few boundaries. After the turn of the century, its rules were adjusted to make the game playable on a strictly recreational basis evolving into the current game of lacrosse. For many years, Indians from nearby Caughnawaga, Canada East (Quebec), competed in sporadic, informal matches. Then, this year in Montreal, Canada East, a group of sports enthusiasts founded the Montreal Lacrosse Club, the 1ˢᵗ **lacrosse club in the world**.

1856: Elkanah Billings (1820-1876) of Bytown (Ottawa), Canada West (Ontario), came from a socially prominent family. He studied in Ottawa and Potsdam, New York, USA, before attending the Law Society of Upper Canada. After being called to the Bar in 1844, he practised law in Ottawa and Renfrew, Canada West, for eight years. His intense interest in fossils led him in 1852 to abandon law for three years and become the editor of the *Ottawa Citizen* writing a series of scientific articles with a concentration on geology and palaeontology, something that had interested him for many years. His first scientific paper on fossils at Trenton, Canada West, in 1854 won him first prize in an essay competition at the Universal Exposition in Paris, France. Sir William Edmond Logan (1798-1875) of Montreal, Canada East (Quebec), took note of Elkanah's work and later secured increased funding for the Geological Survey of Canada which also noticed his accomplishments. It particularly observed Elkanah's launching of *The Canadian Naturalist and Geologist* in 1856, a new monthly periodical. William used this new funding to hire additional staff including Elkanah who became **Canada's 1st palaeontologist**. His first challenge was to identify and arrange a massive backlog of fossils that the Geological Survey had collected over a period of 20 years. Elkanah published descriptions of some 526 new species of fossils by 1863 aptly demonstrating his value to our country in his new career.

Limestone bedrock meets the granite of the Canadian Shield at Grass River Provincial Park in Manitoba. This designated wilderness area has over 150 lakes and plenty of woodland caribou. It also happens to contain the **world's most southerly evidence of permafrost**.

_1857_: The **1ˢᵗ province to provide education for the deaf and the speech-impaired** was Nova Scotia.

_1858_: Henry Ruttan (1792-1871) of Adolphustown, Canada West (Ontario), was a sheriff in Cobourg, Canada West. He became fed up with sweating to death in the stifling heat of railway passenger cars left sitting on a railroad siding in the hot sun. So, Henry invented the **1ˢᵗ air conditioned passenger vehicle in the world**. Unlike today's more sophisticated air conditioning systems, Henry simply directed a flow of air from a ventilating cap on the roof over a shallow, cold water tank.

_1858_: Something very strange happened during the building of the Caribou Trail in British Columbia this year! Frank William Laumeister (1826-1891) decided that it was well worth paying $6,000 to purchase 28 camels on the assumption that a mule could only carry 136.1 kg _(300 lb.)_ while camels could handle 453.6 kg _(1,000 lb)_ each. The problem was that the camels, the **1ˢᵗ and only herd of camels in Canada**, stank so badly that even the mules belonging to "Dirty Harry" Strousse panicked at the first whiff of these strange creatures. Undeterred, even when his camels had trouble crossing the rocky terrain, Frank logically fitted them all with leather shoes! Actually, Frank kept his camels for several years although some escaped and who knows what became of them all. The last camel-sighting in British Columbia occurred in 1925.

_1859_: A tour this year by an English cricket team which played matches in Montreal, Canada East (Quebec), and Hamilton, Canada West (Ontario), was the **1ˢᵗ time that a team from another continent visited Canada for sports competition of any kind**.

<u>1859</u>: The 1ˢᵗ **knitting factory in Canada with powered knitting machines** was a mill in Ancaster, Canada West (Ontario).

<u>1859</u>: Living in Sarnia, Canada West (Ontario), Amelia Frances Howard-Gibbon (1826-1874) of Littlehampton, Sussex, England, became an historic artist with her drawings sketched in the children's book *An Illustrated Comic Alphabet*, the 1ˢᵗ **Canadian picture book ever published**. Printed in 1859, it finally was published in 1966 and is currently in the Osborne Collection of Early Children's Books in the College Street Branch of the Toronto Public Library in Ontario. It is the **oldest known picture book by a Canadian artist**. The Amelia Frances Howard-Gibbon Medal, an award in her commemoration, is given annually to encourage the publication of well-illustrated children's books in Canada. The Canadian Association of Children's Librarians has presented this award every year since 1971 to the artist who best illustrated a book published the previous year.

Eskimo ice cream is a rare delicacy often offered to a visiting tribe. It is made from combining ground up meat, reindeer tallow, blueberries, and chunks of whitefish. The tallow is melted and while still warm, mixed with the other ingredients by hand in the snow until it is frozen. Meat is added until it is impossible to stir the concoction any more. Eskimo ice cream tastes particularly great served with meat and bread and is thoroughly enjoyed by the Inuit.

_1860:_ The Hamilton Works in Hamilton, Canada West (Ontario), paid 7¢ a kg *(16¢ a lb.)* for steel imported from England to build a boiler weighing 4697.4 kg *(10,356 lb.)*, without the copper tubes, for the 0-6-0 *Scotia*. This was a new engine built for the Great Western Railway of Canada. It was the **1ˢᵗ engine in North America to have a boiler made entirely of steel**.

_1860:_ Sir Kazimierz (Casimir) Stanislaus Gzowski (1813-1898) of St. Petersburg, Russia, and Thomas C. Patteson of England petitioned Queen Victoria (1819-1901) of London, England, through the Toronto Turf Club to grant a plate for a horse race in Canada West (Ontario). Casimir was president of the club. Her Majesty granted the petition in 1860 and offered "a plate to the value of Fifty Guineas" as an annual prize. The **1ˢᵗ Queen's Plate in Canada** was run at the Carleton Racetrack in Toronto, on June 27, 1860, when 4,000 fans cheered the flashy thoroughbred, *Don Juan*, owned by Edward Meade Bagot (1822-1886) of Rockforest, County Clare, Ireland, to a triumphant finish making *Don Juan* the **1ˢᵗ ever winner of the Queen's Plate**. This is **North America's oldest continuously held turf event**. It is now held in late June on a 2-km *(1.2-mi.)* track at the 31.6-hectare *(78-acre)* Woodbine Race Track in Toronto—the **largest raceway in North America**. King George VI (1895-1952) of Norfolk, England, with his queen consort Elizabeth I (1900-2002) of London, England, was the **1ˢᵗ reining monarch to attend the Queen's Plate**, at Woodbine Race Track in 1939. Queen Elizabeth II (b. 1926) of London, England, and Prince Philip (b. 1921) of Corfu, Greece, attended the 100ᵗʰ running in 1959. This annual event remains among the most popular horse races on the continent. The stables of successful distiller and politician, Joseph Emm Seagram

(1841-1919) of Fisher Mills, Canada West, **founder of the Canadian Racing Association** and president of the Ontario Jockey Club, owned or bred an unprecedented 15 Queen's Plate winners.

_1860:_ Theodore August Heintzman (1817-1899) of Berlin (Kitchener), Canada West (Ontario), moved first to New York City, New York, USA in 1849, then to Buffalo, New York, and finally to Toronto, Canada West, in 1859. There, he crafted the **1ˢᵗ Heintzman pianos in the world** in 1860 which soon were sold across Canada and around the world.

> The Destroying Angel _(Amanita virosa)_ is a mushroom that is so poisonous that it should not even be touched. It causes death usually within several hours for 90% of those who eat one. It is considered the **deadliest plant in Canada**.

_1860:_ **Niagara Falls was illuminated for the 1ˢᵗ time** the evening before the famous tightrope walker Jean-François Gravelet (1824-1897) of St. Omar, France, known professionally as "The Great Blondin", walked crossed the Niagara Gorge. He came to entertain a very special visitor, Prince Edward Albert (1841-1910) of London, England, Prince of Wales (1841-1910). Today, more than 24 multi-coloured searchlights, each nearly 1 m _(3.3 ft.)_ in diameter, illuminate the falls every night throughout the tourist season. These **high-powered electric lights were turned on for the 1ˢᵗ time** on May 25, 1925. Seasonal lights also bathe the surrounding buildings and park areas from November through February during the Niagara Falls Festival of Lights.

One of the lookout structures, the Skylon Tower, even becomes the **world's largest Christmas tree** when lights are strung from top to bottom every Christmas.

1861: Richard Mott Wanzer (1818-1900) of Ithaca, New York, USA, moved to Hamilton, Canada West (Ontario), and became founder in 1860-1861 of the R.M. Wanzer & Co. Sewing Machine Company which manufactured the **1st sewing machine made in Canada**. His plant attained a production level of 1,000 sewing machines per week until financial difficulties forced it into bankruptcy.

1862: Greenbacks are banknotes printed in a special, permanent green ink which foils photographic forgers. The most commonly known greenbacks are those American bills printed by the U.S. Treasury. Well, Americans can thank American-born Canadian geologist and chemistry professor Thomas Sterry Hunt (1826-1892) of Norwich, Connecticut, USA, for making their bills possible. While working at the Geological Survey of Canada and teaching at Laval University and McGill University in Montreal, Canada East (Quebec), he invented this special ink used to print the **1st greenbacks ever printed in the world**, the first of which were distributed in 1862 in Canada, not in the United States. At that time, the pigment was known as the Canada Banknote Printing Tint.

1862: **Passports were required for the 1st time to enter the USA from British North America**, on December 17th.

1862: The police in Horton, Nova Scotia, transmitted to the Halifax, Nova Scotia police the **1st telegram sent to a police department in Canada warning of criminals headed their way**. The notice warned the police that two horse thieves were heading to Halifax and sure enough, the crooks were arrested the moment they arrived there. This was the **1ˢᵗ known case in Canada of using a telegram to combat crime**.

_1862:_ Mount Allison University in New Brunswick was the **1ˢᵗ university in Canada to admit women as students**.

_1863:_ The jerker rod system was invented in the Oil Springs, Canada West (Ontario) district by John Henry Fairbank (1831-1914) of Rouses Point, New York, USA, one of the founders of Petrolia, Canada West, and a pioneer in the Canadian oil industry. A single source of steam powers one pumping engine which oscillates a system of linked poles carrying the power to as many as 200 widely separated oil wells. Once the oil is pumped from the ground, it has to be collected. The **1ˢᵗ oil pipeline in North America** was built from Petrolia to Sarnia, Canada West. You can still see the jerker rod system operating in the Oil Springs district today.

_1863:_ Early medical doctors in Canada were generalists with even medicine and surgery coming under one discipline. The formation of medical specialization was very gradual. But in 1863, Dr. Abner M. Rosebrugh of Toronto, Canada West (Ontario), became the **1ˢᵗ Canadian medical doctor to specialize in eye and ear diseases**. Dr. Rosebrugh completed postgraduate work in New York City, New York, USA, and London, England, then opened an eye and ear infirmary in Toronto. In 1864, he invented the **1ˢᵗ ophthalmoscope in the world** which he used to photograph the fundus, the part of the eyeball opposite the pupil. Today, more than fifty per cent of Canadian physicians are engaged in a wide range of medical specializations.

1863: The branch of zoology which deals with insects is entomology. Henry Holmes Croft (1820-1888) of London, England, was a professor of chemistry at King's College, University of Toronto, in Canada West (Ontario). In 1863, he established and became the first president of the **1st Entomological Society of Canada**, one of the largest and oldest professional societies in Canada. James Fletcher (1852-1908) of Rochester, Kent, England, became the **1st Dominion Entomologist** in 1884.

1864: Although individuals from many countries emigrated to Canada over the centuries, it was in this year when the **1st group of Polish immigrants settled in Canada**. Most of them were farmers who settled on land in Renfrew County, Canada West (Ontario), between and west of Round Lake and Golden Lake. They named their settlement Wilno after a city of the same name in their native country.

1864: Doctors in Toronto, Canada West (Ontario), developed the **1st retinal photography in the world** by connecting an ophthalmoscope to a camera to photograph the retina of a cat, a first step in photographing the inside of the living human eye. Retinal photography is a technique essential worldwide today in evaluating and treating patients with eye diseases.

The Northern Red-bellied Snake *(Storeria occipitomaculata occipitomaculata)* seldom exceeds 30.5 cm *(12 in.)* in length. It feeds primarily on slugs, earthworms, and beetle larvae. Living from Saskatchewan to the Maritimes, it is the **smallest native species of snake in Canada**.

1864: Coldwater, Canada West (Ontario), was once part of an Ojibwa reserve, site of the **1ˢᵗ Indian log school in Canada**, on which the current Coldwater Memorial Library is located. Built in 1833, the Coldwater River grist mill constructed for the Indians still operates. Coldwater Canadiana, an historical society, operates an arts and crafts and antique shop in a cosy log cabin homestead built in 1864 by Archibald Woodrow, a Scottish immigrant settler. And there is a monument commemorating Coldwater native George Gray (1865-1933) who was the **1ˢᵗ athlete in the world never defeated in 17 years of shot put competition in Canada, the United States, England, and Ireland**. During this time, he won 188 medals and trophies, all firsts, and held 20 world records in track and field events.

1865: Five-pin bowling was not invented by Canadian Thomas F. Ryan (1872-1961) until 1909. But ten-pin bowling was very popular during the Cariboo Gold Rush. This year, Major William Downie (1819-1894) played in the **most expensive bowling match in Canada**. The reason for the expense was that he used imported bottles of champagne for bowling pins!

1866: One valuable source of food at this time was the extremely common passenger pigeon (*Ectopistes migratorius*) which is estimated to have numbered between five and nine billion and comprised one-quarter of the entire bird population of North America. Unfortunately, we ate too many of them as they now are extinct! However, Major W.R. King viewed the **largest flock of birds in the world to have ever been recorded**, at Mississauga, Canada West (Ontario), this year. The major reported that one primary flock took fourteen hours to pass overhead and that smaller flocks of younger or weaker birds followed for several days thereafter. Calculations totalled some 3,717,120,000 pigeons in this flock!

Estevan, Saskatchewan, is considered the sunshine capital of Canada. It enjoys an average of 2,500 hours annually, the **greatest number of hours of sunshine per year in Canada**. Adding to this record is a second one for the **highest annual number of hours per year in Canada with clear skies**. Estevan averages 2,979 hours of clear sky each year with clear skies defined as between zero and two-tenths sky cover. Regina, Saskatchewan, enjoys an average of 2,365 hours of sunshine each year making it the **sunniest of Canada's capital cities**.

1866: Alexander Buntin (1822-1893) of Renton, Scotland, started a wholesale paper and stationary business in Hamilton, Canada West (Ontario), in 1848. He was joined soon thereafter by his brother, James Buntin (d. 1861). Alexander later moved to Montreal, Canada East (Quebec), to establish a similar business while James expanded the Hamilton firm to Toronto, Canada West. After James died, his nephew, David Gillies and his sons joined the firm, then known as Buntin, Gillies & Co. Not only was this a highly successful business but it also was responsible for the **1st paper bag created and produced in Canada**. The thriving business was later purchased by C.W. Graham (d. 1936) until his death after which N.E. Wainwright took over in 1939 followed by the Howard Smith Organization in 1941. Butin, Gillies & Co. certainly played an instrumental role in the development of Canada's pulp and paper industry.

1867: A federal parliament was patterned after the British system, being comprised of the British Monarch, represented by a Governor General, being the head of government along with a legislature consisting of an upper house and a lower house. Approval by the British Government was followed by royal assent given by Queen Victoria (1819-1901) of London, England, on March 29, 1867, with the new *Act* being implemented on July 1st. This brought into reality the Dominion of Canada and the **1st Dominion Day in Canada** celebrating the birth of our new nation.

1867: Student George Eulas Foster (1847-1931) of Wakefield, Carleton County, New Brunswick, later lectured in Fredericton, New Brunswick. He established at the University of New Brunswick the **1st student newspaper in Canada** called the *University Monthly,* although it only survived for one year. However, it was renamed *The Brunswickan* in 1882 and remains the official student publication at UNB to this day. The **oldest continually published student college newspaper in Canada** is the *Dalhousie University Gazette.* Founded in 1869, it provides four pages of news for five cents or an annual subscription rate of fifty cents.

1867: Sir John Alexander Macdonald (1815-1891) of Glasgow, Scotland, became the first president of the Ottawa Rowing Club, **Canada's oldest continuing rowing club**.

1867: The **1st real dining car on a railroad in North America** was a combination kitchen-diner-sleeper called the *President* used on the Great Western Railway. It preceded the restaurant car, the *Delmonico,* of the Chicago and Alton Railroad, by a year.

_1869:_ Mrs. Mary Taylor lived in Huron County, Ontario. On June 29th, she received the **1st patent in the world for a new method of manufacturing cheese from sour milk**.

A popular Indian game called **snow-snake** involves sliding a straight wooden rod with a weighted head resembling that of a snake over a field of snow. Players also may slide them down specially constructed runways. Snow-snakes range from 1.2 to 2.7 m _(4 to 9 ft.)_ in length, are made from maple, ash, oak, or hickory, and are highly polished to make them slide faster.

_1870s:_ Manitoba became a province of Canada in 1870. The railway extended from the Atlantic Ocean to Vancouver, British Columbia, by 1885. Winnipeg, Manitoba, soon became the immigration gateway to the Canadian west as the federal government strongly encouraged new immigrants to settle there. But before that time, settlers arrived from Europe by paddle boats along the Red River travelling by ship first to the east coast of the United States, then to the Midwest by train. From there, they boarded stern wheel paddle boats which sailed from North Dakota, USA, to Winnipeg. Today, these river boats still carry 120,000 travellers annually. They also became the **1st cruise ships in Canada to employ female captains**.

_1870:_ Fish had always had an impossible challenge from waterfalls and dams when instinctively swimming upstream each year to spawn. James Wyeth King of Shubenacadie,

Nova Scotia, solved the problem when he invented the **1st fish ladder in the world**. He patented it under the trade name King Fish Ladder. A collection of steps, or weirs, at a gradual slope enable fish to swim upstream either by jumping over the weirs or by passing through underwater openings known as orifices.

_1870:_ In the 1870s, baseball teams from Pittsburgh, Pennsylvania, USA; Columbus, Ohio, USA; Lynn, Massachusetts, USA; Rochester, New York, USA; and Manchester, England, joined with the London Tecumsehs and the Guelph Maple Leafs from Canada to form the **1st North American baseball minor league** known as the International Association. Quite by surprise, the league title in 1877 went to the London Tecumsehs, the **1st Canadian team to win the International Association championship**.

The Reverend E.J. Devine loved the railroad. He designed the **1st automatic electric signal for railways in the world**.

_1871:_ Opening in May, the Glasgow & Cape Breton Coal & Railway Company operated a 0.9-m _(3-ft.)_ gauge railway line using a Fox Walker 0-4-0 tank engine built in Bristol, England. This was the **1st steam worked narrow gauge railway in North America**. The Toronto and Nipissing Railway opened for traffic between Toronto and Uxbridge, both in Ontario, on July 12th. This was **North America's 1st public narrow gauge railway**. By 1884, this 1.1 m _(3'6")_ gauge line was converted to standard gauge. Advantages of a narrow gauge railway include being less costly to build as it is operated with smaller equipment, and being able to negotiate sharper curves.

1873: On December 2, 1873, after William Augustus Leggo (1830-1915) of Quebec City, Quebec, and Georges-Édouard Desbarats (1838-1893) of Montreal, Quebec, invented the half-tone graphic reproduction process, their newspaper, the *Daily Graphic* published the **1ˢᵗ dated American half-tone** and the **1ˢᵗ half-tone published in any daily newspaper**. Two years later, the weekly *Grip* was founded becoming the **1ˢᵗ paper in Canada to make its own engravings**. The *Grip* established another record in 1905 making the **1ˢᵗ 4-colour printing plates in Canada**. This revolutionised the printing of advertising and illustrations in consumer magazines forever.

1873: There is an actual community on the south shore of the St. Lawrence River, inland from Rivière-du-Loup, Quebec, by 59.5 km *(37 mi.)*, which bears the unusual name of Saint-Louis-du-Ha! Ha!, Quebec. Incorporated in 1873, its name originated both in honour of St. Louis and in memory of Louis Marquis, the first settler. The expression "ha ha" implies "dead end" or "one way." On the north shore, the Saguenay River has a tributary, Ha! Ha! River, with a bay, Ha! Ha! Bay. Sure enough, the city of Saint-Louis-du-Ha! Ha! holds the record as being the **1ˢᵗ and only place name in the world with an official designation that includes two exclamation marks**!

1874: Lawrence House in Maitland, Nova Scotia, was home to shipbuilder William Dawson Lawrence (1817-1886). This elaborate two-and-a-half storey, 19ᵗʰ-century frame home displays shipbuilding artifacts from the days when its original owner built the **largest full-rigged wooden**

ship ever launched in Canada on the Minas Basin just below his home. This three-masted vessel, known as the *W.D. Lawrence*, was 75 m *(246 ft.)* in length and weighed 2459 metric tonnes *(2,710.6 tons)*.

<u>1874</u>: John Hamilton of Fredericton, New Brunswick, a strong, versatile employee of the Fredericton Railway Company, developed the **1st railway flanger in the world for snow removal**. It was able to be raised or lowered by a lever in the cab. It consisted of a pair of iron blades attached to the locomotive pilot that rode close to the rails. This device became standard equipment on the old *Number 2* locomotive. But in later years, it was abandoned because of problems it had with stop signs when they were installed. However, it was patented first but under the name Miller Flanger after Henry Miller, the railway's branch engineer.

<u>1875</u>: Born in Wooden Mills, Scotland, Jennie Kidd Gowanlock (1841-1921) moved with her family to settle near Stratford, Ontario. She married a Toronto, Ontario, publisher, Edward Trout, in 1865 and decided to make medicine her career. Canadian medical schools were still refusing to admit female students so Jennie graduated in 1875 from the Woman's Medical College of Pennsylvania in the USA. She passed her Ontario College of Physicians and Surgeons registration examination that same year. Dr. Jennie Trout became the **1st Canadian woman ever licensed to practise as a doctor in Canada**. She operated a highly successful medical practice in Toronto. She then helped endow the Women's Medical College in association with Queen's University in Kingston, Ontario, in 1883 so that other young women also wishing to make medicine their career would not have to leave the country in order to complete their studies.

> Sir William Osler (1849-1919) of Bond Head, Ontario, was a professor of medicine at McGill University in Montreal, Quebec, in the late 1800s. Through his research there, he become the **1st in the world to identify that asthma is an inflammatory disease of the bronchia**.

_1875:_ Widowed at the age of 38, Elizabeth McMaster (1847-1903) of Toronto, Ontario, a mother of four children, was concerned with the care of sick youngsters. Through her incredible faith, $10 in coins to place an advertisement in a Toronto, Ontario newspaper, and help from a ladies' hospital committee, she rented an 11-room house on Avenue Street in Toronto's downtown on March 23rd. Food, furniture, money, equipment, and additional helpers soon appeared to help her establish the **1st Canadian hospital devoted exclusively to the care of sick children**. A badly-scalded three-year-old girl became the first patient in one of six cots in a rented space at Number 21 Avenue Street, the first Hospital for Sick Children. It is world-famous for its medical research, and is the **largest paediatric medical centre in North America**. It received worldwide acclaim for its standards of hospital practice and medical discoveries that have benefited children around the world. It is affiliated with the University of Toronto. It is also the world's second largest hospital-based paediatric research facility.

_1876:_ Fort Henry, on Point Frederick in Kingston, Ontario, was the sight of the Royal Military College of Canada, the **1st military college in Canada**. This new college, established on June 1st of this year, offers education in military tactics, fortifications, engineering, and science related to the military profession at a level far more intensive than was provided previously in Kingston; Toronto, Ontario; and Montreal and Quebec City in Quebec. Background on the fort and the college is provided through displays of weapons and regimental plate in the college museum. The Royal Military College of Canada attained university status in 1959 while Collège Militaire Royale/Royal Military College in Saint-Jean became the **1ˢᵗ institution in Canada to train French-speaking officer-cadets for the Canadian Armed Forces**.

The **most northern treeline in the world** is found in Kluane National Park. This park covers an area of 22 000 km² *(8,494.3 mi.²)* in the south-western corner of Yukon between north-eastern British Columbia and the edge of the Alaskan panhandle.

1878: What was 6.1 m *(20 ft.)* long, with one tentacle measuring 10.7 m *(35 ft.)*, for a total length of 16.8 m *(55 ft.)*, and weighed 2.2 metric tonnes *(2.4 tons)*? Hint? It ran aground in Thimble Tickle Bay, Newfoundland, on November 2ⁿᵈ of this year. It was the **world's largest known invertebrate ever recorded**. It was discovered, still alive on shore, by resident Stephen Sherring and two other fishermen. Give up? It was the world's largest octopus or Atlantic giant squid *(Architeuthis dux)*. The largest suckers on the ends of the tentacles of this cuddly specimen were 10.2 cm *(4 in.)* in diameter. It also had the **largest eye of any known animal–living or extinct**–measuring 50.1 cm *(20 in.)* across.

1880: The largest weighed 1.8 kg *(3 lb. 14 oz.)* while the smallest, a girl, weighed only 1.1 kg *(2 lb. 8 oz.).* They were two of the three girls and two boys born to Adam and Jeanette Murray in Little Egypt, Pictou County, Nova Scotia, on February 15th. Unfortunately, the lives of the **1ˢᵗ reported quintuplets born in Canada** ended in tragedy when three lived only one day and the remaining two died within two days.

1880: A position as a druggist's assistant as a youth was followed by studies in pharmacology for Alexander Dougall Blackader (1847-1932) of Montreal, Quebec and a position as professor of pharmacology and therapeutics at McGill University in Montreal. With his intense and devoted interest in paediatrics, he developed this year at the Montreal General Hospital, the **1ˢᵗ children's clinic in Canada**.

1880: Tracks were laid across the frozen St. Lawrence River between Longueuil and Montreal in Quebec each November and removed the following April during the 1880s. This was the **world's 1ˢᵗ and only disappearing railway**.

1880: The York-Sunbury Museum at Fredericton, New Brunswick, displays the stuffed remains of **Canada's largest frog**. It lived in the 1880s and weighed in at 19.1 kg *(42 lb.).* It was raised by its owner on a diet of whisky, bugs, and buttermilk. Unfortunately, it finally croaked when someone dynamited near its pond at Killarney Lake, New Brunswick. Incidentally, the Canadian Frog Jumping Championship is held each August at St. Pierre, Manitoba.

1881: The **1ˢᵗ multi-sport club in Canada**, the Montreal Amateur Athletic Association, was incorporated by an *Act* of Quebec Parliament in 1881. It was an amalgamation of the

Montreal Swimming Club, the Montreal Lacrosse Club, and the Montreal Bicycle Club.

1881: A rather strong, soft cheese was **1**st made at a Trappist monastery near the village of Oka, Quebec, in 1881. The famous and well-known **Oka cheese is uniquely Canadian**!

1881: A Toronto, Ontario, cabinetmaker made the **1**st **laminated piano and organ keyboards in the world**. In 1881, he began laminating cellulose nitrate or celluloid sheet onto the keyboards. Lawrence Redmond, a chemist from Petrolia, Ontario, had a pioneering role in the development of phenolformaldehyde polymers in 1909-1910 paving the way for compression-moulding presses.

1881: From 1878 to 1881, Lewis Skaife used the **oldest existing hockey stick in Canada**, now displayed at McGill University in Montreal, Quebec.

1882: The Canadian Wheelmen's Association was formed in St. Thomas, Ontario, in 1882. From the sport of cycling comes the **oldest continuing sports governing body in Canada**. The Association divides cyclists into three categories: Class A—strict amateurs; Class B—employees of cycle firms; and, Class C—true professionals, cycling as a livelihood. This Association became the **1**st **Canadian sports governing body to control both amateur and professional divisions of a sport**.

1882: The Canadian co-founder of the Christian and Missionary Alliance Church, Albert Benjamin Simpson (1843-1919) of Cavendish, Prince Edward Island, worked with evangelist Dwight L. Moody (1837-1899) (Moody Bible

Institute, Chicago, Illinois, USA, 1887) to establish the **1ˢᵗ two Bible schools in North America** as part of a strong involvement in Christian education by the Evangelical Protestant churches in Canada. The **1ˢᵗ permanent Canadian Bible school** was established in 1894 as the Bible Training School, known later as the Ontario Bible College. Bible schools, institutes, and colleges prepare students for Christian ministries through biblical and practical training.

1883: With power to the plant supplied by two Corlis engines, it was on April 6ᵗʰ of this year when the new weave shed at the Canada Cotton Mill in Cornwall, Ontario, became the **1ˢᵗ plant in Canada to use electrical lighting**. This enabled the plant to operate 24 hours a day and thereby increase its output dramatically.

> Bedford Basin in Halifax, Nova Scotia, covers an area of 15.5 km² *(6 mi.²)*. It is the **largest deep water harbour in the world**. In fact, it is large enough to hold the entire combined navies of all the countries in the world!

1883: Ada Marean was a teacher in Toronto, Ontario. She taught a class of 80 children and had seven teachers-in-training assisting her. In the Louisa Street School this year, she opened the **1ˢᵗ kindergarten in Canada established as part of a public school system**. In 1885, Ontario became the **1ˢᵗ jurisdiction in North America to authorize kindergarten for all of its elementary schools**.

1883: When two lacrosse teams of Caughnawagas and Montreal Lacrosse Club players combined with six Toronto

Lacrosse Club players for the 1883 tour, their bright blue uniforms included a special crest. They were known as the "Canadian Gentlemen" and they wore a white maple leaf crest encasing the letter "C" emblazoned on their jerseys. This was the **1st time in history that a maple leaf was used in association with Canadian sport**. Dr. William George Beers (1843-1900) of Montreal, Quebec, led the tour of Great Britain over a period of three months.

1883: In Newark, New Jersey, USA, Joe Laing of Montreal, Quebec, became the **1st Canadian to win the U.S. Single Sculls Championship**.

1883: Founded in 1883, the Royal Canadian Regiment was the **1st regular infantry regiment in Canada**. More than 700 exhibits of memorabilia displayed in Wolseley Hall, Canadian Forces Base London, Ontario, describe the history of the regiment from its role in the North West Rebellion of 1885 to recent peacekeeping assignments around the world.

1883: The Niagara Gorge of the Niagara River below Niagara Falls, Ontario, was the construction site of the **1st cantilever bridge in North America**. The bridge is 150 m *(164 yd.)* long. Cantilever bridges often have only two towers that support the span between them. It was also the longest cantilever bridge in the world until the Firth of Forth bridge was opened in Scotland. Canada regained this title in 1917 with the opening of the Quebec Bridge (Pont de Québec) across the St. Lawrence River connecting Quebec City, Quebec, with Lévis, Quebec.

1884: Most electricity was generated initially by wood- or coal-burning steam engines providing relatively inexpensive electric power. The University of Ottawa and Parliament

Buildings in Ottawa, Ontario, were lighted electrically in 1884 with generators powered by steam engines. Then, in 1885, the City of Ottawa became the **1ˢᵗ city in the world to have all its streets lit by electricity**. Small hydroelectric plants were opened near factories in Ottawa, Peterborough, and Georgetown, all in Ontario, in the late 1880s. A plant built in Georgetown in 1888 was the **1ˢᵗ plant in the world to run on hydroelectric power**. But the greatest change came with the development of the huge power potential of Niagara Falls in 1903.

1885: Agronomist and prairie agriculturalist Angus Mackay (1841-1931) moved from his native Pickering, Ontario, to farm in Saskatchewan in the early 1880s, an area now known as Indian Head, Saskatchewan. Drought had always been a major problem to prairie farmers. But Angus discovered that cultivating land and leaving it fallow for a year allows it to store moisture lost in normal crop cultivation and to yield a good crop the following year. Thus, Angus became the **1ˢᵗ man in the world to introduce "summer fallow"**. In 1888, he was appointed to create the first Dominion Experimental Farm in the Canadian west.

1885: A special Canadian Pacific Railway train arrived at Pacific Tidewater in Port Moody, British Columbia, on November 8ᵗʰ. It was the **1ˢᵗ railway ever to travel across Canada from coast to coast**. Construction of the railroad required 12,000 men, 5,000 horses, and 300 dog sled teams.

1886: Businessman and ornithologist Thomas McIlwraith (1824-1903) of Newton upon Ayr, Scotland, published several papers on birds in Canada West. He was credited with instructing wildlife artist Major Allan Brooks (1869-1946) of Etawa, India, in the proper preparation of bird skins. He was best known for his 1886 treatise on Ontario birds, the **1ˢᵗ major annotated provincial bird book in Canada**. Thomas also was one of 25 founders of the prestigious American Ornithologists' Union and served on its council. His memory has been honoured by the McIlwraith Field Naturalists of London, Ontario.

1887: On November 2ⁿᵈ, the Canada Atlantic Railway began using the **1ˢᵗ railway passenger cars in Canada fitted with electric lights**. On November 10ᵗʰ, it began eliminating the danger of fire from stoves by **heating railway passenger cars for the 1ˢᵗ time in Canada using steam from the locomotive**. The railway equipped its entire passenger fleet with this new heating system by October 1891. In so doing, it became the **1ˢᵗ railway in Canada to use steam exclusively to heat all its passenger cars**.

1887: The city of Sault Ste. Marie, Ontario, was incorporated this year. Its coat of arms is "Ojibwa Kitche Gumeeng Odena" meaning "Ojibway Town next to Big Body of Water". While most mottos for coats of arms traditionally are written in Latin, this is the **1ˢᵗ and only coat of arms in Canada to include an Indian saying**. In addition to these native words, it includes a British crown, a Canadian beaver, maple leaves, a lock-keeper, a native, a Canadian ship canal and lock, pine and hemlock trees, and a Canadian steamer.

1887: Lawyer, journalist, and politician Honoré Mercier (1840-1894) of Saint-Athanese, Quebec, was the premier of Quebec from January 27, 1887, to December 21, 1891. He invited his fellow premiers to Quebec City, Quebec, on October 20, 1887, to discuss their grievances with Ottawa, Ontario, in the **1ˢᵗ Interprovincial Premiers Conference**

in Canada. Other attendees included Edward Blake (1833-1912) of Adelaide Township, Ontario, Sir Oliver Mowat (1820-1903) of Kingston, Ontario, Arthur Sturgis Hardy (1837-1901) of Mount Pleasant, Ontario, and Sir George William Ross (1841-1914) of Nairn, Ontario. The only absentees were the premiers of British Columbia and Prince Edward Island, and Prime Minister Sir John Alexander Macdonald (1815-1891) of Glasgow, Scotland, who was invited but declined to attend. They adopted 21 resolutions for free trade with the USA, and other reforms.

1887: Approximately 2.9% of Canada is located in 42 national parks, national wildlife areas, and bird sanctuaries covering a total area of 291 693.4 km² *(112,623.2 mi.²)*. The **1ˢᵗ bird sanctuary in North America** was created in 1887 in an area of 1011.7 hectares *(2,500 acres)* set aside at Last Mountain Lake in Saskatchewan to protect breeding grounds for wild fowl. It is often frequented by multitudes of migrating sandhill cranes in addition to the near-extinct whooping crane. The park provides a wide range of camping and recreational facilities. It also has attracted some 108 species of birds, 50,000 of which were banded since 1990 alone. On average, it bands 3,400 birds of 76 species annually.

1888: Canada's Governor General Lord Stanley of Preston (1841-1908) of London, England, spoke on September 11, 1888, at the opening of the Toronto Industrial Exhibition, the forerunner of the Canadian National Exhibition (CNE). In so doing, he participated in the **1ˢᵗ known sound recording in Canada**. His speech was preserved on a wax cylinder in 1888 and re-recorded in 1935. The whereabouts of the original wax cylinder is unknown today. The voice of the Governor General can be heard over the background hum and foreground static referring to "this wonder of the age, the phonograph". His speech entitled, "A Message to the president of the United States of America", is the **oldest existing sound on record in the world**.

_1888:_ Perhaps Canada's best-known contribution to the world of photography was an invention by John R. Connon (1862-1931) of Elora, Ontario, who patented the **world's 1st panoramic camera**. Revolving on a tripod, this camera utilizes an ingenious system of automatic controls to advance the film at the proper speed as the lens takes in the changing scene over a continuous 360° circle, all on one exposure of film 0.8 m _(2.5 ft.)_ long. This system is much less expensive to use and more accurate than the old multiple exposure and splicing system. This remains a major advantage even today for photographing large groups or scenes.

Cap Tourmente provides protection for the most important resting and feeding area during fall migration for the Greater Snow Goose. It was the **1st Canadian wetland to be included in the list of Wetlands of International Importance**.

_1888:_ The **1st platinum in the world** was discovered in the nickel-copper ores of Ontario. By the end of WWI and the 1950s, Canada became the **world's major source of supply of platinum**.

_1891:_ **Canada's 1st college football game** was played on October 22nd in Toronto, Ontario, on the lawn of the University of Toronto (U of T) between that university and McGill University in Montreal, Quebec. The two teams endeavoured to play against each other annually thereafter.

In Canadian college football, McGill beat Queen's University in Kingston, Ontario, 3-2 in 1898 in the **1ˢᵗ Canadian intercollegiate football game played under the Canadian Intercollegiate Athletic Union (CIAU)**.

_1891:_ The magazine _Canada's Municipal World_ was founded in St. Thomas, Ontario, to promote effective municipal government. It is the **oldest continuously published monthly municipal magazine in the world**.

_1892:_ Inventor Thomas Ahearn (1855-1938) of Ottawa, Ontario, had already made streetcar travel comfortable in winter inventing his electric car-heating system. Equally concerned with streetcar safety, Thomas also invented the **1ˢᵗ electric sweeper in the world for removing snow from the streetcar tracks and switch points**.

_1892:_ Originally, tea leaves were sold solely in bulk and never in individual packages. This all changed when in 1892, Montreal, Quebec-born wholesale tea merchant Peter Charles Larkin (1856-1930) introduced the **1ˢᵗ individual packaging of tea bags in the world** through his Toronto, Ontario-based company, the Salada Tea Company, named after a Ceylon Tea Garden. Peter was known as the Tea King of America, until the family company was sold in 1957, as he was the **largest tea distributor in both North and South America**.

_1892:_ Thomas Ahearn (1855-1938) of Ottawa, Ontario, always took pleasure in surprising people with his inventions. He made history once again when on August 29ᵗʰ he hosted a gourmet dinner for fifty electrical engineers gathered at the Windsor Hotel in Ottawa to inspect his recently invented electrical heaters. Only after his guests had finished this sumptuous meal did he inform them that they had just eaten the **1ˢᵗ meal in the world cooked entirely by electricity**. Thus came to be what we still know today as the electric stove. The meal included "Saginaw Trout with Potato Croquettes and Sauce Tartare", and "Strawberry Puffs" for dessert.

1893: William Carrol of Hamilton, Ontario, opened his first grocery store on the corner of Emerald and Wilson Streets in Hamilton. He expanded to 6 stores by 1903 and eventually to a grocery chain empire of 114 stores. In so doing, William created the **1ˢᵗ chain of grocery stores in Canada**.

1893: The first Stanley Cup hockey game was played at the Victoria Rink in Montreal, Quebec, in 1893 where 5,000 spectators watched the Montreal Amateur Athletic Club defeat Ottawa, Ontario, 3 to 1. The dimensions of this rink were 56 m x 24 m *(183.7 ft. x 78.74 ft.)*. This size became the **1ˢᵗ standard for North American ice hockey rinks** for decades. Today, a regulation hockey rink in Canada should adhere as nearly as possible to the dimensions 61 m x 26 m *(200 ft. x 85 ft.)* with a corner radius of 8.5 m *(28 ft.)*. The end boards should be 3.4 m *(11 ft.)* from the goal line. There should be 19.3 m *(64 ft.)* between each goal line and the nearest blue line. The two blue lines should be 15 m *(50 ft.)* apart. All hockey rinks outside North America follow the specifications set out by the International Ice Hockey Federation which are slightly different to ours and are given in metric units.

1893: As is the case throughout Atlantic Canada, hearty fishermen are a common sight providing a vital service to our country. The plant in Blacks Harbour, New Brunswick, opened this year and operated by Connors Bros. Limited, is the **largest sardine** and **herring canning operation in the British Commonwealth**. It is also the **world's largest producer of canned sardines** marketing to well over forty countries. Early in 2000, the company continued its expansion purchasing the assets of the Stinson Seafood Company of Maine, USA, thereby adding the leading U.S. sardine brand, Beach Cliff, to its product line.

1894: Artist, artisan, art gallery owner, and politician John Craig (1804-1854) of Ireland moved to York, Ontario, early in 1928. He became the **1ˢᵗ artist of importance in stained glass in Canada**. Designing painted altar windows for the second of St. James' Church between 1831 and 1833 was his most notable commission.

1894: T.H. Estabrooks and M.R. Miles, wholesale general merchants in Saint John, New Brunswick, began importing black teas from India and Ceylon rather than the more common teas from China and Japan. In 1894, they first blended the **most popular tea in Canada**, Red Rose Tea. It also exported in quantity to the United States. They registered the Red Rose trademark officially on October 16, 1899. Brooke Bond Canada Limited acquired the company in 1932. Saint John today is known as "The Home of Red Rose".

1895: The bicycle and the automobile were responsible for much of the growth in rubber production. This year, Dunlop Canada Ltd. manufactured the **1ˢᵗ car tire made in Canada**.

1896: Lutie Desbrisay (1871-1948) was born in Charlottetown, Prince Edward Island, and trained at the Salvation Army Officers' Training College at Saint John, New Brunswick. She was commissioned to Amherst, Nova Scotia, and was the

1st woman colonel in the world in the Salvation Army. She gained more than 500 converts when she successfully organized mission work in Bermuda and later organized hospitals in six other Canadian cities.

_1896:_ Whether or not a goal had been scored in an ice hockey game was a prime source of contention in the early days because the goal consisted of nothing more than two vertical sticks. To resolve this problem, Niagara players from the Southern Ontario Hockey Association fastened fishing nets to the goal posts. This was the **1st hockey goal net in the world**. Then on December 30, 1899, the **1st use in the world of official ice hockey goal nets** was at Montreal, Quebec's Victoria Rink after which goal nets were adopted quickly across our country.

_1897:_ The Canadian film industry began in Manitoba in the fall of 1897 when a Brandon farmer, James Freer (1855-1933) of Bristol, England, made the **1st Canadian films**, depicting life on the prairie. Entitled _Ten Years in Manitoba_, it also was the **1st advertising film ever made**. The Canadian Pacific Railway (CPR) showed these films throughout the United Kingdom in 1898-1899 to promote immigration to Canada. After their incredible success, the federal government sponsored a second tour by James in 1902, and the CPR began financing directly the production of immigration films.

_1898:_ The _S.S. Moyie_ enjoyed a very colourful career with the Canadian Pacific Railway sailing on Kootenay Lake in British Columbia. She was launched in 1898 and by her retirement as a sailing vessel in 1957, she was the **last operating passenger sternwheeler in Canada**. She provided services as a passenger excursion vessel and at times supplied local and freight services plus tug and barge duties hauling a range of commodities. The *S.S. Moyie* is 49.3 x 9.2 x 1.6 metres *(161.7 x 30.1 x 5.1 ft.*) in size, was licensed to carry up to 250 passengers with freight or 400 passengers without freight, and could travel approximately 22.5 km/hr *(14 mph)*. The Kootenay Lake Historical Society purchased and restored her in their dedication to preserving and maintaining the elegance of this magnificent vessel. Today, the *S.S. Moyie* is a very special museum in Kaslo, BC, providing a unique means of promoting the area's local history. She is also the **oldest intact passenger sternwheeler in the world**.

1898: Approximately 56.3 km *(35 mi.)* from Hamilton, Ontario, the Cataract Power Company built a hydroelectric generating plan sending current to the city on August 25th for the first time. This new system of power generation was less expensive than the steam and thermal electricity generated in Toronto, Ontario. The power from Cataract was used for street lighting, the electrified streetcar system, and industrial plants. It was the **1st major electric power service for industry in Canada**.

1898: Residents of Donald, British Columbia, were furious when they learned that they were to be relocated 128.7 km *(80 mi.)* away to Windermere, British Columbia, while their church was heading off in the opposite direction, to Revelstoke, British Columbia. Led by Rufus Kimpton in defiance of this order, they dismantled every bit of their church and smuggled it by rail and ferry to their new home making it **Canada's 1st and only stolen church**. However, en route, an equally enterprising flock of Anglicans from Golden, British Columbia, stole the church's bell. So, today there exists in Windermere the church of St. Peter's the Stolen while Golden is home to St. Paul's of the Stolen Bell!

_1899:_ The single figure skate blade was subject to cracking or breaking from the impact of a hard shot. In Winnipeg, Manitoba, in 1899, the **1ˢᵗ "Tube" skates in the world** were developed and introduced. Considered a lighter and more durable skate, it was not accepted and widely used in the east until after 1901, the year the Winnipeg Victorias once again won the Stanley Cup. They defeated the Montreal Shamrocks from Quebec who had won in the two succeeding years, after which the eastern teams started wearing tube skates.

> Only a few thousand white and Inuit people make remote Labrador their permanent residence. Known as **liveyeres**, the word supposedly a derivation of the English "live here", these residents are usually English-speaking. In summer, tens of thousands of semi-settled fishermen, usually French-speaking, come to fish off Labrador's coast and are known as **habitants**.

_1899:_ The reason that wooden bridges are sometimes covered is to save the beams and planks from the effects of the weather. The inexpensive roofing and siding reduce the cost of maintenance and snow shovelling. An unprotected wooden bridge will only last 10 to 15 years, while a covered one will last from 70 to 80 years. The **longest covered bridge in the world** was completed on December 1, 1899, at Hartland, north-west of Fredericton, New Brunswick, originally as a toll bridge. Its seven spans extend 390.8 m _(1,282 ft.)_ over the Saint John River. The bridge was rebuilt in 1920. Covered bridges are often known as "kissing bridges". By the way, horses also prefer them over uncovered bridges.

_1900:_ College girls began to play hockey at McGill University in Montreal as early as 1894. Then in 1900, three teams from Montreal, Quebec City, and Trois-Rivières, all in Quebec, organized and competed. This was the **1ˢᵗ known hockey league in the world for women**. Unlike games a few years earlier, spectators were allowed to watch!

_1900:_ Until now, telephones required their own internal battery to operate. On April 13ᵗʰ, Ottawa, Ontario, became the **1ˢᵗ Canadian city to receive telephone service on a common battery system**. Power for the phones was provided, as it is today, from the telephone company with no need for batteries at home.

_1900:_ The **1ˢᵗ two ice hockey rules changes in Canada** occurred this year. A player was allowed to stop the puck with his hand, and the puck now was thrown down in a face-off instead of being placed between the players' hockey sticks.

_1900:_ Although the idea first originated in Montreal, Quebec, the **1ˢᵗ Canadian chapter of the Imperial Order Daughters of the Empire (IODE)** was established on February 1ˢᵗ at Fredericton, New Brunswick. Mrs. John Black became its first president, 37 women registered initially, and the chapter was named Governor Carleton. This was a women's patriotic and philanthropic organization. The group's first accomplishment was to raise $858.40 for the Patriotic War Fund in support of the Boer War in South Africa. Before long, over 700 chapters appeared in Bermuda, India, various other British Commonwealth countries, and the United States.

_1900:_ The firm of Pratte et Cie in Montreal, Quebec, began making pianos in 1889. One of its instruments won a Grand

Prix Award at the Paris World Exposition in France, in 1900. That same year, it produced the **1st Canadian player-piano**.

1901: On October 24th, Annie Edson Taylor (1838-1921) of Auburn, New York, USA, became the **1st person to go over the Canadian Niagara Falls and survive**. She accomplished this feat in a wooden barrel which would have reached a speed of 352.8 km/h *(219.2 mph)* at the time it reached the end of her free fall. There have been 16 known attempts to go over Niagara Falls in a barrel or some sort of contraption, of which 6 daredevils died and 10 survived.

1901: French-speaking Métis Antoine "Tony" Gingras (1875-1937) of St. Boniface, Manitoba, was an exceedingly agile hockey player. He was a top scorer playing right wing for the Winnipeg Victorias in Manitoba. When the Victorias went all the way to the national championship in 1901 against the Montreal Shamrocks in a best of three series, Tony became the **1st French Canadian hockey player ever to win the Stanley Cup**. After Tony retired from the sport, he became a hockey coach to minor league teams at l'Union Canadienne of St. Boniface and St. Boniface College and a hockey scout for the Montreal Canadiens.

1901: Pakenham, Ontario, is home to a unique stone bridge having a length of 81.7 m *(268 ft.)*, width of 7.6 m *(25 ft.)*, height of 6.7 m *(22 ft.)*, and piers 2.4 m *(8 ft.)* thick. Its abutments at each end are 5.5 m *(18 ft.)* and the largest stone is 2.7 m *(9 ft.)* long and 0.8 m *(2.5 ft.)* square. It was built by O'Toole & Keting of Ottawa, Ontario, and weighs 5 metric tons *(5.5 tons)*. This is the **1st and only 5-span stone bridge of its kind in North America**.

1901: Speed trials and tours were the form of early automobile racing in Canada. F.S. Evans set a record of 3 hrs, 20 min, driving an automobile the 60 km *(37.3 mi.)* between Toronto and Hamilton, both in Ontario, in 1900. The **1ˢᵗ official automobile race in Canada** took place in Winnipeg, Manitoba, in 1901, won by the driver of a 12-horsepower Ford.

1901: An electricity transmission line was built between Niagara Falls, Ontario, and Niagara Falls, New York, USA, this year. This enabled the beginning of the **1ˢᵗ electricity trade between Canada and the U.S.** Engineer and provincial cabinet minister Adam Beck (1857-1925) of Baden, Ontario, introduced a bill which was passed through the Ontario legislature on May 14, 1906, creating the Hydro Electric Power Commission of Ontario. It was known since July 1974 as Ontario Hydro and as Hydro One since April 2001. It enables the inexpensive production of electricity at Niagara Falls, Ontario. Acting as chairman for the remainder of his life, Adam had created the **1ˢᵗ nationalized electric utility in the world** which grew ultimately into the **largest publicly owned power authority in the world**. The first Ontario Hydro Electric Power Commission transmission line brought electricity to Berlin (now Kitchener), Ontario, on October 11, 1910. Adam and his assistant, Dr. Thomas H. Hogg (1884-1958) of Chippewa, Ontario, also introduced literally hundreds of important technological innovations to this industry. In 1921, Ontario opened Sir Adam Beck No. 1, the **world's largest power plant**.

1902: A special Grand Trunk Railway train travelled between Chicago, Illinois, USA, and Portland, Oregon, USA, for the American Association of General Passenger and

Ticket Agents on October 13th. En route, professor Ernest Rutherford (1871-1937) of Nelson, New Zealand, from McGill University set up a wireless telegraphy station between Toronto, Ontario, and Montreal, Quebec. It enabled him to give the **1st demonstration in the world of wireless communication between a station and a moving train**.

> **Nova Scotia's fungy** or fungee (pronounced fun-jee) is a deep-dish blueberry pie also known as blueberry grunt. Pockets of heated air are driven out of the gelatinous mass of the cooking blueberries giving a plopping sound or grunt.

1902: The Canadian Pacific Railway sponsored a series of films depicting Canadian life to show in Britain to promote immigration to Canada. The series, called *Living Canada*, was produced this year by the Bioscope Company of Canada, **Canada's 1st film production company**.

1902: A few permanent symphony orchestras were formed across the country before WWI in: Toronto, Ontario; Montreal, Quebec; Vancouver, British Columbia; Regina, Saskatchewan; Winnipeg, Manitoba; Edmonton, Alberta; Saskatoon, Saskatchewan; and Moose Jaw, Saskatchewan; along with amateur orchestras in other cities. None lasted all that long, creating a major problem for early Canadian composers. In 1902, 25 players including Léonidas Dumas, Joseph Talbot, and Raoul Vézina (1882-1954) of Quebec City, Quebec, formed the Quebec Symphony Orchestra (QSO)/Orchestre symphonique de Québec (OSQ). Joseph Vézina (1849-1924) of Quebec City became music director of this, the 1ˢᵗ **symphony orchestra in Canada still active today**. The group expanded over the years to some 40 players and changed its name to Société symphonique de Québec (SSQ). WWI completely disrupted the orchestra's activities. It was forced to cease giving any concerts between March 1918 and March 1919 because of the Spanish flu epidemic and a lack of funding. The orchestra bounced back, though, and has continued to delight music fans to this day. Its home is the Grand Théâtre de Québec in Montreal, where the décor is dominated by a 1080 m² *(12,000 ft.²)* mural by Jordi Bonet (1932-1979) of Genevieve, Quebec. The group has featured numerous world-renowned performing artists over the years. It also has won several major awards for its stunning performances.

1902: On May 18ᵗʰ, the **last recorded passenger pigeons in Canada** were a pair observed at Penetanguishene, Ontario. The last living specimen, named Martha, died in the Cincinnati Zoological Gardens in Cincinnati, Ohio, USA, on September 1, 1914.

1903: Militia engineering companies had existed ever since the War of 1812 with America. Yet engineering courses were instituted at Royal Military College for militia candidates only in 1884. In 1903, ex-cadet, Lieutenant Colonel Paul Weatherbe formed the 1ˢᵗ **Corps of Royal Canadian Engineers**.

1903: Electricity soon replaced acetylene for lighting but the 1ˢᵗ **oxy-acetylene torch in the world was invented** in 1903 by Thomas "Carbide" Willson (1860-1915) of Princeton, Ontario. It provided a temperature of 3 315.6 °C *(6,000° F)*, sufficient for welding and cutting steel very quickly and inexpensively.

1903: This year, Hydro-Québec placed in service a 50 kV line 135 km *(83.9 mi.)* from the Shawinigan, Quebec, powerhouse to Montreal, Quebec, the **1st long high-voltage transmission line in North America**.

1903: After completing production of *Living Canada*, a series of 35 films depicting Canadian life, the Bioscope Company of Canada produced *"Hiawatha," the Messiah of the Ojibway* in 1903, the **1st drama film made in Canada**. This production soon led to other railway companies with both federal and provincial governments sponsoring similar releases.

One of the greatest problems initially in processing photographic film was to do so while avoiding scratching the film. The problem was resolved by Gunter Schmidt of Toronto, Ontario, who invented the **1st system of using an air or water cushion for photographic film during processing**. His machinery soon became standard industrial and commercial film processing equipment around the world designed for processing 35mm and 75mm motion picture film. The 75mm format maintained a 1.33:1 aspect ratio but was only an experimental film size later replaced by the 70mm format used for instance in today's IMAX movies.

1904: The Royal Montreal Golf Club in Montreal, Quebec, hosted the **1st Canadian Open Golf Championship** this year. John H. Oke (b. 1880) of Northam, England, member of the Royal Ottawa Golf Club, was the winner with a thirty-six hole score of 156. The Canadian Open is the third oldest national golf championship in the world behind the British and the United States Opens. The Rivermead Cup was the trophy at the Canadian Open until 1936. It was replaced by the Seagram Gold Cup from 1936 to 1970, and the Peter Jackson Trophy after 1971.

1904: Having been granted the same rank and seniority in the Canadian Militia as he was in Britain, Sir Percy H.N. Lake, C.B., C.M.G. (1855-1940) became the **1st brigadier general in Canada** on March 2nd. He was promoted both in Britain and Canada on March 23, 1905, to major general, the **1st major general in Canada**. He was on loan to Canada as an Imperial officer and later appointed inspector general. His tour of duty with the Canadian Militia extended until November 1, 1910, after which he returned to England.

1904: Baritone and choirmaster Joseph Saucier (1869-1941) of Montreal, Quebec, first studied music with his renowned father, a pianist, organist, and teacher. He also studied under Montreal piano instructor, Dominique Ducharme (1840-1899) of Montreal, Quebec, performing publicly as a pianist at the age of 10. Eight years later, he pursued a singing career and began studying voice with Achille Fortier (1864-1939) of Saint-Clet, Quebec, and Paul Wiallard. It was not long before Joseph was singing with various choirs and performing as a soloist at Gesù and St. James Cathedral as well as with the Montreal Symphony Orchestra. He was the organist and choirmaster at St-Louis du Mile-End Church in Montreal by 1897. This was the same year he left Montreal to study voice with August-Jean Dubulle at the Conservatoire de Paris. Joseph sang successfully in concerts in London, England, and Paris, France, then returned to Canada in 1902. The following spring, he accepted the position as choirmaster at Immaculée-Conception Church. Two years later, he was the **1st French Canadian artist to make a recording in Canada**. Joseph served as president of the Académie de musique du Québec twice, in 1907-1908 and in 1911-1912. Then, he was choirmaster at St-Louis-de-France Church in Montreal from 1927 to 1936. His recordings include "O Canada", "Minuit Chretien", and Tchaikovsky's "Sérénade de Don Juan, Op. 38, No. 1".

_1904:_ Thomas "Carbide" Willson (1860-1915) of Princeton, Ontario, moved his family to a summer estate on 1.86 km² _(460 acres)_ at Meech Lake in the beautiful Gatineau Hills north of Ottawa, Ontario. He invented and patented the **world's 1st party line system**. He installed a telephone to keep in touch with business in the city.

_1904:_ The University of Toronto established the **1st Canadian department of astronomy** in 1904. Dr. Clarence Augustus Chant (1865-1956) of Richmond Hill, Ontario, was instrumental in 1935 in the U of T acquiring the David Dunlap Observatory. It is the site of the **largest optical telescope in Canada**. And in 1971, the university inaugurated the **1st Canadian telescope operating in the Southern Hemisphere**, at Las Campanas in Chile.

_1905:_ Until 1905, psychiatric patients were treated in asylums. That year, the Toronto General Hospital became the **1st hospital in North America to treat psychiatric patients in a special unit created specifically for that treatment**.

_1905:_ Each of the pillars that support the soaring arches of St. Mary's Church in Church Point, Nova Scotia, are 18.3 m _(60 ft.)_ high and 61 cm _(2 ft.)_ in diameter, cut from the woodlot of one of its parishioners in 1905. With three bronze bells in the 56.4-m *(185-ft.)* steeple weighing a total of 1696.4 kg *(3,740 lb.)* and seating capacity for 750 worshipers, St. Mary's is the **biggest and tallest wooden church in North America**. Equally noteworthy is its collection of stained glass. Some 40 metric tonnes *(44.1 tons)* of ballast rock have been placed at its base in order to maintain stability of the steeple in the strong winds of St. Mary's Bay.

Another Canadian inventor who worked his genius in the USA was George A. Long of Montreal, Quebec. He became an apprentice pattern-maker at the Pratt & Whitney plant in West Hartford, Connecticut, USA. Of his nearly 200 patented inventions, most of which contributed to the world's telephone industry, perhaps his most famous was that of the **1ˢᵗ workable pay telephone in the world**. He eventually became president of the Gray Telephone Company for whom he developed this unique new equipment.

1906: The mace of the Saskatchewan legislature in Regina, Saskatchewan, was inscribed with a unique engraving, Canada's motto, "From Sea to Sea". This was the **1ˢᵗ time Canada's motto was used officially**.

1906: On January 16ᵗʰ, Britain relinquished her military bases at Halifax, Nova Scotia, and Esquimalt, British Columbia, still the most important bases of the Royal Canadian Navy to this day. Control of the bases was transferred to Ottawa, Ontario, the **1ˢᵗ time Canada controlled its military bases**. However, actual control of Canada's military forces was not put into effect until the end of WWI.

_1906:_ Until now, the Grand Trunk Railway ran all its trains on the left side on double track sections. On July 22nd, it changed all its crossovers, switches, and semaphore signals in Ontario and Quebec, the **1st time that the Grand Trunk Railway changed from left to right hand running**.

_1906:_ The Diamond Flint/Dominion Glass Company in Montreal, Quebec, produced the **1st machine-made beer bottle in Canada** in 1906.

_1906:_ Two auto dealers in Winnipeg, Manitoba, McCulloch and Boswell, invented the **1st cooled engine in the world**. It was water-cooled in the summer and air-cooled in the winter. Unfortunately, this concept was so advanced for its time that their new car never made it to market.

_1907:_ Journalist and social activist Joséphine Dandurand (née Joséphine Marchand) (1862-1925) of St. John, New Brunswick, and Caroline Dessaulles Béique (née Caroline Dessaulles) were two of the founders of the **1st Fédération nationale Saint-Jean Baptiste in Canada** this year. The Fédération was created for francophone, Roman Catholic women providing pure milk, better maternal and child care, and improvements in the legal status of women living in Quebec. Joséphine fought for improved salaries for women teachers, for higher education for women, and for home economics schools.

_1907:_ Saint John, New Brunswick, was home to film mogul Louis Burt Mayer (1885-1957), who was born in Minsk, Belarus, but moved to Saint John with his family at the age of three. It was also home to distinguished actors Walter Pidgeon (1897-1984) of East Saint John, New Brunswick, and Donald Sutherland (b. 1934). In May of 1907, the New

Brunswick musicians at the Nickel Theatre became famous. Under the direction of Walter Golding (1877-1945) of Saint John, they were the **1ˢᵗ musicians** and **1ˢᵗ orchestra in North America to accompany silent moving pictures**.

_1907:_ Primarily a sailing and paddling club in the early years, the Regina Rowing Club formed in Saskatchewan, the **farthest inland rowing club in the world**.

> Giant herds of barren ground caribou comprised of up to 100,000 individuals move incredible distances from season to season in search of food. In the summer, they head for the high tundra of the Canadian Arctic in search of tough northern vegetation such as sedges and reindeer moss, a type of lichen. Each herd has its own calving ground, not used by any other herd. After bearing their young, they return south to the northern edge of the forest region in the autumn. These round trip treks cover a distance of up to 2253.1 km _(1,400 mi.)_, the **longest migrations of any land mammal in the world**. These caribou also are the **only North American deer in which both sexes grow antlers**.

_1908:_ A group of women students established the **1ˢᵗ Society of Independent Spinsters in Canada** at the University of Alberta this year. They found that university life could be quite lonely so the purpose of this new organization was to give each other support.

_1908:_ Governor General Earl Grey (1851-1917) of London, England, anxious to cultivate the arts in Canada, encouraged

George Hedley Vicars Bulyea (1859-1928) of Gagetown, New Brunswick, the lieutenant governor of Alberta, to organize the **1ˢᵗ international music festival in North America** in Edmonton, Alberta. Two English-born musicians in Edmonton, Vernon Barford (1876-1963) of Berkshire, England, organist, choirmaster, and conductor, and Howard Stutchbury (1874-1957), baritone and choirmaster, were the chief organizers of the Alberta Musical Competition Festival. Two adjudicators from Winnipeg, Manitoba, joined some 2,000 supporters on May 5th, listening to thirty individual and group contestants compete in a performance of the combined choruses (about 200 singers) and 50 instrumentalists. The event became a highlight of the festival every year thereafter.

1908: Scandinavians and Inuit of Canada are believed to have raced harnessed dog teams, usually huskies, long before the **1ˢᵗ recorded formal sled dog race** which took place in 1908 at the All-America Sweepstakes.

1908: To help raise funds for Canadian Lung Association programmes to improve lung health, the **1ˢᵗ Canadian Christmas Seals** have been printed every year since 1908.

1908: Robert Samuel McLaughlin (1871-1971) of Enniskillen, Ontario, manufactured the **1ˢᵗ commercially built car in Canada** in Oshawa, Ontario, in 1908. The McLaughlin Motor Co. Ltd. held a 15-year contract to build McLaughlin bodies fitted with U.S. Buick engines—hence its name, the *McLaughlin-Buick.* They built 1,098 cars by 1914 when the company merged with Chevrolet Motor Co. of Canada to form General Motors of Canada Limited (GM Canada). Robert later became chairman of GM Canada and held the position until his death, shortly after his 100th birthday. Production of *McLaughlin-Buicks* continued until the 1920s.

1908: What do you get when you cross White, Wyandotte, Leghorn, Rhode Island Red, Cornish, and White Plymouth Rock chickens? Why, the Chantecler, or Chanticleer chicken of course. Its name derives from Chanticleer, the cock in the medieval *Reynard the Fox*! It was bred between 1908 and 1918 by Brother Wilfred of the Trappist monks at Oka, Quebec. This new breed of white poultry became the **1st all-Canadian chicken**!

1908: Until the 1960s, the greatest social concern in Canada was to opiates, particularly heroin, although prior to this century, the use of psychotropic drugs was not considered a serious social problem or criminal offence. This is surprising as more Canadians were dependent on opiates at the turn of the century than at any time before or since. In 1908, Canada became the **1st Western nation to prohibit, under criminal law, the importation, manufacture, and sale of opium**. At that time, little scientific knowledge was known about these drugs. Thus, this decision was inspired essentially by racial prejudice, particularly against Asians, and moralistic commitment.

1909: General Motors of Canada Limited in Oshawa, Ontario, invented the **1st hand-operated windshield wiper in the world**.

1909: In the *June Bug*, the third airplane built by the Aerial Experiment Association, Canadian John Alexander Douglas McCurdy (1886-1961) of Baddeck, Nova Scotia, **flew the 1st figure eight in history**, a major triumph in the early days of aviation.

1909: Lethbridge, Alberta, began in the 1870s as a coal mining town. It is known for the CPR railway bridge which spans the Oldman River valley and the Indian Battle Park there. This bridge extends over 1.6 km *(5,327.6 ft.)* and is 95.7 m *(314 ft.)* high. It is the **longest and highest trestle bridge in the world**. The Canadian federal government designated it a National Historic Site in 2005.

1909: On August 2, 1909, Frederick Walker (Casey) Baldwin (1882-1948) of Toronto, Ontario, became the **1st passenger to be carried by an airplane in Canada** when he joined John Alexander Douglas McCurdy (1886-1961) of Baddeck, Nova Scotia, who flew his airplane at Petawawa, Ontario. The same year, Dolly MacLeod flew some 4.8 km *(3 mi.)* aboard the *Silver Dart* at Baddeck Bridge with Casey becoming the **1st female in the world to fly in an airplane**.

1909: Joseph-Elzéar Bernier (1852-1934) of L'Islet, Quebec, was captain of the government steamship *Arctic* near Melville Island in the Northwest Territories. On July 1st, he placed a metal plaque at Parry Rock. This was the **1st time that Canada formally claimed sovereignty over the entire Arctic Archipelago**.

> Scottish merchants trading under the name of *The Northwest Company* engaged agents known as **Coureur de bois** to establish fur trading posts from Ottawa, Ontario, to the Rocky Mountains. This term also referred to those unlicensed traders who hunted through the forests for furs.

1909: At Scarborough Beach near Toronto, Ontario, the **1st flying exhibition in North America for paying spectators** took place.

1910: Private businesses had established electrical engineering generating plants in every province by 1890. The power grid was funded by the government in Ontario and privately in Quebec. Producing electricity was one thing, but then a method of distribution was necessary before it could be used. By necessity, the first customers to use electricity lived in or near the cities. Berlin (Kitchener), Ontario, was the **1ˢᵗ municipality in Canada to be connected to the provincial public power grid**.

1910: Shelton Brooks (1886-1975) was born in Amesburg, Ontario, of black and Indian parents. This accomplished pianist and performer **wrote Sophie Tucker's most famous songs**, "The Darktown Strutters' Ball" and "Some of These Days". Shelton's fame for writing songs and skits for vaudeville performers including Al Jolson (1886-1950) of Asa Yoelson, Seredžius, Lithuania; Sophie Tucker (1886-1966) of Tulchyn, Ukraine; and Nora Bayes (1880-1928) of Joliet, Illinois, USA, emerged in Chicago, Illinois; Detroit, Michigan; and New York City, New York, all in the USA.

Abitibi-Consolidated, Inc., a company now based in Montreal, Quebec, is the third largest producer of lumber in the world, second largest producer in the world of pulp (used to make newsprint), and the **largest newsprint manufacturer in the world**.

1910: The Detroit River Tunnel between Windsor, Ontario, and Detroit, Michigan, USA, was completed in 1910 using ten prefabricated elements 80 m *(262.5 ft.)* in length. The total length between portals was 2552.1 m *(8,373 ft.)* comprised of two steel tubes joined into a rectangular section with concrete. The navigation depth over the tunnel is 12.5 m *(41 ft.)*. This was the **1st immersed-tube tunnel in Canada** and until 1914, the largest such tunnel in the world.

1910: Under the sponsorship of the now extinct newspaper *Montreal Daily Witness*, the **1st model airplane contest held in Canada**, known as the Boys' Model Aeroplane Competition, took place on July 4, 1910, in Montreal, Quebec, in conjunction with a full-sized air show. Boys from all parts of Canada provided excellent workmanship in their models. Their designs, not surprisingly, were predominantly of Wright biplanes and Blériot monoplanes, although some were unique designs of these inventive young competitors. A carefully constructed Blériot XI replica brought the grand prize of $50 to J.H. Parkin of Toronto.

1911: Members of Parliament and Canadian Pacific Railway officials had been strong supporters of developing natural reserves in Canada since 1887, protecting these areas from "sale, settlement, or squatting." Similar action was taken in Eastern Canada beginning in 1904 with the establishment of the St. Lawrence Islands National Park of Canada. The Dominion Parks Branch was formed, the **1st distinct bureau of national parks in the world**, under the authority of the Department of the Interior in 1911. The *National Parks Act* was passed in 1930 providing the requisite legislative protection for national park lands. The objective of Parks Canada is to have at least one national park located in each of Canada's 39 natural regions. This achievement necessitates the creation of 14 additional national parks. The current national parks system encompasses approximately 291 693.4 km² *(112,623.2 mi.²)* but when finished will cover just over 3% of Canada.

1911: Most people would be surprised to learn that more than half of the prairie province of Saskatchewan is covered with forest. Within the total 355 000 km² *(137,066.3 mi²)* of the province's forest, **North American's largest white birch forest** is included in the 140 000 km² *(54,054.3 mi²)* considered commercially viable. Prince Albert, Saskatchewan, saw construction of the first sawmill in the province in 1877. The **largest sawmill in the British Commonwealth** opened for business in Big River, Saskatchewan, in 1911. Today, the mill can produce 1 million board feet of lumber a day.

1911: Lester Patrick (1883-1960) of Drummondville, Quebec, and Frank Patrick (1885-1960) of Ottawa, Ontario, constructed two covered skating arenas in Victoria and Vancouver, both in British Columbia and both with artificial ice, and formed the Pacific Coast Hockey Association in 1911. It also was known as The Patrick League and was responsible for introducing many innovations to pep up play and make hockey more interesting to spectators. Owners built higher ranks of seats to attract more fans who finally could identify individual players easily after the Patricks became the **1st in the world to put numbers on the hockey players' backs**. The offside rule proved rather boring, disallowing a player to skate ahead of his team-mate who had control of the puck. So, the Patricks divided the ice surface into three parts by painting the **1st two blue lines in hockey** and permitting forward passing in the centre zone between the blue lines. The Patrick League became the **1st to permit a goalie to leap, jump, or dive to stop the puck** and **introduced the assist to hockey scoring**.

1911: Pilot George Mestach (d. 1920) of Belgium was flying over Quebec City, Quebec, on September 1, 1911, when he dropped a number of messages from his Blériot monoplane addressed to various officials of the exhibition being held there between August 30th and September 5th. These were the **1st messages known to be dropped from an airplane in Canada** and were eagerly picked up by excited onlookers.

> As common as the bicycle throughout southern Canada, the dog sled or **komatik** is the usual mode of land transport in the North, apart from skidoos. This open Inuit sled, also spelled *ka(h)motik, kamutik, kumotik,* or *commetik,* is usually pulled by six or eight dogs.

<u>1912</u>: The Winnipeg Art Gallery (WAG) in Manitoba was established back in 1912, was the **1st civic art gallery in Canada**, and has become the largest art gallery in Western Canada. It moved into new premises in 1953, then into its own new building opened on September 25, 1971, by Her Royal Highness Princess Margaret, Countess of Snowdon (1930-2002) of Glamis Castle, Scotland. It contains 8 exhibition galleries, an auditorium, an elegant penthouse restaurant overlooking a rooftop sculpture garden, a library, a variety of meeting rooms, and The Gallery Shoppes. In October 1995, the WAG opened its new Studio Building to house its art classes. The WAG established itself as one of Canada's leading art museums and has a strong international reputation. The Gallery's collection contains over 20,000 works of art from 16th century Flemish tapestries to 20th century videos, extensive European works, and of particular interest, the **world's largest collection of contemporary Inuit art**. Since its inception, the Gallery has developed the **longest continuous association with Inuit art, relative to collection and research, of any other public art**

museum in the world. This group of contemporary, historical, and decorative art includes 6,700 sculptures, 2,500 prints, 1,100 drawings, and 20 textiles, all of which are being expanded upon regularly. In March 1998, the Gallery also became the **1ˢᵗ recipient of the annual Canada Council for the Arts' York Wilson Endowment Award**. It was established to enable an eligible Canadian art museum or public gallery to purchase an original artwork that will enhance its collection significantly. The WAG used its award funds, which can be worth up to $10,000, to purchase *Rotterdam Pioneers New Technologies for a Subterranean Eco-Suburb, and Environment with Clean Air, Clean Water, and Abundant Daily Sunshine* by Winnipeg artist Eleanor Bond.

1912: Initially, the Stanley Cup hockey game was always played in 30-minute halves. On March 12ᵗʰ, Quebec beat Moncton, New Brunswick, 9-3, a win which moved Quebec on its way to sweep the **1ˢᵗ Stanley Cup game played in three 20-minute periods**.

1912: On January 3ʳᵈ in Victoria, British Columbia, the New Westminster Royals defeated the Victoria Aristocrats 8-3 in a hockey game organized by Frank Patrick (1885-1960) of Ottawa, Ontario. This was the **1ˢᵗ Canadian hockey game played on artificial ice**.

1912: Swimmer George Ritchie Hodgson (1893-1983) of Montreal, Quebec, a member of the Canadian Sports Hall of Fame, received little formal training as a swimmer but practised in the summer at his family's cottage in the Laurentians and in winters at the Montreal Amateur Athletic Association pool. At the age of only 18, he defeated the world record holder, Sid Battersky of Britain, over the

1.6-km *(1-mi.)* distance representing Canada at the Festival of the Empire Games in 1911. He also set world records at the Stockholm Olympic Games in 1912 winning gold medals in the 400 m *(1,312.3 ft.)* freestyle and 1500 m *(4,921.3 ft.)* freestyle competitions becoming the **1ˢᵗ Canadian Olympic swimming champion**. Simultaneously, he was the **1ˢᵗ Canadian to win 2 Olympic gold medals**. George again represented Canada in the 1920 Olympic Games.

1913: George B. Dorey of Montreal, Quebec, was granted the **1ˢᵗ patent in the world for a rail car brake**. His invention in 1913 was only one of over 175 patents George held which deal exclusively with solving the problems of transporting and unloading bulk cargoes efficiently and inexpensively by freight car. He also received a U.S. patent for this rail car brake in 1941. Most of George's patents applied to railway car equipment, particularly ore hoppers.

1914: The armoured cruiser *HMS Good Hope* met her end off Coronel, Chile, on November 1ˢᵗ. The **1ˢᵗ casualties in the Royal Canadian Navy** were four midshipmen: Midshipman William Archibald Palmer RCN (20) of Ottawa, Ontario; Midshipman John V.W. Hatheway RCN (19) of Granville, Nova Scotia; Midshipman Malcolm Cann RCN (19) of Yarmouth, Nova Scotia; and Midshipman Arthur Wiltshire Silver RCN (20) of Halifax, Nova Scotia.

1914: The *Sunfish* was the **1ˢᵗ flying boat to be owned or flown in Canada**. It was purchased in 1914 from the American Curtiss Aeroplane & Motor Company, Ltd. by W.A. Dean of Toronto, Ontario. He obtained the services of Colonel Theodore C. Macaulay (1887-1965), an expert airman, to pilot the craft. Theodore was well known as an instructor and flyer. He flew the plane extensively from the waters of Lake Ontario throughout the vicinity of Toronto and its neighbouring cities. His most publicised achievement occurred on May 15th when he flew the well-known sports writer, Lewis (Lou) Edwin Marsh (1879-1936) of Campbellford, Ontario, who was then with the *Toronto World*, on a return flight from Toronto to Hamilton. Thus, Lou became the **1st passenger to be flown from one Canadian city to another.**

1914: Actress Marie Dressler (1869-1934) of Cobourg, Ontario, starred in the movie *Tillie's Punctured Romance* along with Charlie Chaplin (1899-1977) of London, England, Mabel Normand (1894-1930) of Boston, Massachusetts, USA, and Mack Swain (1876-1935) of Salt Lake City, Utah, USA. Shown first in New York City, New York, USA, on December 21st, the film was based on Marie's vaudeville act. It was directed by fellow Canadian Mack Sennett (1884-1960) of Danville, Quebec. This was the **world's 1st six-reel, feature-length, silent film comedy.**

1914: Until now, women in the Canadian military worked solely in the field of medicine. More than 2800 women served during WWI with the Royal Canadian Army Medical Corps. The majority served in hospitals overseas, on board hospital ships, in several theatres of war, and with field ambulance units in combat zones. However, Canadian women also began forming paramilitary groups. They wore military-style uniforms and trained in small arms, drill, first aid, and vehicle maintenance. This was the **1st organization of Canadian women in a military capacity other than nursing.**

1914: Reginald Aubrey Fessenden (1868-1932) of East Bolton, Quebec, immediately volunteered his services to the

Canadian government with the outbreak of World War I in Europe. Of the many Canadian inventions instrumental in the success of the Allies in WWI, one in particular remains in use worldwide to this day. Reginald developed the **1ˢᵗ visible bullet in the world**, known today as "tracer bullets".

_1915:_ Dr. Cluny MacPherson (1879-1966) of St. John's, Newfoundland, attended McGill Medical School in Montreal, Quebec, in 1896, then returned to practice in his hometown. A doctor, inventor, businessman, and justice of the peace, Cluny was decorated in May this year for his development of the **1ˢᵗ effective gas mask in the world** known as the Macpherson Gas Helmet. It became the most important protective device of World War I when the German Army released poison gas at Ypres in 1915 before attacking the Canadian-held front line. Cluny's invention became the standard mask issued to all Allied soldiers saving thousands of lives and changing the course of the War against the German troops.

Romeo Lebault of Oka, Quebec, designed **Canada's most unusual exercise track for horses**. A half-hour swim in his 3.4-m _(11-ft.)_-deep swimming pool holding 318 226.3 litres _(70,000 Imperial gallons)_ of water gives a horse the same exercise as a man would gain jogging for 30 km _(18 mi.)_.

_1915:_ When a gap appeared in the line at Ypres, Belgium, during World War I, the Canadian 13ᵗʰ Battalion Quebec Regiment (Royal Highlanders of Canada) moved up reserves. With his company machine gun under heavy fire, Lance

Corporal Frederick Fisher (1895-1915) of St. Catharines, Ontario, moved forward and covered the retreat of a battery. He obtained four more men in his gun team to replace those lost in the attack but he was killed under heavy fire while bringing his machine gun into action. Frederick was awarded the Victoria Cross posthumously on June 23rd for his bravery. He became the **1ˢᵗ Canadian-born man to win the Victoria Cross while serving in the Canadian Army**.

_1915:_ Prior to the 1960s, most Canadian universities offered credit courses in dramatic literature and criticism but left the practical work to student drama societies, departments of extension, and intercollegiate festivals on an extracurricular basis. Combined McGill University personnel and alumni in the University Dramatic Club of Montreal staged one of the earliest stage productions, _Arms and the Man_, in 1907 for the first Earl Grey Musical and Dramatic Competition, held in Ottawa, Ontario. Similar dramatic activity occurred during the winter of 1914-1915 at the University of Alberta. However, it was the University of British Columbia Players Club which became the **1ˢᵗ all-student drama society in Canada**, operating from 1915 to 1958. Almost all Canadian universities had established a student drama society within the next ten to fifteen years.

_1916:_ Investment counsellor Helen Cleveland of Minneapolis, Minnesota, USA, moved to Toronto, Ontario, with her family as a young girl. She graduated from Havergal College wanting to enter the workforce so joined CIBC Wood, Gundy and Company from 1916 to 1956. There, she established **Canada's 1ˢᵗ women's department for an investment firm**. The department was staffed by women and served thousands of female clientele exclusively. She lectured to women on investment for forty years spearheading a lecture series on investment at the Toronto Museum after WWII. Helen retired in 1956 and became the **1ˢᵗ woman in Canada granted an Investment Counsel licence** and the **1ˢᵗ woman member of the Investment Counsel Association**. This truly was a remarkable accomplishment considering only 15 men held such a licence at that time.

<u>1916</u>: Saskatchewan was the **1ˢᵗ in North America to give rural municipalities the power to collect taxes to build and operate their own hospitals**.

<u>1916</u>: The International Game Fish Association ratified the Fresh Water and Salt Water All-Tackle Class World Records set in July this year when Canadian W.J. Cook caught the **1ˢᵗ 6.5 kg *(14 lb. 8 oz.)* Brook trout in the world caught with a casting rod**.

<u>1916</u>: New technological developments have always been well represented at the CNE since its inception initially as the Toronto Industrial Exhibition in 1879. It became the Canadian National Exhibition in 1904. The coming of the automobile was no exception. Automobile shows held there became popular very quickly. With its growing national prominence, the CNE's auto exhibit became known in 1916 as the National Motor Show. This was the **1ˢᵗ auto show in North America to feature the coming year's models**. The Automotive Building was constructed in 1929 to address increased demand for exhibit space. It provided 11,148.4 m² *(120,000 ft.²)* of exhibit space on two levels and cost $1,000,229 to build, an exorbitant price at that time.

<u>1917</u>: Louise McKinney (1863-1935) of Frankville, Ontario, helped strengthen Prohibition and improve conditions

for women and immigrants. She worked for the Women's Christian Temperance Union (WCTU) and women's suffrage. She became in 1917 the **1ˢᵗ woman in the British Empire to sit in a provincial legislature**. Louise was defeated from her Alberta legislative position in 1921 but continued working for the WCTU and women's rights. She also became active in the formation of the United Church of Canada.

_1917_: By 1917, Allied Forces needed all the shipbuilding yards they could create. Canadian Vickers constructed twenty-four submarines for Britain, Russia, and Spain. When first delivered, they became the **1ˢᵗ submarines ever to cross the Atlantic under their own power**.

_1917_: Dedicated conservationist Gordon Hewitt (1885-1920) of Macclesfield, England, emigrated to Canada in 1909 and was appointed Dominion Entomologist. He recognized the dangers of indiscriminate hunting of migratory birds. These birds also faced problems from environmental damage, pollution, and the depletion of our natural resources. The carrier pigeon had already been hunted to extinction. Gordon was instrumental in the signing in 1916 and ratification in 1917 of the **1ˢᵗ international treaty in the world for the conservation of wildlife**. The _Migratory Birds Convention Act_ resulted from a long and complicated process of negotiation with the United States and Britain to protect migratory birds common in North America. This convention implemented the Treaty for International Protection of Migratory Birds signed in 1916.

_1917_: Prior to WWI, the federal government raised money primarily from customs duties on imports and from excise duties on items like tobacco and alcohol. The **1ˢᵗ federal income tax and corporation taxes were introduced** on July 25, 1917, as "a temporary war-time measure", in order to finance Canada's role in war. Federal sales taxes, including the Manufacturers' Sales Tax, were initiated in 1920. The *Income Tax Act* was enacted on June 30, 1948. The Federal Sales Tax was replaced by the Goods and Services Tax (GST) in 1991.

1917: In his King Street West factory in Hamilton, Ontario, Robert Newbiggin built the **1st phonograph in Canada**.

1918: The federal government introduced the **1st Daylight Saving Time programme in Canada** this year in an effort to lengthen the working day during the long winter months. The process involves turning clocks forward one hour on the first Sunday in April and turning them back one hour to Standard Time on the last Sunday of October every year. Currently, Saskatchewan is the only province in Canada which remains on Standard Time year-round. United States President George Walker Bush (b. 1946) of New Haven, Connecticut, USA, signed an *Energy Bill* in August 2005 that would extend Daylight Saving Time starting in 2007 by four weeks each year. In 2007, Ontario became **Canada's 1st province to synchronize clocks with the USA**. Beginning that year, daylight saving time began on the second Sunday of March and ended on the first Sunday in November instead of the previous period extending from the beginning of April to the end of October.

1918: No, it was not Snoopy who **shot down the Red Baron** in WWI. German flying ace Baron Manfred von Richthofen (1892-1918) of Breslau, Germany, was known as the Red Baron after becoming the ace of aces during the War, credited with shooting down 80 Allied planes. Canadian flying ace Captain Arthur Roy Brown (1893-1944) of Carleton Place, Ontario, flew with the 209th Squadron of the British Royal Flying Corps. He was credited with 12 victories, including that of shooting down the Red Baron's Fokker triplane during a dogfight on April 21, 1918. A dogfight involves two planes fighting "one-on-one" in the sky. Bullets from Roy's plane did clip the triplane. However, some military historians believe that Australian anti-aircraft artillery from the ground brought ultimate demise to the Red Baron. Roy actually went into a profound depression soon after the dogfight. After suffering a flying accident, he left the Royal Air Force.

1918: Of the many varieties of plastics available today, casein plastic is another thermosetting material. The **1st casein plastics in Canada** were used in Montreal, Quebec, around 1918 for manufacturing buttons. This particular plastic is also known by various names including galalith, aladanite, and erinoid.

1918: The government introduced the **1st food grading system in Canada** with the *Canada Fruit and Vegetable Act.*

1918: Molière's *Les Femmes savantes* was the first production of the University College Alumnae Dramatic Club, an all-female, non-professional group which founded the Coach House Theatre in Toronto, Ontario, the **"oldest Little Theatre group in Canada"**. Gradually attracting male participation, the group produced plays in a coach house, a garage, and even a synagogue. In 1972, it changed its name to the Fire Hall Theatre and moved to an abandoned firehall on Berkeley St. in Toronto. Presenting the works of Canadian, American, and European playwrights in both classical and experimental genres, this theatre group was virtually the only non-commercial playhouse in Canada from the 1920s to the late fifties.

1919: Arthur Edward Iutzi of Bright, Ontario, patented the **1st automatic automobile transmission in the world** in 1919. He invented a pendulum device that automatically shifted the car's transmission into a lower gear going uphill and into neutral going down.

1919: It is often amazing how some inventions originate. The **Canadian Good Roads Association was formed** in 1914 to unify and invigorate the campaign for better roads. However, it was in 1919 when Public Works Minister Frank Campbell Biggs (1872-1942) of Brantford, Ontario, was inspired with an idea from Robert Hunter of Galt, Ontario, who was painting parking spaces in a public garage. Frank immediately had a solid white line painted on four dangerous curves near his farm near Clarkson, Ontario, the **1st middle-of-the-road stripes in the world**, to separate more readily the vehicles travelling in opposite directions. Engineer J.D. Millar wanted to resolve the frequent problem of fog blown in from Lake St. Francis making driving difficult for motorists travelling Route 2 near the Quebec-Ontario border. He did so in 1930 by painting the **1st dotted white division lines on a highway anywhere in the world**. Within three years, these dotted lines had become standard in North America. Frank later became minister of the Department of Highways.

1919: Reginald Aubrey Fessenden (1868-1932) of Sherbrooke, Quebec, **invented the 1st television set in North America** this year.

1920s: The **1ˢᵗ silk trains in North America** were operated by the Canadian Pacific Railway in the 1920s. They raced across Canada from Vancouver, British Columbia, to the market cities of Eastern Canada and the United States. Their only passengers were armed guards because of their precious silk cargoes worth up to $6,000,000. The goods were sealed in special containers to protect them from moisture and thieves. The trains travelled faster than the fastest passenger trains. Speed was essential not only because of the high value of the cargo but also because of the daily changes in market prices for silk.

1920: The House of Commons appoints the chief electoral officer, an independent administrator in Canadian federal elections. Colonel Oliver Mowat Biggar (1820-1903) of Kingston, Ontario, became Canada's **1ˢᵗ chief electoral officer**.

Corunna Bolduc was employed at St. Joseph's Hospital in Sudbury, Ontario. She was the **1ˢᵗ blind person in North America to become a darkroom operator**.

1920: Singer, pianist, and actor Hector Pellerin (1887-1953) of Montreal, Quebec, was known for his exceptional baritone voice. He studied piano and organ with well-known Canadian composer Alexis Contant (1858-1918) of Montreal and organist Joseph-Daniel Dussault (1864-1921) of Charlesbourgh, Quebec. His career began with accompanying silent films around 1907 followed by some acting, then recording in 1916. Hector specialized in interpreting French popular, cabaret, and romantic songs by French songwriters. He recorded over 140 wax cylinders and 78-rpm discs between 1916 and 1928. He also sang on some of the very first radio broadcasts in Canada, particularly at CKAC from 1933 to 1943 in Montreal. This was the **1ˢᵗ Canadian city with scheduled radio broadcasts**, beginning in May, 1920. CKAC also was the **1ˢᵗ French-language radio station in Canada**.

_1920:_ Until this year, our one cent coins were much larger than they are today. In 1920, the Mint issued 6,901,626 large one cent pieces and 15,472,153 small ones made of bronze. The small ones were the **1ˢᵗ small one cent coins minted in Canada**. They were struck May 18ᵗʰ and put into circulation on May 21. The Royal Canadian Mint produced the last Canadian penny in May 2012.

_1920:_ On January 10ᵗʰ, the Montréal Canadiens played the Toronto St. Patrick's in Montreal, Quebec, winning 14-7, the **highest aggregate score ever in a professional hockey game**. This record was tied on December 11, 1985, when the Edmonton Oilers beat the Chicago Blackhawks, 12-9, at Chicago, Illinois, USA. On the home ice of the Quebec Bulldogs on March 3, 1920, the Montréal Canadiens pounded their opponents to a 16-3 victory, the **most goals ever scored by one team in one single professional hockey game**.

_1920:_ **Native peoples were given the right to vote in a Canadian election for the 1ˢᵗ time** although Status or Treaty Indians had to relinquish their treaty rights and registered Indian status to do so. It wasn't until 1960 that the **First Nations people living on reserves were granted the right to vote and the right to run as candidates in federal elections without having to give up their status under the _Indian Act_**.

1921: Passing took the emphasis away from kicking when the **forward pass was 1ˢᵗ introduced to Canadian football** this year. Being a better projectile, the elongated football evolved from this rule change and was soon adopted in the U.S. game. In a game against Edmonton, Alberta, on September 21, 1929, Gerry Seiberling threw the **1ˢᵗ legal forward pass in Canadian football**. Ralph Losie of the Calgary Altomah-Tigers made the **1ˢᵗ reception of a forward pass in Canadian football**.

1921: The Peace Arch was built on the international boundary between Canada and the United States—Douglas in British Columbia and Blaine in Washington State, USA. It was dedicated on September 6ᵗʰ. Its purpose was to commemorate the lasting peace between the two countries. Its dedication was to commemorate the signing of the Treaty of Ghent on December 24, 1814, which ended the War of 1812 between Great Britain and the United States. Donations from school children in both countries were used to purchase the land surrounding the monument. In 1939, Canada officially dedicated Peace Arch Park covering an area of 16.2 hectares *(40 acres)*. The Peace Arch, the **world's 1ˢᵗ international peace monument**, is the park's centrepiece rising 20.4 m *(67 ft.)* in height. The park is nestled between two mountain ranges and includes dry, rolling hills of the prairie, mountain peaks nearly 3000 m *(9,842.5 ft.)* high, plus three Waterton Lakes, each over 150 m *(492 ft.)* deep. This spectacular setting encompasses a great variety of plant and animal life including antelope, coyote, mountain goats, bighorn sheep, grizzly bears, and marmots.

1921: Shelburne, Nova Scotia native and medical student John Augustus Larson (1892-1965) invented the **1ˢᵗ polygraph (lie detector) in the world**. The unit simultaneously and continuously records a person's pulse rate, breathing rate, perspiration secretion, and blood pressure. The results can determine relatively accurately whether or not a person is lying.

_1921:_ Between July and August of this year, the **1ˢᵗ dog in the world suffering from diabetes to receive continuous daily injections of insulin** was a hound treated at the faculty of medicine, University of Toronto.

_1921:_ The **1ˢᵗ automatic automobile cowcatcher in the world** was invented in 1921 by Louis Balogh of Fort Erie, Ontario, and Ilona Pakozdy of Niagara Falls, Ontario. They developed a rather complex safety device that triggered the instant the front bumper hit anything. It automatically and simultaneously would apply the automobile's brakes and lower a cowcatcher.

_1922:_ The government initiated the **1ˢᵗ licensing of private commercial radio stations in Canada** this year. On July 1, 1927, the Diamond Jubilee of Confederation witnessed the **1ˢᵗ national radio broadcast in Canada**.

_1922:_ The good features of streetcars, which drew their power from overhead lines, was combined with those of motorbuses, which ran on rubber tires, producing the trolleybus. The **1ˢᵗ trolleybuses in Canada** operated in Windsor, Ontario, beginning on May 5ᵗʰ when the Lincoln Road route was first opened. A similar route was opened in Toronto, Ontario, in June of that year. Trolleybuses continue to be used there to this day.

_1922:_ Andrew Bonar Law (1858-1923) was born in Rexton, New Brunswick, educated in Scotland and England, and amassed a large fortune as a partner in one of the largest iron manufacturing and exporting firms in Glasgow, Scotland. He retired from business and went to England to became a Member of Parliament in 1900. He succeeded Arthur Balfour (1848-1930) of Whittingehame, East Lothian, Scotland, as leader of the Conservatives, served as colonial secretary from 1915 to 1916, and eventually held a series of important cabinet posts including Chancellor of the Exchequer from 1916 to 1919. From then until 1921, Andrew was Lord Privy Seal. On October 20, 1922, Andrew became the **1ˢᵗ and only prime minister of Great Britain born outside the British Isles**. Unfortunately, he was forced because of poor health to resign his position after serving for only 209 days, and died in 1923.

1922: Swiss guides built Abbott's Hut in 1922, the **highest building in Canada**. Sitting at 2950.5 m *(9,680 ft.)* on the Continental Divide between Alberta and British Columbia, the hut lies in Alberta while its outhouse is in British Columbia!

1922: On June 29ᵗʰ, the **largest Lake Sturgeon recorded in the world** weighed 141 kg *(310.9 lb.)*, was 241 cm *(7 ft. 11 in.)* long, and was caught in Batchewana Bay, Lake Superior, Ontario.

1923: On July 9ᵗʰ in Calgary, Alberta, Guy Weadick persuaded six local ranchers to join him in what he billed as "the half mile of hell". They participated in the **1ˢᵗ chuck wagon race at the Calgary Stampede**, still one of the most popular events there to this day.

1923: Fleeing from Pennsylvania, USA, to Canada early in her life via the Underground Railroad, former slave Susan

Augusta Maxwell (1806-1923) led a very event-filled life before passing away on February 11th in Richmond Hill, Ontario. Susan was **Canada's oldest citizen**, having lived to the ripe young age of 117!

1923: Republican Warren Gamaliel Harding (1865-1923) of Corsica, Blooming Grove, Ohio, USA, 29th president of the United States of America, addressed a crowd of 40,000 in Stanley Park, Vancouver, British Columbia, during his ten-hour visit on July 26th. Warren was the **1st U.S. president to make an official visit to Canada during his term of office**. He died of food poisoning one week later in San Francisco, California, USA. It seems that he ate tainted Alaskan crab aboard the ship that took him to Vancouver on a return trip from Alaska, USA.

1923: The **1st hockey radio broadcast in the world** was given by Norm Allen who called the plays from Toronto's Mutual Street Arena on February 8th. On March 14th, Peter Parker of CKCK Radio in Regina, Saskatchewan, made the **world's 1st play-by-play radio broadcast of a professional hockey game** when Edmonton, Alberta, defeated Regina 1-0.

1924: Laurentide Air Service Ltd. carried out general air service in both Quebec and Ontario. It launched a passenger and freight service to the Rouyn gold fields in Quebec, operating from bases at Larder Lake and Haileybury, both in Ontario. On September 11th, they sold special stickers for mail flown that day when they established the **1st regular Canadian airmail service in Canada**. That year, Laurentide planes carried 1,004 passengers, 35 743.1 kg *(78,800 lbs.)* of express and freight, and over 15,000 letters and telegrams.

_1924:_ One of the first toolmakers in Canada to make and work with moulds for thermoplastics was engineer Arthur A. Burry. He designed and built the moulds for a jewel box that he blow-moulded from celluloid sheeting and tube stock in Toronto, Ontario. This was the **1ˢᵗ blow-moulded product for the quality commodity market in Canada**. Construction of the jewel box involved cementing the four blow-moulded legs to the double-walled base. Then the double-walled cover was hinge-fastened mechanically to the base. The entire box was designed in a Chinese motif and was a great seller for the company.

_1925:_ Winnipeg, Manitoba, is considered Canada's year-round festival capital with more than 130 days of annual festivals. This year saw the founding of Le Cercle Molière, **Canada's oldest continuously active theatre**, highly regarded nationally for its excellent performances of the highest calibre.

_1925:_ On November 4ᵗʰ, a Canadian National Railway oil-electric car 18 m _(59.1 ft.)_ long carrying 57 passengers arrived at Vancouver, British Columbia. It had just completed a record-setting 67-hour trip from Montreal, Quebec, averaging 70 km/h _(43.5 mph)_. By never shutting the engine down during the entire journey, this became the **longest non-stop train voyage in the world made by a single engine**.

_1925:_ A Canadian was the **1ˢᵗ in the world to coin the term "Groceteria"**. An advertisement in the _Canadian Labor Advocate_ for Kirkham's Grocerteria in 1925 printed this new word for the first time. Derived from the combination of groce(ry), for a self-service grocery store, with (cafe)teria, the second "r" was dropped and the word "groceteria" emerged.

One of Canada's favourite waterfowl is the **Canada goose**, *Branta Canadensis*. This large grey goose has a black head and neck with white cheek patches. It flies in an impressive V-formation and has an unforgettable honking cry as it passes overhead.

1925: Principally a cornet player and singer, Jimmy "Trump" Davidson (1908-1978) of Sudbury, Ontario, made his first public appearance at the age of 12. He played trumpet in Sudbury's Canadian Legion Band. He formed the Melody Five in 1925, the **1st jazz-style group in Canada**. Jimmy went on to form several Dixieland big bands, travelled internationally, appeared at Toronto's Palace Pier in Ontario for many years, and was heard regularly on the radio. Jimmy performed well into the 1970s. He even had his own CBC programmes including Trump Davidson's Dixieland and Dixieland Downbeat.

1925: Another important contribution to science by Gordon Merritt Shrum (1896-1985) of Smithville, Ontario, was his research into the Northern Lights. In 1925, he became the **1st person in the world to create the necessary conditions in the laboratory to see the aurora green line and explain it**. His many scientific efforts resulted in the establishment of Simon Fraser University in Burnaby, British Columbia, of which he later became its chancellor.

1926: Vimy Ridge Memorial Park in Winnipeg, Manitoba, is home to **Canada's 1st monument dedicated to women who served in World War II**. Vimy Ridge in Northern France was the **1st allied offensive success on the Western Front in World War I**.

Uniquely Canadian

Uniquely Canadian — Volume I, Volume II, Volume III, Volume IV, Volume V, Volume VI — Donald Allen Gillmore

6 Volume Hardcover Set

1880 - 1899   Chapter 6

Uniquely Canadian

was later renamed the National Council of Women of Canada. It maintained close ti Order of Nurses (VON), the Imperial Order Daughters of the Empire (IODE), children a Canadian Association of Consumers.

1888: H. Swanzy (1841-1910) and W. Green (1847-1919) of Ireland climbed Mt. Bonney in the Rogers Pass, British Columbia, 3048 m *(10,000 ft.)* using rappels in descent in the **1ˢᵗ technical mountaineering ascent in Canada**, in 1888.

1888: The buildings at Ridle in St. Catharines, Ontario, atmosphere of English public sc the shaded campus to the crick It is **Canada's largest residen for boys**, becoming co-educationa

1888: Long before skating blades were riveted to skating boots, James Al 1893) of Kings County, New Brunswick, invented the **1ˢᵗ clamp skate in C** company, located at Jones Creek near Saint John, New Brunswick, was fa thousands of clamp skates, hockey skates, roller skates, and the popular long reacher long distance skating. After he also invented the **1ˢᵗ Long Reacher skate in the** forerunners of today's speed skates, this elongated blade ice skate with its blade in skate designs became popular worldwide resulting in the increased popularity of mat covering distances of 80.5 km *(50 mi.)* or more. Skating from Saint John to Fred Brunswick, and back was particularly popular. Several New Brunswick skaters won W Championships and James himself set a world record skating 1887 km *(117 mi.)* in ten with which we are more familiar today eventually took over in popularity.

Also spelled *larugan* or *larigan*, the Canadian **larrigan** is a unique n cowhide. It has uppers reaching almost to the knee and the soles gene They are tanned usually with linseed oil to provide weatherproofing and v are common footwear in Northern Canada.

1888: Dr. Donald Campbell Meyers graduated from Trinity Medic became **Canada's 1ˢᵗ neurologist**. He established the Dr. Hospital in 1898, a private sanatorium, devoted to neurasthenia a the Weir Mitchell Cure, which operated until 1920. He also government in 1905 to establish the "Nervous Wards" at the Toronto General Hospi neuroses in patients. In 1911, the wards were closed when the hospital moved to its pre to the university campus.

1888: Ernest A. LeSueur (b. 1869) of Ottawa, Ontario, made numerous outs to the industrial chemistry industry. He developed the **1ˢᵗ successful elec world for the manufacture of caustic soda and chlorine from salt 1ˢᵗ in the world to conceive the principle upon which the electrolytic cell operates**. And he also invented the **1ˢᵗ method in the world of ev content of liquid air**. This was very important in the development of many of today's

1889: The Ontario Canoe Company construct the **1ˢᵗ racing war canoe in Canada**, for Toronto Canoe Club.

124

Chapter 17   2000 - 2012

Uniquely Canadian

Glasgow, Scotland. It is the **1ˢᵗ and only year-round College of Piping and Celtic Performing Arts in North America**. In addition to bagpipe courses, instruction is offered in Scottish-style snare drumming, Highland dancing, and step dancing. It is also a **world leader in promoting Celtic festivals, concert series, plus stage and related events.**

2001: Big White Ski Resort in British Columbia operates four high-speed quads and nine lifts for skiers and snowboarders. It also has three state-of-the-art snowboard parks and half-pipes built to competition standards plus 25 km *(15.5 mi.)* of cross-country ski trails. It boasts one of the largest International Ski Schools offering lessons designed for all ages and abilities. Its on-mountain accommodations are augmented by 17 bars and restaurants, international cuisine, and take-out food. Big White's greatest service, however, is in often being the **1ˢᵗ ski resort in North America to open with all natural snow**, as happened in the 2001-2002 season. Its longer than average ski season runs from mid-November to mid-April attracting enthusiasts from around the world.

2001: St. Marys, Ontario, is the home of the Baseball Hall of Fame & Museum and is also home to Canada's elite in women's baseball. Beginning July 4ᵗʰ, Team Canada began the **1ˢᵗ Women's World Series of Baseball in the world** beating Australia 8-2. Captain Stephanie Topolie of North Bay, Ontario, scored three times and drove in two hits leading her team to victory. The team had three hits from the Game MVP (Most Valuable Player) Melanie Harwood of Tottenham, Ontario, and the victory run from Kate Psota of Burlington, Ontario. Japan defeated Australia 5-4 in Game 2 while a strong USA club defeated Canada 6-2. On July 8ᵗʰ, Canada lost to Australia 0-1 taking the bronze medal while the USA team won the 2001 championship beating Japan 9-1.

2001: Lance Matthews, working in Mansfield, Ontario, **invented a new medical crutch that frees both hands of people suffering from lower leg injuries or disabilities**. He calls it the iWALKFree and is helping thousands of amputees and others around the world with this unique device. He received the Ernest C. Manning Innovation Award for his work.

2001: Boyd Wesley Benjamin of Vuntut Gwitch'in First Nation of Old Crow, Yukon, was a talented lad who learned to play the fiddle, jig, and cook. After graduating from high school, he became a ramp attendant for Air North Airlines. In addition to his daily duties refueling aircraft and handling baggage and cargo, Boyd began completing his first training flight and soon thereafter his private pilot licence. This year, he became the **1ˢᵗ member of the Vuntut Gwitch'in First Nation to be accepted into the First Nation Technical Institute to train as a pilot**. He completed a successful year of pilot training in this school in Deseronto, Ontario, receiving a scholarship to attend the renowned aviation programme at Mount Royal College. Next came training as a flight attendant with Air North in Whitehorse, Yukon. Boyd expanded his flying skills obtaining a commercial helicopter pilot licence. Indeed, he had fulfilled his lifelong dream to fly. In 2008, he received the First National Aboriginal Achievement Award in the Special Youth division.

2001: Emanuel Sandhu (b. 1980) of Toronto, Ontario, began studying ballet at the age of 3 and figure skating when 8 years old. After completing high school, he graduated from Canada's National Ballet School. He relocated to Burnaby, British Columbia, where he continued his training in figure skating. Emanuel is fluent in English, French, and Italian which combined with his East Indian/Italian heritage have given him a unique look and style on

2001: In Brampton, Ontario, on July 1ˢᵗ, Industrial Thermo Polymers Ltd. made the **world's longest pool toy ever measured**. It was 1609.34 m *(5,280 ft.)* long.

165

Contents

Full 4-colour throughout the hardcover set

More than 7,100 stories

Over 12,700 firsts or uniquely Canadian treasures

Canada Map, Flag, National Coat of Arms

List of Floral and Animal Emblems

Provincial/Territorial Flags and Coats of Arms

National Anthem, Statistics

Each Volume 21.0 cm x 29.7 cm

(8.27" x 11.69") in size

Laminated covers for increased durability

Stronge hardcover binding

Volumes lay flat when open

Silk bookmark in each volume

Each Volume is printed using

environmentally friendly soya-based inks

This Book Can Help You If . . .

- ✂ *You are a **Student** searching for new ideas and research material;*
- ✂ *You are a **Teacher** looking for inspiring student assignment topics;*
- ✂ *You are a **Parent**, **Grandparent**, or **Relative** in need of a great idea for family gifts (birthday, graduation, religious holiday, special event);*
- ✂ *You are a **Corporate or Government department** looking for the perfect, unique Retirement Gift, Performance Reward, or Customer/Client/Visitor Gift;*
- ✂ *Your **Club** or **School** could use a **75% profit Fund-Raising** plan;*
- ✂ *You would like some interesting reading while on the bus, taking a cab, waiting in a doctor's office, eating lunch, or relaxing on vacation.*

FREE With Each 6-Volume Hardcover Set

- ✂ *1 UC Pocketbook*
- ✂ *1 paper pocketbook bookmark*
- ✂ *1 Full Colour UC Poster (A4)*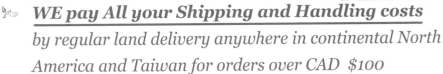
- ✂ ***WE pay All your Shipping and Handling costs** by regular land delivery anywhere in continental North America and Taiwan for orders over CAD $100*
- ✂ *Shipping faster or elsewhere worldwide available at competitive prices*
- ✂ *Full 60-day Satisfaction Guarantee*

Excellent Financial Options

Pay by

Variable **Volume Discounts** offered

Wide variety of very profitable
Fund-Raising opportunities!

Gift Certificates available!

For Further Information and

TO ORDER

www.FirstInCanada.ca

<u>1926</u>: Harold Anthony Oaks (1896-1968) of Hespeler, Ontario, designed and built the **1ˢᵗ portable nose hangar in the world**. It is used by bush flying operators worldwide to service aircraft engines outdoors in severe temperatures.

<u>1926</u>: The **1ˢᵗ Canadian Legion in Canada** was formed this year, originating from a number of World War I veterans' organizations. It followed the lead of Field Marshal Earl Haig (1861-1928) of Edinburgh, Scotland, the creator of the British Empire Service League. Hundreds of thousands of members from all Canada's wars support veterans' interests with government assistance and engage in public service work. The group took the title "Royal" in 1960.

> Robert Oliphant of Victoria, British Columbia, published **Canada's tiniest book printed with movable type**. Entitled *Short Works*, all 28 pages of the book are only 1.75 mm x 0.95 mm *(11/16 in. x 3/8 in.)* in size, about half the size of a normal postage stamp!

<u>1927</u>: A 42-year-old Canadian woman identified only as Mrs. H. checked into Ontario Hospital in London, Ontario, in 1927 to be treated on June 10ᵗʰ for a "slight abdominal pain". What turned out to be the **worst reported case in the world of compulsive swallowing** astounded Dr. S.G. Chalk and Dr. H.O. Foucar. They removed 2,533 objects, including 947 bent pins, from her stomach!

<u>1927</u>: Fenton A. Roth, an electrical engineer at Port Arthur Shipbuilding in Ontario, perfected a unique timing device in 1927 that worked on the principle of the stopwatch. Four

canvas "clocks", each 1.2 m *(4 ft.)* square, surrounded an electrical mechanism operated by the official time-keeper at a hockey game. The clock was suspended over the centre of the hockey arena so that hockey spectators and players alike could watch every minute of the game ticked off. The **1ˢᵗ electronic four-sided hockey arena stop clock in the world** was installed in 1931 in both the Montreal Forum in Montreal, Quebec, and in Maple Leaf Gardens in Toronto, Ontario, to be followed by other indoor rinks around the world.

1927: Why was the 89-day trip in 1927 by George Scott of Amherst, Nova Scotia, and Frank Elliot (d. 1985) of Amherst from Halifax, Nova Scotia, to the West Coast the **strangest journey ever across Canada by car**? They never filled their Model T Ford's gas tank once. Instead, they persuaded 168 passing motorists into towing their vehicle. They really had little choice as their car had no engine! George and Frank won a $1,000 bet on October 15 to complete this trip successfully. This also was the **longest tow in world history**, a distance of 7659 km *(4,759 mi.)*!

1927: Elizabeth Graham played hockey goaltender at Queen's University in Kingston, Ontario, in intercollegiate games. She wanted to protect her face so wore her mask of choice, a fencing mask. Elizabeth was the **1ˢᵗ person to wear a goalie mask in a hockey game**.

1927: Pioneer broadcast executive Ernie Bushnell (1900-1987) of Lindsay, Ontario, trained as a singer at the Toronto Conservatory of Music. He turned to announcing and then station management. Ernie was hired in 1926 by Radio CJYC, owned by the Jehovah's Witnesses, to procure sponsors and programmes. The following year, Ernie introduced the **1ˢᵗ singing commercial in the world**, a new kind of commercial for the "Toronto Wet Wash Laundry Show." From 1929 to 1933, he managed CFRB and CKCN in Toronto, Ontario. He then established **Canada's 1ˢᵗ advertising agency for radio**. Ernie worked to the vice-president's chair with the Canadian Broadcasting Corporation (CBC) from 1945 to 1958, became assistant general manager in 1953, then retired as a vice-president. Ernie was honorary chairman of Bushnell Communications Ltd. in 1983.

1928: The wonder horse *Gratton Bars* was bred by Archie Pedden of Strathroy, Ontario, in 1923. Canadian harness racing driver Gid Litt drove *Gratton Bars*, the **1ˢᵗ horse in the world to win three 0.8-km *(1/2-mi.)* heats**, in London, Ontario, in 1927. In one three-week period the following year, *Gratton Bars* became the **1ˢᵗ horse to win the top three pacing stakes in North America**. The $25,000 Derbies at Windsor, Connecticut; Toledo, Ohio; and Kalamazoo, Michigan, all in the USA, were considered the "original triple-crown of pacing".

1928: Nat (Nathaniel Ryal) Bailey (1902-1978) of Saint Paul, Minnesota, USA, established White Spot in Vancouver, British Columbia, **Canada's 1ˢᵗ drive-in restaurant**. By 2013, more than seventeen million guests dined at White Spot each year. It serves more full service than any other casual dining establishment in British Columbia. Not only is White Spot committed to excellence in taste and freshness but also established **Canada's 1ˢᵗ restaurant carhops**. It set another record by installing the **1ˢᵗ stainless steel kitchens in Canada**. Certainly the ambiance and quality of White Spot restaurants provide an inviting dining experience for the entire family.

_1928:_ This year, the T. Eaton Company offered its customers "a selective literary service" creating **Canada's 1ˢᵗ book club**. They sold to their membership a monthly selection of titles, chosen by a committee of literary authorities and announced in advance of publication, at an average price of $2.00. The Eaton Book Club had 5,000 members but only functioned for four years.

_1928:_ The Canadian Post Office issued a new 2¢ stamp with a bust of King George V (1865-1936) and the words "Postes" and "Postage" printed on it. This was **Canada's 1ˢᵗ bilingual stamp**.

_1928:_ Colonel William Eric Phillips (1893-1964) of Toronto, Ontario, incorporated the Duplate Safety Glass Co. of Canada in Oshawa, Ontario, in 1928. That year, it manufactured the **1ˢᵗ safety glass interlayers in Canada using cellulose nitrate**, and later cellulose acetate. In the 1930s, Duplate developed the **1ˢᵗ high test vinyl butyraldehyde safety glass interlayer in automobile windshields in the world**. Duplate also formed Fiberglas Canada Ltd., a pioneer in manufacturing reinforced plastics. Smith & Stone Ltd. manufactured thermostats and thermoplastics while H.J. McIntyre also worked in plastics manufacturing. Duplate bought H.J. McIntyre in 1938, then Smith & Stone in 1944 and changed its name to Duplate Canada Ltd.

_1928:_ The Old Fraser River Bridge was constructed this year in Quesnel, British Columbia. Along the banks of the Quesnel River and the Fraser River at Ceal Tingley Memorial Park, it joins the River Front Trail Walk, the North Trail, and the West Trail. This bridge is now a footbridge, but not just any footbridge as it is the **world's longest wooden truss**

footbridge, being 274.6 m *(901 ft.)* in length. Today, it is reserved for pedestrians who enjoy a walk, run, rollerblading, or a bike ride along the banks of the rivers.

1928: On April 27ᵗʰ on Prince Edward Island, motorists **switched to driving on the right-hand side of the road for the 1ˢᵗ time**.

1928: The government of Prince Edward Island in 1928 created the **1ˢᵗ advertising licence plates in Canada**. It advertised P.E.I. as the home of "Seed Potatoes and Foxes." Although it realised the benefits of using licence plates as miniature billboards on vehicles crossing North America, the lack of romance in this initial slogan initiated its change the following year to "Garden of the Gulf". In 1966, "Garden Province" was adopted in P.E.I. In the province's centennial year, it was changed to "The place to be in '73". Since its inception, this new concept has expanded to include pictorial emblems and advertisements in many instances. Licence plate advertising has become a standard throughout North America and in many other parts of the world.

1929: On March 20ᵗʰ in Vancouver, British Columbia Telephone Company established the North-West Telephone Company as a subsidiary of the parent company. This was the **world's 1ˢᵗ radiotelephone company**.

1929: Although the telephone had been around for some time, its use did have some restrictions, particularly when it came to moving vehicles. On May 5ᵗʰ, a score of reporters from Canadian, American, and European news services came to witness the **1ˢᵗ two-way simultaneous telephone conversation in the world held from a moving train**. It was made possible through the use of a combination of telephone and radio technology with variations in radio wave frequency allowing for contact with different trains. J.C. Burkholder, known as "The Electric Kid", perfected the first two-way train telephone circuit at 3:45 aboard the Canadian National Railway's "The International Limited" as it sped at 95.6 km/h *(60 mph)* from Toronto, Ontario, to Montreal, Quebec.

1929: Brooklyn-born carnival operator James Wesley (Patty) Conklin (1892-1970), born Joe Renker, joined with the original J.W. Conklin (1892-1920) also of Brooklyn, New York, USA, owner of Clark and Conklin Shows in the midwestern USA. He took his adopted father's name and headed to Canada where he joined in a partnership with Speed Garrett (c. 1880-1933) of Boise, Idaho, USA, as operators of the Conklin & Garrett Shows in Western Canada in 1924. They founded Conklin Shows Ltd. in Winnipeg, Manitoba, in 1929. They became the **largest midway concessionaires in the world**. Operating as far east as the Maritimes by 1932, the current Conklin head office settled in Brantford, Ontario, since 1937. Patty was successful that year in bidding for the midway franchise to the Canadian National Exhibition in Toronto, Ontario. In 1955, he set a new industry trend purchasing the 1ˢᵗ **European spectacular ride in North America**, the "Wild Mouse". Conklin & Garrett Shows supplies midways to numerous country fairs throughout Ontario and Quebec including the Western Ontario Fair in London, Ontario, the Amusement Park at Crystal Beach, Ontario, and ten other county fairs. They have all been managed since 1970 by Patty's Toronto-born son, J. Franklin (Jim) Conklin (b. 1933). He was joined a few years later by third-generation Frank Conklin (b. 1959).

1930: Found at White Head Island in New Brunswick, a great white shark 11.3 m *(37 ft.)* long was discovered. This was the **largest specimen of the world's largest carnivorous fish ever found.**

1930: Born of Canadian parents, Dr. James Kenneth Wallace Ferguson (1907-1999) of Tamsui, Formosa (Taiwan) moved to Canada. He held numerous teaching and research positions throughout his career. James was serving in WWII with the Royal Canadian Air Force when he collaborated with Fred Frye of the University of Toronto in developing the **1ˢᵗ rubber oxygen mask in the world for pilots.** It continued in common use until development of a new design later in the USA in the 1930s.

1930: We sometimes look back on the 1930s primarily as financially impoverished times. It was Saskatchewan farmers who **1ˢᵗ coined the expression "Dirty Thirties".** The term originated from the description of the farmland ravaged by erosion, fields stripped of topsoil, and dust storms so thick that they turned the sky black.

1930: Until this year, clockwork and weight mechanisms powered the world's lighthouses. Then, the **1ˢᵗ lighthouse in the world powered by electricity** was tested at Musquash, New Brunswick, and at Cranberry Island and Guyion Island, Nova Scotia. Compact electric motors supplied both light and rotary power.

1931: Ontario-born James Speers (1881-1955) was a racehorse breeder. In 1923, he built his own racetrack at St. Boniface, Manitoba, and at the Polo Park Track in Winnipeg, Manitoba, the following year. In 1931, he introduced the **1ˢᵗ pari-mutuel betting to Canada** and the **1ˢᵗ daily double system to North America**. He also became Canada's leading breeder of racehorses at his racing empire in St. Boniface.

_1931:_ The **1ˢᵗ television signals to go on the air in Canada** were broadcast by radio station CKAC in Montreal, Quebec. VE9EC was owned jointly by CKAC and _La Presse_. The picture was about 40 mm x 40 mm _(1.6 in. x 1.6 in.)_ and in red and black. Douglas West founded Canadian Television Ltd. (CTL) a year later. He and his chief engineer, Leonard Spencer of CKAC, produced **Canada's 1ˢᵗ live TV broadcast**. The programme included a violinist, a singer, and a cartoonist. Doug and Leonard began broadcasting programmes twice a week but the company had a short lifespan. With only about 20 television receiver sets in the country at the time, the entire project was definitely ahead of its time. CTL did hire a young engineer, J. Alphonse Ouimet (1908-1988) of Montreal, to work with them. He later became president of the Canadian Broadcasting Corporation (CBC).

_1931:_ Working at McGill University in Montreal, Quebec, this year, Dr. William Chalmers (1905-1994) of Edinburgh, Scotland, discovered a process to produce acrylics by polymerizing specific materials into a hard, transparent solid. These **1ˢᵗ acrylics in the world** are technically referred to as polymerized methyl methacrylate, the process for which William was granted a patent. They are known more commonly as "Plexiglas", "Perspex", and "Lucite". These products make up a large part of our everyday items today from automobile tail lights and dishes to paper weights.

_1932:_ The **1ˢᵗ Royal Canadian Mounted Police (RCMP) Marine Section** was created this year through the transfer to it of the men and vessels of the Preventive Service, National

Revenue. This included acquiring the RCMP schooner *St. Roch*. The RCMP this year could provide the **1ˢᵗ effective patrol of Canada's Arctic territory**.

1932: The Governor General, Sir Vere Brabazon Ponsonby (1880-1956) of London, England, 9ᵗʰ Earl of Bessborough, inaugurated the **1ˢᵗ Trans-Canada telephone system** by speaking to the lieutenant governor of each province by telephone. Made on January 25ᵗʰ, these were the **1ˢᵗ trans-Canada phone calls** ever made.

1932: It is no wonder that the judges were startled this year at the Arlberg-Kandahar downhill race when George Jost became the **1ˢᵗ Canadian to win a major European downhill ski title**. He also was the **1ˢᵗ skier in the world to use the low crouch style in international competition**.

Canadian Violet Milstead flew more than 50 types of aircraft and was known as the "Bush Angel". She became the **1ˢᵗ Canadian to teach bush pilots how to fly**. More than 100 such pilots benefited from Violet's vast knowledge and experience in the field of aviation. In 1995, she was inducted into the Bush Pilot Hall of Fame.

1932: Novelist W.E. Daniel Ross (1912-1995) of Saint John, New Brunswick, was described by the *New York Times* as "one of the most formidable writing factories in this or any other hemisphere." He is considered **Canada's most prolific, most read writer**. Specializing in romantic fiction, gothics, Westerns, and mysteries, Dan's works appear under such pseudonyms as W.E.D. Ross, Marilyn Ross, Clarissa Ross, Jane Rossiter, Rose Dana, Dan Roberts, Ruth Dorsett, Ellen Randolph, Rose Williams, and Tex Steele. He published over 325 mass market paperback books and more than 600 short stories in 22 countries and 13 languages specializing in mystery, plays, and romance. One novel he actually completed in just five days. His book *China Shadows* sold over 2 million copies.

1932: Waterton Lakes National Park of Canada 525 km² *(202.7 mi.²)*, once a Blackfoot stronghold, was established in 1895. It is situated on the Alberta/Montana, USA, border some 276 km *(171.5 mi.)* southwest of Calgary, Alberta, on land divided by the 49th parallel. It was combined with Montana's Glacier National Park in 1932 creating Waterton-Glacier International Peace Park, the **world's 1st international peace park**. The parks were designated Waterton-Glacier International Peace Park World Heritage Site in 1995.

1933: A fire injury to his hands at age 18 while putting out a fire on his sister's clothes ruined his promising career as a concert pianist. Yet **Percy Faith** (1908-1976) of Toronto, Ontario, became an internationally renowned conductor, arranger, and composer of popular music. He gained national recognition as a composer and arranger for CBC Radio (1933-1940). His big break began in 1940 when he joined NBC Radio as music director of the "Carnation Contented Hour". Percy recorded more than forty-five albums as musical director of Columbia Records' popular music division. He arranged three early hits of Tony Bennett (b. 1926) of Astoria, New York, USA. He also conducted pop concerts for various symphonies and composed numerous film scores. His biggest success was "The Theme from a Summer Place" which was the number one song in 1960.

1933: The **world's 1ˢᵗ comic book**, issued in 1933, was never sold directly to the public! *Funnies on Parade*, featuring Joe Palooka, Mutt and Jeff, and Hairbreadth Harry was offered as a gift premium by Canada Dry.

1933: Generations of movie buffs will remember the gigantic gorilla *King Kong* who carried to the modernistic peak of New York's Empire State Building, a beautiful screaming woman named Ann Darrow. That woman was played by **Vina Fay Wray** (1907-2004) of Cardston, Alberta, known in her day as "a great screamer." Fay moved to Los Angeles, California, USA, at a young age and landed her first bit part in a Universal Studios Western in 1923. Her role in Erich von Stroheim's (1885-1957 of Vienna, Austria) *The Wedding March* made her a star. Although *King Kong* (1933) was Fay's greatest film, she appeared in a host of others including *Gasoline Love* (1923), *The Hounds of Zaroff* (1932), and *Hell on Frisco Bay* (1955). She enjoyed playing opposite many renowned leading men including Gary Cooper (1901-1961) of Helena, Montana, USA, Ronald Colman (1891-1958) of Richmond, Surrey, England, William Powell (1892-1984) of Pittsburgh, Pennsylvania, USA, and Fredric March (1897-1975) of Racine, Wisconsin, USA.

H. Blanchette invented the **world's 1ˢᵗ automatic butter-wrapping machine**, manufactured by Gosselin Limited in Drummondville, Quebec, and still distributed worldwide today.

1933: Iron moulder and frustrated inventor George Brown Barclay (1863-1940) of Illinois, USA, moved his family to the district of Meadowbrook, Alberta, to homestead in 1905.

They had little success at farming so moved to Calgary, Alberta, in 1913. While George worked as a well-driller, Elsie Ellen Barclay (née Elsie Ellen Wilson) (d. 1932) of New Forest, Ontario, was a seamstress. Mary Belle Barclay (1901-2000) and Elsie Catherine Barclay (1902-1985), their two daughters, became school teachers in Calgary and in various rural schools throughout their lengthy careers. Catherine taught French and became well known for her work in the Banff School of Fine Arts in Alberta while Mary specialized in natural science. In 1933, the two sisters founded the Canadian Youth Hostels Association at Bragg Creek, Alberta. This was the **1ˢᵗ official youth hostel in North America**.

_1934:_ Helen Alice Kinnear (1894-1970) of Cayuga, Ontario, graduated from the University of Toronto in 1917 and Osgoode Hall Law School in 1920. She was called to the Bar on October 21, 1920, then joined her father's law firm and carried on the practice after his death. Her outstanding ability was highly respected and in 1934, she began to establish several national and international accomplishments. That year, she became the **1ˢᵗ woman in the British Empire to be appointed King's Counsel (K.C.)**. The following year, Helen became the **1ˢᵗ woman to plead a case before the Supreme Court of Canada**. In April, 1943, Helen was appointed judge of Cayuga County Court becoming the **1ˢᵗ woman appointed in the British Commonwealth as county judge**. That same year, she was the **1ˢᵗ federally appointed Canadian female superior court judge**. Recognition for these important undertakings was given through the Helen Kinnear Prize in Criminal Procedure and the Helen Kinnear Prize in Family Law awarded by Osgoode Hall Law School. Helen had lived in Port Colborne, Ontario, from 1904 to 1943. In her honour, the city opened a children's centre in her name. She was awarded an Honorary Doctor of Laws degree in 1953. She also served on two Royal Commissions reviewing various aspects of the Criminal Code. Canada Post issued a commemorative stamp in 1993 to honour her achievements.

1934: On October 6, Halifax, Nova Scotia, set up a radio transmitter at their local police station to send radio messages to their police vehicles. This made Halifax the **1ˢᵗ city in Canada to introduce radio patrol cars to their fleet**. At 4 p.m. three days later, the **1ˢᵗ radio equipped police car in Canada** went on patrol.

1934: A 41-year-old woman in Kingston, Ontario, weighing only 52.2 kg *(115 lb.)* experienced one of the most unique losses in weight imaginable. On June 21ˢᵗ, staff of the Kingston General Hospital removed a tumour weighing 25 kg *(55 lb.)*, the **largest tumour ever surgically removed from a human body**.

1934: The Nash company opened for business in Windsor, Ontario, in 1936, merging with Hudson to form American Motors in 1954. Its makers concentrated their advertisements of the *Nash-LaFayette* four-door sedan, first built in 1934, on it being roomier and more comfortable than other cars in its price range. It was more importantly the **1ˢᵗ car in the world with a seamless, all-steel body**. The *LaFayette* was discontinued in 1939.

1934: Archibald Lang Fleming (1883-1953), a native of Greenock, Scotland, began his theological studies at Wycliffe College in Toronto, Ontario. In 1909, he established a mission at Lake Harbour, Nunavut, on Baffin Island with the Reverend J.W. Bilsby. Archibald was ordained in 1913, returned to Lake Harbour for a couple years, then served at Saint John, New Brunswick, and other churches in Eastern Canada before being appointed archdeacon of the Arctic in 1927. From 1933 until his resignation in 1948, he was Anglican bishop of the Arctic diocese. He was soon known as The Flying Bishop because of his long journeys by air. On July 12, 1934, Archibald became the **1ˢᵗ Bishop in the world to cover 2096 km (1,302.4 mi.) in a one-day preaching blitz in the Arctic**. He embarked from Aklavik, Northwest Territories, and touched down at such far-flung locales as Coppermine, Nunavut; Fort McMurray, Alberta; and Cameron Bay, Nunavut.

_1935:_ At age 17, Edna (Miller) Lockhart Duncanson (1916-2006) of Avonport, Nova Scotia, in the Annapolis Valley was visiting her sister in New York City, New York, USA. When she began playing catch with a friend, she fell in love with the sport of baseball. Obviously talented, she began playing the following day with the New York Bloomer Girls. Edna became the **1ˢᵗ Canadian female professional baseball player** when she officially signed with the team in 1935. She was the **1ˢᵗ and only Canadian player in the U.S. Women's Pro-Baseball League**. In her retirement years, she returned to live near her birthplace in the Gaspereau Valley.

_1935:_ The internationally renowned pianist Émiliano Renaud (1875-1932) gave a series of courses on CFCF Radio in Montreal, Quebec, based on a manual distributed by _La Presse._ The piano lessons extended for thirty weeks. They were the **1ˢᵗ music lessons in North America given over the radio**. Émiliano used excerpts of works played live as specific examples to illustrate his courses.

1935: Horst Wendland of Dollard-des-Ormeaux, Quebec, holds two unique records. His Kreuger Flat Top, turned out on January 24th, was the **world's 1st beer can**. Horst also owned the **largest collection of beer cans in Canada**, a total of 3,360 different beer cans!

1936: Joan Miller (1909-1988) of Nelson, British Columbia, won a best actress award at the Dominion Drama Festival in 1934. She was well aware that the success of her acting career hinged on her moving abroad so Joan moved to England. A BBC producer asked her to play the part of the switchboard operator on *Picture Page.* This attractive young actress became the **1st person to appear on the BBC's 1st television programme**, broadcast on November 2, 1936. She was paid £12.10 per week. Joan was also chosen many years later to be the **1st person in the world to appear on the 1st transatlantic television programme**. It was telecast between London, England, and New York City, New York, USA.

1936: A message dated November 19, 1899, was thrown overboard off the coast of Sweden from the *S.S. Crown Princess Cecelia*. Found in Victoria, British Columbia, on December 9, 1936, it is **Canada's oldest known message in a bottle**.

1936: From July 5th to 17th, 1,180 Canadians, primarily infants and the elderly, died from weather-related causes in Manitoba and Ontario. Of that total, 400 drowned in an attempt to cool down as the temperature exceeded 44°C *(111.2°F)* during what became the **longest and deadliest heat wave in Canadian history**. People weren't the only casualties of this unusual summer weather. Bridge girders twisted as did the steel track on railroad lines. Sidewalks buckled and not only did the crops dry up but fruit actually began to bake right on the trees!

_1936:_ This year, St. Michael's Hospital in Toronto, Ontario, established the **1ˢᵗ School of Medical Records in Canada**. It also became the **1ˢᵗ Canadian hospital approved by the Canadian Dietetic Association for the training of dieticians**.

_1936:_ Champion paddler and member of the Canadian Sports Hall of Fame, Frances Amyot (1904-1962) of Ottawa, Ontario, won the Canadian Canoe Association intermediate singles in 1923 and six senior national titles in Canadian Single-Blade Paddling Championships, plus one double-blade title, throughout his canoeing career. He captained, managed, and coached **Canada's 1ˢᵗ Olympic canoeing team** in Berlin, Germany, in 1936. The Canadian canoe team won a gold medal in the 1000 m _(3,280.8 ft.)_ single-bladed singles, setting a 5:32.1 record, a silver medal in the 10 000 m _(32,808.4 ft.)_ single-bladed tandem, and a bronze medal in the 1000 m _(3,280.8 ft.)_ single-bladed tandem. Frances was the **1ˢᵗ Canadian to win Olympic gold in canoeing**.

_1936:_ A number of political parties were part of the Canadian social credit movement in Quebec, usually at the provincial level but at times affiliated with the federal Social Credit Party of Canada. Louis Even and Gilberte Côté-Mercier (1910-2002) founded the **1ˢᵗ Union des électeurs in Canada** in accordance with the créditiste movement. Louis and Armand Turpin ran as part of the nationwide New Democracy movement in the 1940 federal election. Evan placed third in the riding of Lac St. John-Roberval with 17% of the vote while Armand won 31.8% of the vote in Hull. The party unsuccessfully ran more candidates in the Quebec provincial elections of 1944 and 1948. But things improved in a 1946 federal by-election when Réal Caouette (1917-1976) of Amos, Quebec, won a seat in parliament. He lost it in the next general election, though. The Union des électeurs ran 56 candidates in the 1949 federal election although none were successful and the party faded away.

_1937:_ John Buchan, 1ˢᵗ Baron Tweedsmuir of Elsfield (1875-1940) of Perth, Scotland, inaugurated the **1ˢᵗ Governor General's Literary Awards** this year. Since their inception, they have become the most valued national literary awards in the country. The Canadian Authors Association launched the awards initially as non-monetary prizes for the best works of fiction, non-fiction, poetry, and drama written in English or translated into English from French. In 1959, the Canada Council for the Arts assumed responsibility for these awards including funding, administering, and adjudicating them. They also added prizes for works written in French. The Council then converted its Prizes for Children's Literature and Translation into Governor General's Literary Awards in 1987. The initial prize in 1951 was $250 which rose to $15,000 in 2000. Numerous other presentations and prizes are also given bringing the total value of the awards to more than $300,000 annually. Since 1988, the BMO Financial Group has sponsored the Governor General's Awards. Applications are very substantial with, for example, the 14 independent juries assessing 1,488 submissions from publishers in 14 categories in 2005.

_1937:_ The most famous and prestigious road bicycle race in the world is Le Tour de France. It also is referred to as La Grande Boucle, Le Tour, or The Tour. This long-distance race began in 1903. Professional cyclists race through France and nearby countries over a period of three weeks every July. Pierre Gachon, riding for the British/Canadian combined team in 1937 was the **1ˢᵗ North American cyclist to race in Le Tour de France**. He retired after stage 1 of the race.

_1938:_ Near Boissevain, Manitoba, is the International Peace Garden which opened in 1938 to commemorate peaceful relations between Canada and the United States. With the Chapel of Peace as its centrepiece in an area covering 2442.4 km² _(943 mi.²)_, this is the **world's largest garden dedicated to world peace**.

_1938:_ The French established a fort and fishing base at St. Anns, Nova Scotia, located in the Cape Breton Highlands on St. Anns harbour, just west of Sydney, Nova Scotia, in 1609. When they left after the fall of Louisbourg in 1758, the area was settled by industrious Scots who established a large shipbuilding industry, a plaster quarry, fishing, and farming. Today, one can visit the Giant Angus McAskill Highland Pioneers Museum or purchase traditional Scottish crafts and hand-woven tartans made in St. Anns. The Gaelic tongue and the lore of the clans also live on as St. Anns has the **1ˢᵗ and only Gaelic college outside of Great Britain**. Here, students may learn the Gaelic language, music, bagpipes, dance, arts, crafts, weaving of tartans, and Gaelic customs.

_1938:_ Slovaks in Ontario wanted to keep the songs, music, and traditions of their homeland alive. To help accomplish this goal, they organized this December the **1ˢᵗ Slovak Radio Club in Canada**. Initially, CKTB in St. Catharines, Ontario, broadcast weekly programmes. After 1953, CHVC in Niagara Falls, Ontario, took on this responsibility. Unfortunately, the club was unable to meet its broadcasting expenses and was forced to dissolve in 1965.

A meteorological phenomenon not uncommon during a Canadian winter and particularly in the Arctic is called a **white-out**. It occurs during a heavy snow storm or when the light on a cloudy day is balanced between the sky and that reflected off the snow on the ground. The result is a constant whiteness over the terrain totally removing the visibility of any landscape or shadows. It makes it literally impossible for a person to retain any sense of direction.

_1938:_ The Stork Derby, as it was called by the newspapers, ended on May 30th, the culmination of the **strangest baby boom in Canadian history**. When Charles Miller (1856-1927) died, he had willed his fortune to the mother in Toronto, Ontario, who could give birth to the most children in the ten years following his death. Ten years later, four mothers divided up Millar's $568,000 estate—Annie Smith, Kathleen Nagle, Lucy Timleck, and Isabel Maclean. Every penny of it was certainly needed to help support these four families— each of which now included ten children!

_1938:_ Singers and orchestras from all over Canada performed in _A Musical Portrait of Canada_ on October 23, 1938. This was the **1st major Canadian production broadcast to a worldwide audience**.

_1939:_ After a career as a character dancer in Russia and the Far East, Boris Vladimirovich Volkoff (1900-1974), born Boris Baskakov in Tula, Russia, moved to Toronto, Ontario, from the USA in 1930. Boris was a graduate of the Bolshoi Dance School. He is considered the **Father of Canadian**

Ballet. He founded the Boris Volkoff School of the Dance which won the Tanz-Spiele Medal representing Canada at the 1936 Berlin Olympiad in Germany. He launched the Volkoff Canadian Ballet in May, 1939, **Canada's 1ˢᵗ ballet company**. Boris choreographed routines for Canadian skater Barbara Ann Scott (b. 1947) of Ottawa, Ontario. In 1951, he donated his studio and dancers to help the National Ballet of Canada.

> Approximately 3,000 Tlicho (Dogrib) Dene of the Northwest Territories live in the communities of Behcho Ko (Rae-Edzo), Wha Ti (Lac Martre), Gameti (Rae Lakes) and Wekweeti (Snare Lake). Behcho Ko is the **largest Dene community in Canada**.

_1939:_ The Queen Elizabeth Way (QEW), connecting Toronto with Hamilton and Niagara Falls, all in Ontario, became the **1ˢᵗ 4-lane, controlled-access, divided highway in North America** using the latest concepts in highway development. It was built to overcome local traffic bottlenecks and to open Ontario to U.S. motorists entering Canada via the Peace Bridge at Fort Erie, Ontario. Middle Road, the initial name of the Toronto-Burlington section, was completed first. The entire QEW was opened officially on June 7ᵗʰ by Her Majesty Queen Elizabeth The Queen Mother (1900-2002) of London, England. With four lanes of pavement to Fort Erie completed in 1956, the QEW has seen numerous upgrades over the years. The Pennsylvania Turnpike joined the QEW on the American side beginning in 1940, but unlike the QEW, had tolls.

<u>c. 1940</u>: The **origin of the 1ˢᵗ screech in the world** dates back to WWII in Newfoundland. The name itself was derived from "screigh", a Scottish dialect word for whisky. For many years, Newfoundlanders commonly exchanged their salt fish for low-grade Jamaican rum, until the government took over control of the liquor business in the early twentieth century and began selling rum in unlabelled bottles. Downing his first taste in one gulp, a visiting American serviceman let out such a loud howl that many locals came running to see what was the matter. An American sergeant demanded to know the cause of "that ungodly screech". "The screech? 'Tis the rum, me son", replied the serviceman's Newfoundlander host, and this popular Newfoundland drink was born. Of course, the liquor board then began labelling their rum as Screech.

Paper manufacturer Crown Zellerbach on Canada's West Coast has long been a pioneer in new logging methods. They developed the **1ˢᵗ log sorter in the world**. They also were the **1ˢᵗ to use the mobile-spar technique**. This is a means of moving a powerful crane and other log handling equipment into the centre of the forest to handle the cutting of trees more effectively.

<u>1940</u>: Actor and TV host **Raymond Burr** (1917-1993) of New Westminster, British Columbia, acted in movies long before appearing on television screens. His first movie was in *Earl of Puddlestone* in 1940. He portrayed numerous villains in movies like *His Kind of Woman* (1951), *Meet Danny Wilson* (1952), *A Cry In The Night* (1956), and *Rear Window* (1954) directed by Sir Alfred Joseph Hitchcock (1899-1980)

of Leytonstone, London, England. He won two Emmy Awards for his lead role on TV's *Perry Mason* from 1957 to 1966 plus six Emmy nominations and two Golden Globe nominations for *Robert Ironside* from 1967 to 1975. He also starred in *Centennial*, *79 Park Avenue*, and *Unsolved Mysteries*. Throughout his career, Raymond stared in 121 movies and made at least 16 notable television guest appearances.

<u>*1940:*</u> Trans-Canada Airlines became the **1st airline in the world to develop and implement a standard format and numbering control system for the preparation of technical instructions**. Later on June 1, 1956, the Air Transport Association of America adopted this unique principle for all airlines under its administration. In January 1965, Trans-Canada Airlines officially changed its name to Air Canada.

<u>*1940:*</u> During the War years, illicit stills continued to flourish, particularly in the Maritimes. Police dogs like Prince were instrumental in solving large numbers of excise tax cases. He assisted the police in obtaining so many convictions that one Nova Scotian appealed to a higher court against the admissibility of evidence resulting from the dog's work. The **1st case in which evidence produced by a dog was accepted in a Canadian court** resulted from the court's upholding this conviction in February, 1940, one concerning police dog Black Lux, son of Dale.

<u>*1940:*</u> Professionals and do-it-yourself home decorators alike owe Norman James Breakey (1891-1940) of Pierson, Manitoba, a debt of gratitude. He later moved to Toronto, Ontario, where he invented and patented the **1st paint roller in the world**, in 1940. He was unable to convince any Canadian company to back him financially. So Norman

died a poor man while several American companies made major money after infringing on his patent rights. He also invented a device for tapping beer kegs and a supermarket inventory system.

1940: The **1ˢᵗ surveys of nutrition in Canada** were made in 1940 by Fred F. Tisdall (1893-1949) in the northern frontier areas and in outlying districts in Newfoundland. Subsequent studies were undertaken in Newfoundland in 1944 and 1948. They showed marked improvements in general health attributed to improved education resultant from that initial survey.

1940: Duke Neilsen of Woodstock, New Brunswick, played with The New Brunswick Lumberjacks who had been invited to the Boston Sportsmen Show in 1940. A local television station was looking for some low-cost talent so it asked the group to appear on camera making them the **1ˢᵗ Canadian band to appear on television**. These new pioneers obliged, working under the hot lights. Duke eventually went on to play with Don Messer (1909-1973) of Tweedside, New Brunswick. In Boston, Massachusetts, this same year, Duke's was the **1ˢᵗ Canadian band to be televised in the USA**. Duke was inducted into the New Brunswick Country Music Hall of Fame in 1983.

1941: The Royal Botanical Gardens in Burlington, Ontario, is the **largest botanical garden in Canada**. Established this year, it includes extensive collections of lilacs, irises, roses, and many other flowers plus vast nature trails. The garden was also the **1ˢᵗ and only botanical garden in Canada to have a royal charter**. The Gardens is the home of the International Registration Authority for lilac cultivars. It also is home to the **largest lilac collection in the world**, comprised of over 1,000 bushes consisting of 26 wild lilac species native to Europe and southern Europe. Breeders have developed more than 1,600 cultivated varieties. Canadian Isabella Preston (1881-1965) of Lancaster, England, originated the 1st **Preston hybrids**. They are part of over 800 species and cultivars of common lilacs, French hybrids, wild species, and early-bloomers exhibited in the Gardens. Lilacs peak bloom in late May adding astounding colour and scent to the annual Lilac Festival.

_1941:_ Leaside, Ontario, was home to Canada Wire and Cable Co. Ltd. established by Ken Clipsham and his associates. In November of this year, it became the 1st **processor of polyethylene in North America** when it began manufacturing coaxial cable insulated with polyethylene and jacketed with polyvinyl chloride. This product was used extensively for radar systems. Coaxial cable is a unique product incorporating a wire conductor in the centre covered by polyethylene insulation. An outer metal braid becomes both a return circuit for the cable and a shield for the inner elements. The challenge in its manufacture was to provide an insulating material that didn't melt into the metal braids of the shield. Covering all these materials was an outer layer of polyvinyl chloride.

_1941:_ Brigadier John Kelburne Lawson (1887-1941) of Hull, England, commanded the Royal Rifles of Canada and the Winnipeg Grenadiers in Manitoba when they were caught by the Japanese invasion of Hong Kong, China, on December 8th. These were the 1st **Canadian units to fight in WWII**. They had not received training as front-line troops and had almost no air or naval defences as they had not anticipated this invasion. Japanese aircraft destroyed all six Royal Air

Force planes at Kai Tak Airport at 8 a.m. that day. The **1ˢᵗ Canadian casualties of WWII** were two men of the Royal Canadian Signals wounded in the camp at Sham Shui Po as the Japanese 38ᵗʰ Division moved across the frontier of the New Territories. John was the **most senior officer killed in action during the Battle of Hong Kong.** He also was the **highest ranking Canadian soldier killed in action in WWII.**

1941: The **world's longest spans of opening bridges of various types** cross the ship canal between Canada and the USA at Sault Ste. Marie, Ontario. Completed this year, the main span extends 102 m *(336 ft.).* The complex includes the **longest double-leaf railway bridge in Canada** 274.3 m *(900 ft.).* Not only was it the largest lock in the world at the time of its construction but also the **1ˢᵗ lock in the world to generate and employ electricity in the operation of its control valves, mitre gates, and lighting system.**

1941: Flying an airplane through clouds in cold weather causes clear ice to form all over it, a dangerous situation that can cause a plane to stall and crash. In 1940, John L. Orr and T.R. Griffith of the National Research Council developed the **1ˢᵗ method in the world of de-icing airplane propellers in flight**, a system known as the "Rubber shoes" de-icing method. They used carbon to impregnate a rubber shoe covering the leading edge, then passed electricity through it to melt any ice formations enough for the centrifugal force of the propeller to throw off the ice. Canada was asked by the Tizard Mission in Great Britain in 1940 to take over all aircraft de-icing research during WWII. Our work produced the **1ˢᵗ systems in the world for carburettor de-icing, wing and propeller de-icing,** and **windscreen de-icing** by the end of the War. We also developed the

1ˢᵗ stall-warning indicator in the world to warn a pilot when his aircraft was about to stop flying.

Certainly the **oldest art in Canada** is that of totem pole carving. A unique Canadian artist and carver, Indian Princess Kahasolas, also known as Ellen Neel (1916-1966) of Alert Bay on Vancouver Island, British Columbia, was the granddaughter of renowned master totem carver Charlie James (1870-1938) of Port Townsend, Washington, USA. Ellen was instrumental in reviving the art of carving among the Kwakwaka'wakw. She even travelled as far as Stratford, Ontario, to give a demonstration of carving at the Stratford Shakespearean Festival in the summer of 1956. She passed down the skills she learned from Charlie to her children and proudly was **Canada's 1ˢᵗ woman totem pole carver** whose art continues to be enjoyed to this day.

1941: Working at the Fort Qu'Appelle Sanatorium in Saskatchewan, Henry George "Harry" Ferguson (1884-1964) of Growell, County Down, Ireland, was acknowledged as a leader in studies on tuberculosis in Canada. His work from 1938 to 1943 on the protective value of BCG in adults and children was exceptional. He also was the **1ˢᵗ in the world to introduce mass chest X-ray surveys**.

1941: The *Canada Carries On* series of short, documentary films used as theatrical newsreels during WWII chronicled the war effort of the Allies. Stuart Legg (1910-1988) of London, England, wrote, edited, produced, and directed *Churchill's Island* for the National Film Board of Canada.

Narrated by Lorne Greene (1915-1987) of Ottawa, Ontario, this 22-minute, black and white film documented Winston Churchill (1874-1965) of London, England, and the Battle of Britain. In June, 1941, it became the **1ˢᵗ Canadian film to win an Academy Award**.

_1941:_ In WWII, Canada was the **1ˢᵗ of the Western Allies to declare war on Japan, Finland, Hungary, and Romania.** The USA, Britain, and other Allied countries followed the next day, after the Japanese bombed the U.S. base at Pearl Harbor, Hawaii, USA. The Axis powers included Germany, Italy, Japan, Hungary, Romania, and Bulgaria. The Allies included Britain, France, USSR, Australia, Belgium, Canada, Brazil, China, Denmark, Greece, the Netherlands, New Zealand, Norway, Poland, South Africa, Yugoslavia, and the USA.

_1942:_ Ian Fleming (1909-1964) of London, England, was a writer and creator of James Bond novels. Before then, however, he became the **1ˢᵗ graduate of the Special 25 training school for spies** in Port Hope, Ontario, on July 5ᵗʰ. Ian later became a member of MI5. He certainly benefited from this experience in developing the plots for his spy novels.

_1942:_ Between 1940 and 1942, the RCMP supply ship _St. Roch_ became the **1ˢᵗ vessel in the world to navigate the Northwest Passage from east to west.** In 1944, it became the **1ˢᵗ ship in the world to navigate the Northwest Passage in one season**.

_1943:_ Permafrost is prevalent in most of Northern Canada where frost is never out of the ground. However, it wasn't until 1943 that the **1ˢᵗ use in the world of the term** "**permafrost**" occurred describing this geological state. It evolved in English from the combination of "permanent" and "frost".

1943: The Alaska Highway, also called the Alcan Military Highway, joins Dawson Creek, British Columbia, to Fairbanks, Alaska, USA, covering a distance of 2451 km *(1,523 mi.)*. It was constructed in less than one year, between 1942 and 1943, making it the **fastest built highway in North America**. It was constructed to move supplies and munitions quickly north in the event of a Japanese invasion during WWII.

1944: The **1ˢᵗ and only fully-accredited Canadian woman war correspondent overseas during WWII** was Margaret Ecker Francis (1915-1965) of Edmonton, Alberta. Margaret was one of the fifteen representatives of the world's press and radio summoned to a hot room in enemy territory. She also was the **only woman present when General Dwight David Eisenhower (1890-1969) of Denison, Texas, USA, announced the German surrender**. She won the Canadian Women's Press Club award in 1944, 1946, and 1947.

1945: Andrée Maillet (1921-1996) of Montreal, Quebec, wrote the book *Ristontac* this year. It was illustrated by Robert LaPalme (1908-1997) of Montreal and published using new techniques developed after WWII by Éditions Lucien Parizeau in Montreal, Quebec. This is considered to be the **1ˢᵗ quality picture book published in Canada**.

1945: The **1ˢᵗ Soaring Association of Canada (SAC)** was formed in 1944 and given a national charter the following year. It immediately organized **Canada's 1ˢᵗ gliding**

instructor's school at Carp, Ontario. They were inspired in part by the Royal Canadian Air Force. In co-operation with the Air Cadet League, they structured a two-month course which attracted students from across Canada. Two courses of twenty students each produced nearly forty qualified instructors trained on six Slingsby Kadet gliders and launching equipment imported from England. The school did much to promote gliding in Canada.

1945: K. Dock Yip (1906-2001) of Vancouver, British Columbia, was the second youngest son of Yip Sang (1845-1927) of Shengtang village, Taishan County, Guangdong, People's Republic of China, a prominent Chinese merchant there in the 1900s. After graduating from Osgoode Hall Law School in Toronto, Ontario, in 1945, he became the **1ˢᵗ Chinese Canadian lawyer**. He helped to bring about the repeal of the *Chinese Immigration Act* of 1923.

1945: Dick Fowler (1921-1972), a native of Toronto, Ontario, played his entire Major League Baseball career with the Philadelphia Athletics in Pennsylvania, USA, beginning at the age of 20. He served with the Canadian Army for three years, then returned to professional baseball in 1945. That September, Dick became the **1ˢᵗ Canadian to pitch a no-hitter in the major leagues**, playing against the St. Louis Browns at Philadelphia's Shibe Park. By the time he retired in 1952, he had a lifetime record of 66-79, a very respectable 88 hits, and 1 home run. Dick was inducted into the Canadian Baseball Hall of Fame in 1985.

1945: The depth of wet concrete that can be placed in one operation is called a lift. Until concrete hardens, it is in a liquid form which exerts considerable pressure on the forms holding it in place. Different from slip-forming, Ontario

Hydro developed the **1ˢᵗ high-lift concrete pouring technique in the world**. The pouring of the 23.5-m *(77-ft.)* Barrett Chute Dam on the Madawaska River in eastern Ontario in 1945 was the **highest lift of concrete placed in one operation in the world**. Such lifts were commonly comprised of 9174.6 m³ *(12,000 yd.³)* of concrete.

1946: Mennonite Jacob John Siemens (1896-1963) of Altona, Manitoba, was a teacher from 1918 to 1929. Later, he managed the family farm and began taking on organizational responsibilities in his community. This led him to establish the Rhineland Consumers Co-operative Ltd. It was one of 33 co-operatives he organized into the Federation of Southern Manitoba Co-operatives around 1930. Jacob promoted new crops and served as the first president of Co-operative Vegetable Oils Ltd. in 1946. This was the **1ˢᵗ plant in North America to extract oil from sunflower seeds**. The following year, he became vice-president of the Manitoba Sugar Beet Growers Association.

1946: **Canada's 1ˢᵗ major professional basketball team** was founded this year, the Toronto Huskies of the Basketball Association of America. Unfortunately, the team only survived for one year. However, on November 1ˢᵗ, the New York Knickerbockers defeated the Toronto Huskies 68-66 at Maple Leaf Gardens in Toronto, Ontario. The Knickerbockers also were members of the Basketball Association of America. This was the **1ˢᵗ game of the National Basketball Association (NBA)** which evolved out of this previous Association. Thus, the NBA had its basketball origins in Canada.

1946: Harold Russell (1914-2002) of North Sydney, Nova Scotia, lost both his hands in WWII. Yet Harold believed that "It is not what you have lost but what you have left that counts". He became an actor and played the role of a handicapped veteran in *The Best Years of Our Lives* in 1946 becoming the **1ˢᵗ and only actor ever to win two Academy Awards for one performance**. Harold won an Oscar for Best Supporting Actor in addition to a Special Award for "bringing hope and courage to his fellow veterans".

<u>1946</u>: Princess Juliana (1909-1980) of The Hague, the Netherlands, and her consort, H.R.H. Prince Bernhard von Lippe-Biesterfeld (1911-2004) of Jena, Germany, resided at Stornoway in Ottawa, Ontario, from June, 1940, to May, 1945. Canada provided wartime refuge to these members of the Dutch royal family. We also temporarily declared the Ottawa Civic Hospital as Dutch territory in 1943 while Juliana gave birth there to Princess Margriet Francisca (b. 1943) of the Netherlands. Returning to Holland after the War, Juliana served as Queen of the Netherlands from 1948 to 1980. Queen Juliana sent 100,000 tulip bulbs to Ottawa in 1945 in gratitude for the kindness of the citizens of Ottawa. This became in 1953 the genesis of the **1ˢᵗ Canadian Tulip Festival**, the **largest Tulip Festival in the world** which now displays some two million blossoms annually. Some 25,000 new bulbs arrive each year from the royal family blooming throughout Ottawa's parks. The week-long Festival of Spring, the official name of this annual Tulip Festival, is held in late May. It includes concerts and special tour exhibitions with the focus of the Festival being on Parliament Hill. This event attracts thousands of tourists every year to Ottawa. In 1970, Dutch Canadians gave Canada a 1,500-pipe concert organ in celebration of the 25ᵗʰ anniversary of the liberation of Holland.

1947: Superstar hockey player Fred (Cyclone) Taylor (1885-1979) of Tara, Ontario, played for the Ottawa Senators in 1908-1909 in Ottawa, Ontario. He moved to the Renfrew Millionaires in Ontario from 1909 to 1911, then the Vancouver Millionaires in British Columbia from 1912 to 1921. Fred scored 194 goals in 186 games and was the NHL scoring leader five times during his career. At the charter meeting in 1947, he was elected the **1st living member of the Hockey Hall of Fame**.

1947: Vernon, British Columbia, native Larry "King" Kwong (b. 1923) was born Eng Kai Geong to immigrant parents who ran a family grocery store. Larry loved hockey and enjoyed a very successful and lengthy amateur and minor pro career playing in the position of centre. He played with the Vernon Hydrophones in 1939-1941, followed by the Trail Smoke Eaters, Nanaimo Clippers, the Vancouver St. Regis, Red Deer Wheelers, and New York Rovers. In the 1947-1948 season, he played professionally for the New York Rangers in New York City, New York, USA, making him the **1st Chinese Canadian to play in the National Hockey League (NHL)**. Thereafter, Larry played with the Valleyfield Braves, the Troy Bruins, the Trois-Rivières Lions, the Cornwall Chevies, and finally for the Notthingham Panthers in England before retiring from hockey. Perhaps his greatest year was when in 1951 he led the Braves to the league championship having exceeded the 20-goal mark six times. He was presented the Vimy Trophy as the most valuable player in the league.

1947: In addition to her career as freelance newspaperwoman and magazine writer, Isabel Dingman (1898-1960) was also **Canada's 1st syndicated lovelorn advice columnist**, writing under the pen name Elizabeth Thompson. This year, she became the **1st woman in the British Commonwealth**

to hold the position of professor of journalism when she received her appointment at the University of Western Ontario in London, Ontario.

According to students of Canadian English, *eh* is the **most characteristic Canadian expression**. Generally no more than simply a verbal question mark, this colloquial expression sometimes means "What do you say?" or "Wouldn't you agree?" Its pronunciation rhymes with *hay*.

1947: Television was still in its infancy in Canada at this time. On June 3rd in Windsor, Ontario, Canadian General Electric engineers received the **1st official electronic television broadcast in Canada**. U.S. station WWDT transmitted it from their new studios in Detroit, Michigan, USA. The following year, the **1st television manufacturing in Canada** began after which more and more Canadians were soon glued to their new television sets.

1948: Dr. Anne Currier graduated from Ontario Veterinary College in Guelph. As was common at that time, no male veterinarian would hire her. She was forced to go to the United States to begin her career. She returned to Canada and settled in Manotick, Ontario, where she became the **1st woman veterinarian in private practice in Canada**.

1948: International success came to Canadian pair figure skaters who won 7 out of 8 world pair titles between 1954 and 1962. Suzanne Morrow Francis (1930-2006) of Toronto, Ontario, and Wallace Distelmeyer (1925-1999) of Kitchener, Ontario, won bronze medals at the 1948 World Figure Skating

Championships and the Olympics, and in 1994 at both the Olympic Games and the World Championships. In 1948 in Davos, Switzerland, they were the **1ˢᵗ figure skaters in the world to perform "The Death Spiral" in its present day low position at international competition**. This is a circular move whereby the man lowers his female partner to the ice with one arm and swings her in a circle while she is arched backward, gliding on one foot with her head almost touching the ice. Wallace also became the **1ˢᵗ figure skater in the world to win five skating disciplines out of six**. Wallace's wife, Bette Distelmeyer, also gained prominence in the skating world becoming the **1ˢᵗ woman Gold Test skating judge in Canada**.

_1948:_ Boys from the Scout Troupe in Westville, Nova Scotia, established the **1ˢᵗ youth Pipe and Drum Band formed in Canada**. It was for youth aged 12 to 14.

_1949:_ William Francis Giauque (1895-1982) of Niagara Falls, Ontario, won the Nobel Prize in chemistry this year for being the **1ˢᵗ to discover a way of producing temperatures near absolute zero**.

_1949:_ No deaths and very little damage was reported when the **biggest earthquake recorded in Canada** hit British Columbia on August 21ˢᵗ off the Queen Charlotte Islands. The surface wave magnitude registered 8.1 on the Richter Scale.

_1949:_ Goitre was still a serious problem in the 1940s as essentially only the military was using iodized salt. In 1949, **adding iodine to table salt became mandatory for the 1ˢᵗ time in Canada** after which goitre all but disappeared.

1950s: After enlisting in the Royal Canadian Air Force (RCAF) in 1943 and graduating as a pilot the following year, Bert William Mead (b. 1923) of Vermillion, Alberta, enrolled in the Royal Navy as a sub-lieutenant pilot. He transferred to the VX-10 Squadron of the Royal Canadian Navy in 1952. He was responsible for flight testing the **world's 1ˢᵗ successful automatic takeoff and landing system**. This enabled military aircraft to leave or land on an aircraft carrier in most any weather conditions. Bert later became commander of the Air Cushion Vehicle (ACV) Search and Rescue unit in Vancouver, British Columbia. In this role, he became **Canada's 1ˢᵗ qualified air cushion vehicle pilot**.

1950: Some professional hockey goalies were concerned with their being expected to play sixty to seventy games well each year. This year, The Toronto Maple Leafs were the **1ˢᵗ professional hockey team in North America to introduce the two-goalie system** when they had Walter (Turk) Broda (1914-1972) of Brandon, Manitoba, and Al Rollins (1926-1996) of Vanguard, Saskatchewan, sharing goal-tending duties equally. This new system was adopted formally in the 1960s.

1950: Harry Wasylyk (b. 1925) of Winnipeg, Manitoba, and Larry Hansen of Lindsay, Ontario, invented the **1ˢᵗ disposable green polyethylene garbage bag in the world**. The bags were sold first to the Winnipeg General Hospital as their intent was for commercial, not domestic, application. Larry worked for the Union Carbide Company in Lindsay which bought the invention from Harry and Larry. Union Carbide then manufactured the **1ˢᵗ green garbage bags in the world for home use** in the late 1960s under the trade name Glad Garbage Bags.

1950: A mass spectrometer is a scientific device used to measure the quantities of different charged particles. Examples are atomic nuclei and fragments of molecules. Physicist Arthur Jeffrey Dempster (1886-1950) of Toronto, Ontario, built the **1ˢᵗ mass spectrometer in the world** on August 14ᵗʰ.

1951: Actor and director Jean Gascon (1920-1988) of Montreal, Quebec, was a distinguished figure in Canadian theatre. In August this year in Montreal, Jean established the **1ˢᵗ Théâtre du Nouveau Monde in Canada**. In 1960, he was co-founder of the **1ˢᵗ National Theatre School in Canada**. Jean was equally successful both in French and English. He was a very popular artistic director of the Stratford Shakespearean Festival in Stratford, Ontario, from 1969 to 1974. He was director of the theatre at the National Arts Centre in Ottawa beginning in 1977. Jean was forced to retire from the NAC in 1984 for health reasons but continued to teach and occasionally direct opera for the rest of his life.

1951: Elsa Jenkins of Peterborough, Ontario, enjoyed a varied career throughout her life teaching handicrafts with the Canadian Red Cross. She acted as editor and columnist for *Mayfair Magazine*, participated as a panellist on *Court of Opinion*, and filled the job of manager of the women's division of the Canadian National Exhibition. In addition to handling radio appearances, she was also appointed the **1ˢᵗ woman announcer in Canadian television**, in 1951.

1952: Hypothermia is the process of reducing body temperature artificially to slow metabolic processes so that less oxygen is required during cardio-vascular open-heart surgery. Dr. Wilfred Gordon Bigelow (1913-2005) of Brandon, Manitoba, developed the **1ˢᵗ hypothermia technique**

in the world at the Toronto General Hospital between 1948 and 1952. His research began during WWII where he established regional hypothermia for severe wounds of the extremities by means of cooling cabinets. Making complex operations far safer is one of the advantages of hypothermia. Providing the longer period of circulatory control needed in more elaborate intra-cardiac surgery today now depends primarily on extra-corporeal circulation although both techniques can be combined successfully. Bill and his team became the **1ˢᵗ people in the world ever to see inside a living human heart while it was beating**.

_1952_: Inventors Parsons, Dunlop, and Curran of Ottawa brought increased safety and convenience to the world of aviation this year. They invented the **1ˢᵗ Position Homing Indicator (PHI) in the world**, a fully automatic dead reckoning instrument for aircraft. It constantly integrates, computes, and presents position and course information to a pilot without charting or calculation.

_1952_: Strip artiste "Krystyne Kolorful" (b. 1952) of Alberta took ten years to have 95% of her body tattooed, making her the **world's most decorated woman**.

_1952_: Author Thomas B. Costain of Brantford, Ontario, wrote _The Silver Chalice_. It became the **1ˢᵗ Canadian novel to make it to the top of annual worldwide best-seller lists**.

_1952_: The United Jewish People's Order (UJPO) organized the UJPO Folksingers. They organized tours in 1952 and 1953 travelling from Quebec to British Columbia. This was the **1ˢᵗ professional level ensemble to bring the new folk music to audiences across Canada**. This was a unique beginning to a musical era that never truly took off until the 1960s. Yet it offered wonderful insight into folk music in Canada at its very beginning.

_1952:_ The 1ˢᵗ **use of enriched flour in Canada** originated as a direct result of Newfoundland becoming our tenth province. Having used enriched flour for some time, Newfoundland insisted that one condition of its joining Confederation was permission for continued use of enriched flour!

_1952:_ Isabelle Cadel, a resident in Etobicoke, Ontario, is still using her very first microwave oven which she bought back in 1952. It was the most advanced appliance of its kind at that time and is the **oldest working microwave oven in Canada**.

_1953:_ Lake sturgeon _(Acipenser fulvescens)_ can grow to a considerable size. One caught in Lake Superior, Wisconsin, USA, in 1922 weighed in at 140.6 kg _(310 lb.)_ and was 1.8 m _(7 ft. 11 in.)_ long! They also can have a very long lifespan. A smaller one was caught in 1953 in Lake of the Woods weighing only 94.4 _(208 lb.)_. However, it was no youngster. Estimated to have been born in 1801, that made it 152 years old and the **oldest North American lake sturgeon ever recorded**.

_1953:_ Imperial Oil hired John Johnston on a full-time basis this year. This was the 1ˢᵗ **Canadian company to hire an industrial hygienist**.

_1953:_ Completed in 1900, a railway was built across Yukon winding along the original White Pass Trail of the gold-seekers and bypassing the rapids. Prospectors transferred at Whitehorse, Yukon, from the train to a sternwheeler for the remainder of the journey to Dawson City, Yukon. The full 177-km *(110-mile)* White Pass and Yukon Route was completed in 1953. It became the 1st **containerized railway in the world**. To this day, it continues to be the **world's longest commercial narrow-gauge railway**.

1953: Created this year, the Great Seal of Canada designed for the Queen specifically mentioned Canada in a new style and title. This also was the 1st **time that Her Royal Highness Queen Elizabeth II (b. 1926) of London, England, had been designated as Queen of Canada**.

1953: The 1st **private television station in Canada** was CKSO in Sudbury, Ontario, which launched its first telecast on October 20th. It was the first Canadian Broadcasting Corporation (CBC) affiliate so some of their programming was provided by the CBC. CFPL in London, Ontario, followed suit by November 28th as did CBUT in Vancouver, British Columbia, on December 16th. The CBC enjoyed quite the coup this year by being the 1st **broadcaster in North America to televise the coronation of Her Royal Highness Queen Elizabeth II** (b. 1928) of London, England. It beat out its American competitors by flying television footage across the Atlantic from London, England. The 1st **microwave network in Canada** connected CBC television stations in Montreal and Quebec City in Quebec plus Ottawa and Toronto in Ontario. When it extended this network to Victoria, British Columbia, then to Halifax and Sydney in Nova Scotia, this became the **longest television network in the world**.

1954: Having been dormant for more than 10,000 years, the **oldest living plant seeds ever found in the world** were those of the Arctic lupine *(Lupinus arcticus)*. They were unearthed in a system of rodent burrows by Harold Schmidt in frozen silt at Miller Creek, Yukon, in July, 1954. The seeds were germinated in 1966, then radiocarbon dated to at least 8,000 B.C. and more probably to 13,000 B.C.

A very popular cairn design known throughout Canada today is called an inukshuk. It usually is constructed by Inuit. It resembles the outline of a man and has several purposes. It can serve as a landmark or deer hedge in some parts of the Arctic. An inukshuk is also used to frighten caribou herds into moving into certain areas where hunters would wait for them with bows and arrows at the ready. It is not uncommon to see an inukshuk most anywhere in our country today. The **largest inukshuk in the world**, 11.377 m *(37.3 ft.)* high and weighing 82 000 kg *(90.4 tons),* was built in Schomberg, Ontario.

1954: The Canadian Broadcasting Corporation (CBC) operated two mobile units in Vancouver, British Columbia, feeding their signal first to Seattle, Washington, USA, then across America to the National Broadcasting Corporation (NBC). It then fed the signal to its network and back into Canada. They were televising the Empire Games of 1954, the **1ˢᵗ Canadian sports events ever to be televised around the world**.

1954: Don Mills, Ontario, was constructed 11 km *(6.8 mi.)* northeast of downtown Toronto, Ontario, this year under the direction of E.P. (Edward Plunket) Taylor (1901-1989) of Ottawa, Ontario, owner of O'Keefe Breweries. It was named after a mill on the Don River. It was **Canada's 1st comprehensive suburb**. Planner Macklin Hancock designed the community as a series of curved, discontinuous roads, the purpose being to block outside traffic and thereby attract a diverse population—the working class living in the many apartments and working in the nearby mills and factories, and the middle class in the many homes and commuting to downtown Toronto. In addition to the residential structures, the area contained a shopping mall designed by John Burnett Parkin (1911-1975) of Toronto, churches, schools, and green space. The idea quickly caught on in communities across Canada. However, its popularity drove prices upward. The suburb soon became home primarily to a uniform, white middle class.

1954: Roy G. Snyder (b. 1915) of Waterloo, Ontario, was the first full-time employee of the Waterloo Cattle Breeding Association in 1946. He excelled to the position of manager from 1950 to 1963. In 1954, Roy established the **1st artificial insemination centre in the world**, to adopt an all-frozen semen programme. He was instrumental in importing the **1st Charolais bull in Canada** in 1954. He placed the **1st Brown Swiss bulls in Canada** into artificial insemination service. His portrait was hung in the Canadian Agricultural Hall of Fame in the Coliseum of the Royal Agricultural Winter Fair in Toronto, Ontario, in 1982.

1955: The Canso Causeway at Port Hastings, Ontario, serves several purposes. It is 1371.6 m *(4,500 ft)* long, 243.8 m *(800 ft.)* wide at its base, 24.4 m *(80 ft.)* wide on the surface, and 66.5 m *(218 ft.)* deep. It is the **deepest causeway in the world**. Joining mainland Nova Scotia with Cape Breton Island, the causeway carries a two-lane highway, a railway track, and a pedestrian walkway while ships use a navigation lock at the northern end. Meaning "opposite the lofty cliffs", the name Canso originates from the Mi'kmaq word *kamsok*. The Canso Causeway opened this year creating an ice-free harbour 16.1 m *(10 mi.)* long by preventing ice from entering the Strait from the north. The **1ˢᵗ train to cross the Canso Causeway** did so on May 17ᵗʰ.

1955: After logs are sawn into different sizes of lumber at sawmills, the boards must be sorted and graded, a slow and laborious process. Sawmill superintendent George Beale of the Tahsis Lumber Company in British Columbia engineered the **1ˢᵗ Beale timber sorter in the world**. He had it manufactured by Canadian Car in the late 1950s. His invention enables one operator to do the work of three, handling a load of 2.7 metric tonnes *(3 tons)* and timbers 0.5 m *(1.6 ft.)* wide and 12 m *(39.4 ft.)* long. These sorters continue to be used in Canadian sawmills today.

1955: The Rainbow Stage opened in Winnipeg, Manitoba's Kildonan Park on July 7ᵗʰ. It presented operettas and musicals using local performers. The first full-length musical presented there was *Brigadoon* in the fall of 1955. The Rainbow Stage is **Canada's longest running outdoor theatre**.

1955: Stories of amethyst near Lake Superior date as far back as the 1600s. The **1ˢᵗ large amethyst deposit in Canada** was discovered in McTavish Township east of Thunder Bay in 1955. About 1.1 billion years ago during the Keweenawan faulting of the Lake Superior basis, amethyst crystals formed in the cavities of the rock. Amethyst is a variety of the common mineral quartz and forms as beautiful purple crystals. It is found with other minerals including pyrite, galena, sphalerite, fluorite, calcite, chalcopyrite, and native silver. Some have a thin layer of reddish brown hematite just beneath the surface. Amethyst Mine Panorama is the **largest amethyst deposit in North America**. It was discovered in 1955 and production began in 1960. It has continued to this day producing 40% useable amethyst by volume. There is even a large digging area open to the public where you can pick your own amethysts. All types of amethyst are found in this location which is the **largest open pit gemstone mine in North America**. Amethyst is the official gemstone of the Province of Ontario.

_1955_: The **1st time a Mountie had a regular spot on an American network's prime-time schedule** was on _Sergeant Preston of the Yukon_. It starred Dick Simmons (1913-2003) of St. Paul, Minnesota, USA. The next such instance was with the programme _Due South_, starring Paul Gross (b. 1959) of Calgary, Alberta, on CBS in the period 1994-1998. It was the **1st Canadian-produced television series to win a prime-time spot on an American Network**.

_1956_: Thousands of people from across Canada and the United States came to sit on the sunny grass slopes surrounding the outdoor stage in August this year in Tatamagouche, Nova Scotia. Arts and crafts displays plus six concerts comprised this Nova Scotia Festival of the Arts. It was the **1st Festival of the Arts in North America**. It moved eventually to Wolfville, Nova Scotia, then to Halifax, Nova Scotia, but appears to have ceased operation around 1976.

_1956_: Internationally renowned novelist **Arthur Hailey** (1920-2004) of Luton, England, served in the Royal Air Force as a flight lieutenant from 1939 to 1947, immigrated to Toronto, Ontario, in 1947 as a naturalized Canadian, and became a Canadian citizen in 1952. He was an editor for Maclean-Hunter from 1947 to 1953. His suspense drama *Flight Into Danger* (1956) became a 60-minute teleplay shown by CBC TV on *GM Presents*. This launched his popular writing career of more than a dozen highly researched, best-selling novels including *Runway Zero-Eight* (1958) and *The Final Diagnosis* (1959). His only book with a specific Canadian setting, the Ottawa political scene, was *In High Places* (1960). *Airport* (1968) became the basis for three action-suspense movies—*Airport* (1968), *Airport 75* (1974), and *Airport 77* (1976). *Hotel* (1965), *Wheels* (1971), *The Money-Changers* (1975), *Overload* (1979), *Strong Medicine* (1984), *The Evening News* (1990), and *Detective* (1997) were just some of his many successful novels which have sold over 160 million copies in 36 languages. His firm grip on detail and inherent ability as a storyteller dealing with fashionable subjects made Arthur one of Canada's most popular writers.

1956: The St. Catharines Parachute Club in Ontario formed the **1st Parachute Club of Canada** to control and advance sport parachuting. The national club today is known as the Canadian Sport Parachuting Association.

1957: Humane Societies across Canada have many common goals in their endeavour to prevent animal cruelty and abuse and to encourage the compassionate and humane treatment of all animals. These organizations faced no lack of challenges this year in bringing together their many diverse biases to form the **1st Canadian Federation of Humane Societies (CFHS)**. Yet they now view their individual diversities as providing strength to their membership. The specific objectives of CFHS members are: to promote the value of pets; to educate the public about responsible pet ownership; to promote compassion toward animals; and to collaborate with their member humane societies.

1957: As a senior research officer at the National Research Council, Harry T. Stevinson (b. 1915) of Passberg, British Columbia, invented the 1ˢᵗ **Crash Position Indicator (CPI) in the world** in 1957. It is comprised of a small airfoil containing a radio distress beacon which is deployed at the first indication of an impending aircraft accident. The CPI falls clear of the plane, slows down as it tumbles to land, and identifies the location of the crash making rescue operations faster and more efficient.

1957: Electronics scientist Dr. Maurice Levy built the 1ˢᵗ **automatic mail sorter in the world** for the Canadian Post Office this year. He demonstrated it to the Universal Postal Union Congress in Ottawa, Ontario. This new invention, capable of sorting 200,000 letters per hour, attracted worldwide attention yet was abandoned by the new conservative government of Prime Minister John George Diefenbaker (1895-1975) of Neustadt, Ontario.

1957: Steve Pasjack of Vancouver, British Columbia, was a package designer by trade, working in the corrugated carton business. Tired with having to carry awkward cases of beer under his arms, he developed the 1ˢᵗ **tuck-away beer carton handle in the world**, in 1957. The handle disappears so that the cases can be stacked evenly, but it pops up for easy carrying. His simple, yet brilliant invention now is used worldwide making it easier than ever to carry or store that favourite twelve-pack.

1958: In the Valley of the Dinosaurs near Drumheller, Alberta, there is a structure only 2.1 m *(7 ft.)* wide and

3.7 m *(12 ft.)* long. It is a church with no regular congregation, no collection plate, no minister, and room for no more than six worshippers at a time. Known as the "Biggest Little Church in the World", it actually is the **smallest church in Canada**. The idea originated with Reverend E. C. O'Brien of the Pentecostal denomination. Local contractor Trygve Seland built the church almost single-handedly. Robert Gibson provided the architectural design and painted the glass windows. City Council proclaimed August 31 as "Little Church Sunday". Honourable G.E. Taylor, Mr. Robert Gibson, Reverend E.C. O'Brien, Mr. Trygve Seland, and Mayor E.A. Toshach participated in the opening day ceremonies on July 9, 1958; over 1,200 visits were recorded in the guest book. Within the first 10 months after it opened, the chapel record showed over 36,000 visitors, a tribute to its advertisement of accommodating ten thousand people—6 at a time!

1958: Promoting language retention and addressing housing, training, business, and cultural awareness among the Manitoba Aboriginal people has been a life-long passion for Mary Richard (b. 1940) of Camperville, Manitoba. She became the executive director of the **1st Indian and Métis Friendship Centre in Canada**. It is located in Winnipeg, Manitoba, and was created as a result of an Indian and Métis Conference held in 1958. The Centre acts as a referral service on various community services including employment, housing, education, and health. In 2000, Mary became the first chief executive officer of Thunderbird House, a social outreach centre for many low-income people living in north Winnipeg. She is also a past president of the Aboriginal Council of Winnipeg. She was named to the Order of Manitoba in 2000. Three years later, Mary received the

National Aboriginal Achievement Award for Community Development.

1959: Opened this year and operating until its closure in 1990, the Big Four Curling Rink in Calgary, Alberta, was the **largest curling rink in the world**. Forty-eight sheets of ice on two floors accommodated 96 teams and 384 players.

> With half the bridge being Canadian and half American owned, a bridge linking two of the Thousand Islands in the St. Lawrence River is only 15.2 m *(50 ft.)* long—the **world's shortest international bridge**.

1959: All Inuit sculpture, prints, and other art is tagged with a registration number and a co-op name. Co-operatives owned and operated by Inuit were established in Canada's North to arrange the manufacture and sale of the native arts and crafts produced by its members. The **1st Inuit co-operative in the world** was the West Baffin Eskimo Co-operative at Cape Dorset, Nunavut. It is just one of almost sixty Inuit co-operatives in the Northwest Territories, Nunavut, and Northern Quebec today.

1959: During the opening of the Prince Albert Radar Laboratory in Saskatchewan on June 3, 1959, the voice of Prime Minister John George Diefenbaker (1895-1975) of Neustadt, Ontario, was **one of the 1st two voices on the moon**. He and U.S. President Dwight David Eisenhower (1890-1969) of Denison, Texas, USA, had their voices relayed during the opening ceremony.

_1959:_ The **1ˢᵗ Harris Tweed in the world** was invented in Tweed, Ontario. This hand-woven fabric is used to make men's jackets.

_1959:_ The **1ˢᵗ Canadian table tennis teams competed in the World Championships**.

_1959:_ Born of French Canadian and Irish parents, **Kate McGarrigle** (b. 1946) and **Anna McGarrigle** (b. 1944) of St. Sauveurs des Monts, Quebec, grew up with an enthusiasm for blues, jazz, traditional French Canadian folk songs, Broadway show tunes, and country music. Singing together since 1959 in both English and French, both girls can play piano, banjo, guitar, fiddle, ukulele, zither, and button accordion. Kate studied engineering at McGill University in Montreal, Quebec, in the 1960s while Anna studied painting at the École des Beaux-Arts in Montreal. Yet their love of music flourished, and in 1963 they began playing in Montreal's coffee houses and started writing their own songs. By the 1970s, they gained international recognition as songwriters. They performed at the Charley Wakes Folk Festival in Lancashire, England, and at Victoria Palace, both in 1976. One of their songs, "Heartbeats Accelerating", became a major hit when it was recorded by Linda Ronstadt (b. 1946) of Tucson, Arizona, USA, in 1994. Kate and Anna continued to appear in highly successful, sold-out concerts and festivals throughout the world. They also composed and performed music for several movie and television productions and released albums all through the '90s and into the new millennium. They both were honoured as Members of the Order of Canada in 1993.

1960s: Some documents suggest that the Chocolate Siamese cats of the 1800s were actually Tonkinese. Wong Mau, the ancestress of the Burmese, was the first known Tonkinese before the name was even known, first arriving in the USA in 1930. Cat lover Margaret Conroy decided in the early 1960s to cross a seal point Siamese and a sable Burmese. The result was a true Tonkinese with physical and personality characteristics mid-way between those of the Siamese and the Burmese. Margaret asked the Canadian Cat Association (CCA) to register this intermediate hybrid as a new breed of cat in Canada. They approved her request making the Tonkinese the 1st **breed of cat developed in Canada**. In 1984, the CCA was the 1st **cat association to recognize the Tonkinese breed**. The Cat Fanciers' Association (CFA) followed in 1984. Tonkinese cats come in one of four colours— natural, also called sable or seal; champagne, also called chocolate; platinum, also called lilac or frost; and blue. Their patterns may be solid, pointed, or mink. The eyes of solid Tonkinese range in colour from green/gold to yellow/green while those of pointed Tonks range from sky blue to violet. The mink Tonkinese have brilliant, aqua-coloured eyes. This true intermediate breed thrives on human companionship and affection and has become a well-loved cat.

1960: Imperial Oil in Canada was the 1st **company in the world to distribute motor oil in plastic containers**. The intended applications were for outboard motors, lawn mowers, and chainsaws.

1960: In London, Ontario, Wellington Square became **North America's 1st enclosed downtown mall**. It was designed by John Graham and Company and developed by Webb and Knapp. The mall was expanded in 1980 and the name changed to London Eaton Square. In 1989, London

Eaton Square was demolished to make way for London's new Galleria Mall. The concept of enclosed downtown malls soon expanded throughout North America and remains as popular today as it did in the 1960s.

<u>1960</u>: The *Canadian Bill of Rights* recognizes the rights of Canadians to life, liberty, personal security, and the enjoyment of property. It guarantees the legal right to equality, freedom of speech, freedom of religion, freedom of assembly and association, and freedom of the press. The **1st *Canadian Bill of Rights*** received royal assent and became law on August 10th. It remains in effect today as it cannot be overruled by the *Charter of Rights and Freedoms* introduced in 1982.

<u>1960</u>: Messages between the Canadian North and southern Canada had to rely on annual supply ships prior to the late 1920s. Thereafter, radio was introduced. By the 1930s, high frequency radio was used for medical emergencies and business while broadcast radio maintained daily contact with the South. The **1st Inuit-language broadcast in the world** occurred in 1960 to better encourage communication between Inuit and other Canadians. Short wave programming in Inuktitut, particularly on CBC Northern Service short wave, has continued to expand throughout the years.

<u>1960</u>: Gary Johnston (1916-2000) of Alma, Ontario, was a teacher and served in the Royal Canadian Air Force. He attained a B.Sc. in chemistry in 1947 from the Ontario Agricultural College (OAC). He went on in 1951 to earn his Masters degree in crop science and winter wheat. He worked for Agriculture and Agri-Food Canada in 1953 as a research scientist, then moved to the University of Guelph in Ontario where he led a research team during the

1960s. They experimented combining a North American white potato (Norgleam) with a South American yellow (W5279-4). The end result was the **1st Yukon Gold potato in the world** which also became the **1st Canadian potato to be marketed by name**. It has become prized by chefs worldwide, particularly after its introduction to the U.S. market in 1980. For his impressive work, the University of Guelph honoured Gary in 2000 with an Honorary Doctor of Science degree.

_1960:_ On March 8th, the Canadian Curling Championships were held at Fort William, Ontario. Playing for Alberta against Nova Scotia in this brier, Stu Beagle (1917-1999) of Calgary, Alberta, played the **1st perfect championship curling game in the world**, scoring a total of 48 points.

_1961:_ The Six Nations Indian Reserve near Brantford, Ontario, was the birthplace of poetess Emily Pauline Johnson (1861-1913). Her Mohawk name was Tekahionwake. Published in her book entitled _Flint and Feather_, Pauline's work was particularly popular at the beginning of the 20th century. In fact, **no book of poetry by a Canadian has ever outsold her collected verse in _Flint and Feather_**. She made long tours across Canada speaking in theatres, church halls, and schoolhouses where thousands of people flocked to hear her recite her poems. Honouring Pauline as a great national figure, the Federal Post Office issued a special commemorative stamp celebrating her Aboriginal heritage on the centenary of her birth. Pauline thus became the **1st Canadian author, 1st Canadian woman, and 1st Canadian Indian to be honoured with a commemorative stamp**.

_1961:_ Did you know that no two instant potato flakes are shaped exactly alike, or that they are a Canadian invention?

Dr. Edward Anton Asselbergs (1927-1996) of the federal Department of Agriculture developed the **1st instant mashed potato flakes in the world**, in 1961. They are made from dehydrated real potatoes. Edward assigned his patent for instant potato flakes to Salada-Shirriff-Horsey in Toronto, Ontario, to market his new product. He then went on to **develop instant meat, fish, chicken,** and **cheese products**.

_1961:_ In Grigon, France, William Dixon of Brampton, Ontario, became the **1st Canadian to win the world ploughing match**.

_1962:_ Teams from Montreal, Quebec, and West Germany competed in the **1st international team handball competition in the world**, played in Canada.

_1962:_ A total of 705 people have been executed by hanging in Canada. The last two were convicted murderers, Ronald Turpin (1933-1962) and Arthur Lucas (d. 1962) of Georgia, USA, in Toronto, Ontario's Don Jail on December 11th. Commonly called the death penalty, **capital punishment in Canada was abolished** formally by parliament on July 14, 1976, excluding premeditated murder of law enforcement officers. The free vote for abolition was a close one of 132-124. Many people were concerned that without capital punishment, criminals would be more likely to commit murder. Yet statistics showed that the murder rate in Canada actually decreased several years after the death penalty was abolished. In 1976, capital punishment was replaced by a mandatory life sentence without possibility of parole for 25 years for all first-degree murders. A similar amendment was made in 1998 to the _Canadian National Defence Act_ bringing Canadian military law in line with civil law. Today, the United States is the only western industrialized country still practicing capital punishment.

1962: The first of the movies to star Sir Thomas Sean Connery (b. 1925) of Edinburgh, Scotland, as James Bond, Secret Agent 007, was *Dr. No* (1962), also the first movie in this ongoing series. The 1st sinister arch-villain himself, **Dr. No**, was played by the character actor Joseph Wiseman (1918-2009) of Montreal, Quebec. The 1st **Miss Moneypenny** was played in fourteen 007 films over 23 years by another native Canadian, actress Lois Maxwell (1927-2007) of Kitchener, Ontario. As M's spinster secretary, she was always secretly in love with 007. Lois was considered the matriarch of all the actors who eventually came to fill this role, "the one grown-up among sexpots and psychopaths". She was born Lois Hooker but changed her name when a talent scout spotted her acting in the theatre in London, England, and hustled her off to Hollywood at the age of 20. Movie producer Harry Saltzman (1915-1994) of Saint John, New Brunswick, co-produced the first nine James Bond films with Albert R. "Cubby" Broccoli (1909-1996) of New York City, New York, USA. Lois is the **only cast member to appear in 14 James Bond movies**, the most of any single actor.

1962: The real name of yodeller singer Lucille Starr (b. 1938) of St. Boniface, Quebec, is Lucille Marie Raymonde Savoie. She applied her skill yodelling for the character Cousin Pearl in the highly popular television series the ***Beverly Hillbillies***.

1962: The 1962 Grey Cup game on December 2nd made history becoming the 1st **and only professional football match ever played in North America that took a whole weekend to complete!** The Winnipeg Blue Bombers were leading the Hamilton Tiger-Cats 28-27 in the fourth quarter of the game. But the fog on the field became so thick that the contest was stopped until the following day. In spite of nice, bright sunshine and much greater yard gains by the Tiger-Cats, Winnipeg held on to their slim lead winning their fourth Grey Cup in five years.

1963: A native of Hamilton, Ontario, Blaine MacDonald (b. 1937) became the **1st Canadian cartoonist ever to win the famous International Salon of Cartoons**, in Montreal, Quebec. In 1970, he was the **1st Canadian to win the New York City, New York, USA-based Reuben Award**, cartooning's highest honour, for his work in editorial cartooning.

1963: The Université de Moncton in New Brunswick was established in 1963, the result of three smaller Acadian educational institutions in New Brunswick amalgamating. It was the first French-language university founded in Canada outside Quebec. Its law school is the **1st law school in the world teaching common law in the French language**.

1963: Captain Wilson Kettle (1861-1963) of Port aux Basques, Newfoundland, ranks second in the world but **1st in Canada for having the most descendants**. At his death at age 102, his family included a total of 591 descendents— 11 children, 65 grandchildren, 210 great-grandchildren, and 205 great-great-grandchildren!

1963: George Chenier (1907-1970) of Hull, Quebec, was a world class billiards player. He was the North American snooker champion from 1947 right through to 1970. He also was runner-up to world champion Fred Davis (1913-1998) of Chesterfield, Derbyshire, England, on two occasions. Then, on November 14, 1963, he ran the **1ˢᵗ perfect game of 150 points ever registered in the World Pocket Billiard Championship**, beating the champion Irving Crane (1913-2001) of Livonia, New York, USA.

_1963:_ A computerized traffic control device controls the timing of traffic signals according to the number of vehicles passing a particular corner. It detects the vehicles magnetically. The system is also useful in relaying information to the police regarding unusual traffic patterns. Reports indicate a 28% decrease in traffic congestion with these controls. The average rush-hour speed also increases by 5.6 km/h _(3 mph)_. The **1ˢᵗ computerized traffic control system in North America** was installed in Toronto, Ontario, in 1963.

_1964:_ Red Robinson, DJ for CKNW in Vancouver, British Columbia, hosted a live broadcast on August 22ⁿᵈ of the **1ˢᵗ Canadian concert by the Beatles**. The top ticket price was $5.25. Some 20,000 fans filled Empire Stadium to hear this new hit group play songs from their latest album "Something New". Fearing a riot, the police cut the concert short after just 27 minutes.

_1964:_ Colin Kerry of Toronto, Ontario, was the owner of "Rajah", the **1ˢᵗ and only mynah bird insured by Lloyd's of London** in England. This Indian Hill mynah also happened to be the **1ˢᵗ and only talking bird in the world trained to repeat the word "antidisestablishmentarianism"**!

_1964:_ The University of Toronto became a major neurosurgical institution in 1964 specializing in the care of children with neurosurgical disease thanks to Edward Bruce Hendrick (1924-2001) of Toronto, Ontario. He completed his medical residency at the University of Toronto, then became the

1st full-time paediatric neurosurgeon in the world. In 1986, the division of neurosurgery established the annual E. Bruce Hendrick Lectureship in Paediatric Neurosurgery in his honour.

1965: Northern Ontario directors of municipal recreation drew up and approved the **1st complete set of ringette rules in the world**.

1965: Commissioned in Montreal, Quebec, on June 1st for the Canadian Coast Guard, the *CCGS John Cabot* was the **1st icebreaker cable-repair ship in the world**.

1965: The town of Gold River, British Columbia, was built in six months in central Vancouver Island, British Columbia, during 1965 to house employees of the Tahsis Company Ltd. pulp mill. It was reincorporated as the Village Municipality of Gold River on January 1, 1972. With all electricity, telephone, and television cables buried underground, it was the **1st Canadian city to have underground wiring**. Gold River also was the **1st all-electric town in Canada**. The town is located in the Gold River Valley at the junction of the Gold and Heber rivers on Vancouver Island.

1965: George H. Cluthe was the owner of Cluthe Manufacturing Co. in Waterloo, Ontario. He patented one of his inventions this year, the **1st interchangeable head screwdriver in the world**. Its pop-top handle opens revealing five or six different screwdriver bits.

1965: The five-man rhythm and blues group Mandala of Toronto, Ontario, flourished between 1965 and 1969. Mandala was the **1st rhythm-and-blues group in North America to make use of theatrical lighting**. It also set another record becoming the **1st Canadian musical**

group to earn more than $1,000 for a performance in Canada.

<u>1965</u>: The province of Quebec has more than 10,000 maple trees tapped for their liquid gold, some 6.8 million litres *(1.5 million Imperial gallons)* of maple syrup, annually. More than 80% of North America's 16,000 maple-syrup producers are in Canada. Quebec supplies 90% of Canada's maple syrup and 80% of the world's maple syrup and related products. It is the **largest supplier of maple syrup in the world.** The first flowing of maple sap, which is rich in sugar, is called the robin run after which the sap flow often diminishes or stops. The next run, known as the frog run, is less sugary and inferior for making maple syrup. The original antiquated methods of tapping maple trees and sugaring-off, or processing the sap in a sugar shanty, created a major problem in the 1960s when demand greatly exceeded supply. That was the case until Denis Desilets of Laval University's rural engineering department invented the 1st **maple tree vacuum sap-tapping system in the world.** His unique system mechanically transports the sap from tree to evaporator through plastic tubing. The entire system can be operated in one sugar bush by just one person. This system encourages the sap to begin flowing earlier and to continue flowing longer while producing a higher quality product. The maple sap is boiled down and it takes 136.4 to 227.3 litres *(30 to 50 Imperial gallons)* of sap to produce 4.6 litres *(1 Imperial gallon)* of maple syrup or 4.5 kg *(10 lb.)* of delicious maple sugar. So, how much maple syrup does Quebec really produce each year? Well, it's enough to cover piles of pancakes stacked eight high and reaching all the way to the moon!

1966: Scientific advisor and university lecturer Dr. David George Bailey (b. 1945) of Toronto, Ontario, began training at the East York Track Club in 1961 under coach Fred Foot. David set a world record for a 17-year-old in 1962 running a 4:07.5 mile. On June 11, 1966, he became the **1ˢᵗ Canadian to crack the four-minute mile** with a 3:59.1 run at San Diego, California, USA. George then ran the mile in 3:57.7 at the Toronto Police Games in 1967. He won numerous competitions throughout his career before retiring in 1976 after breaking an ankle preparing for the Olympic Games.

1966: Under "Subscription rates" in the publication *The Drum*, it was suggested that "Since many subscribers may live in the 'bush', subscriptions may be paid in either cash or kind." This six-page newspaper was the **1ˢᵗ newspaper in the world produced in English, Inuit, Loucheux Indian, and Slavey dialect**. It was first issued on January 6ᵗʰ by publisher Tom Butters (b. 1925), a graduate of the school of journalism, Carleton University in Ottawa, Ontario. He was formerly the regional administrator at Inuvik, Northwest Territories, for the Department of Northern Affairs. *The Drum* was distributed primarily in Inuvik.

1966: The Prairie Panorama Museum at Czar, Alberta, was first opened this year. A new museum was opened the following year. It now displays more than 1,860 cruet sets of every imaginable design making it **Canada's largest collection of salt and pepper shakers**. It also displays **Canada's largest collection of spoons**, totalling 2,940!

1967: A local German club in Kitchener, Ontario, adopted this year the old European tradition of celebrating the harvest. The event quickly spread beyond the club and today involves 21 festival halls in Kitchener and Waterloo, Ontario, plus another in Cambridge, Ontario. Each hall can accommodate from 400 to 4,000 people, a definite necessity as the **largest Bavarian festival in North America** attracts some 700,000 visitors to the area each year. Oktoberfest brings $18 million dollars of direct spending annually to these communities. The festival features a mix of entertainers including bands and folk dancers, some of whom fly over from Germany just to perform here. Of course, there is also a wide selection of excellent German beers and traditional foods.

_1967_: The Canadair CL-215 built in Montreal, Quebec, was the **world's 1ˢᵗ aircraft built specifically as a water bomber**. It flew for the first time in October. Designed to fight forest fires with water bombing or chemical fire retardants, this unique amphibious aircraft can fly inches above a body of water, scoop up a load of nearly 4923.4 litres _(1,083 Imperial gallons)_ of water in 10 to 15 seconds, then jettison it over a fire in just one second. This plane is designed primarily to combat forest fires in remote areas, to spray crops, and to assist in search, rescue, and patrol situations.

_1967_: On May 25ᵗʰ, the Montreal Stock Exchange in Quebec became the **1ˢᵗ stock exchange in North America to admit female members**.

_1967_: The Canada Games is a series of amateur sports events for Canadian athletes held in different Canadian cities every two years, both in summer and winter. The **1ˢᵗ Canada Winter Games** were held in Quebec City, Quebec, beginning February 11, 1967. Dartmouth, Nova Scotia, hosted the **1ˢᵗ Canada Summer Games** on August 16, 1969.

_1967:_ Clinton Shaw made a 7885.8-km _(4,900-mi.)_ trip from Victoria, British Columbia, to St. John's, Newfoundland, over 225 days in 1967. It was the **world's longest recorded journey on roller skates**.

_1967:_ The Canadian Federation of Amateur Baseball formed the **1ˢᵗ national baseball team in Canada**. They participated in the Pan American Games in Winnipeg, Manitoba.

_1967:_ Lester Bowles Pearson (1897-1972) of Newtonbrook, Ontario, launched the anniversary celebrations of Canada's 100ᵗʰ anniversary of Confederation at one second past midnight on January 1ˢᵗ. He did so by **lighting the Centennial Flame for the 1ˢᵗ time**. The Centennial Flame, located in front of the Parliament Buildings in Ottawa, Ontario, is a gas-fired torch set in a round stone base surrounded by crests of all the provinces and territories. Natural gas bubbles up through water in the centre of the fountain to fuel the flame. Never intended to be extinguished, the Centennial Flame symbolizes Canada's unity from sea to sea.

_1967:_ Hundreds of people witnessed one of Canada's most famous and still unexplained incidents on October 4ᵗʰ. They all saw an unidentified flying object (UFO) fly erratically a distance of some 300 km _(186.4 mi.)_ southwest from Dartmouth along the coast of Nova Scotia. Eventually, it crashed into Shag Harbour, Nova Scotia. Working with writer Don Ledger, one such witness, Chris Styles, co-authored a book in 2001 entitled _The World's Only Government-Documented UFO Crash_. Their research for this book involved interviewing RCMP and military officers involved in the official search for the missing UFO. To this day, the incident remains unexplained in spite of some odd-looking debris thought to be from the wreck brought to the ocean's surface. Chris and Don also discovered that the RCMP records classified the incident as a UFO making this the **world's 1ˢᵗ and only UFO documented by a government**.

1968: On May 31ˢᵗ, Dr. Pierre Grondin (1926-2006) of Montreal, Quebec, and a 27-member surgical team at the Montreal Heart Institute performed **Canada's 1ˢᵗ heart transplant** on retired butcher Albert Murphy (1910-1968). It was only the 18ᵗʰ such operation in the world. Unfortunately, Albert died 46 hours after the operation began. That same year, Dr. Clare Brenton Baker (1922-2010) of Biggar, Saskatchewan, and Dr. James Yao plus a cardiac team of 30 specialists operated on Charles Perrin Johnston under the direction of heart specialist Dr. John Wilson. This was **Canada's 1ˢᵗ successful heart transplant**. Charles lived six years after his operation, the longest time for any heart transplant recipient in the world at that time.

1968: Toronto, Ontario, native Thomas Gayford (b. 1928) started representing Canada on the international equestrian scene participating in the 1959 Pan American Games. Competing in the 1968 Mexico Olympic Games, he brought home **Canada's 1ˢᵗ equestrian Olympic gold medal**. In the 1976 Montreal Olympics in Quebec, Tom designed the jumping course. He served as equestrian team leader beginning in 1978.

1968: The winter Mecca of Rossland, British Columbia, is home to the Red Mountain Ski Club. This world-class ski facility offers outstanding Alpine and cross-country skiing in an area of unsurpassed snow conditions and ideal ski slopes. This year, it hosted the **1ˢᵗ World Cup Races ever held**

in Canada. Rossland is also home to the British Columbia Ski Hall of Fame, and the Rossland Winter Carnival, held the last week in January.

Constructed in the 1960s, Manicouagan No. 5 in Quebec is 46 538 849 hectares *(115,000,000 acres)* in size. British Columbia's Portage Mountain Dam opened in 1968 (renamed the W.A.C. Bennett Dam after completion) covers 25 090 510 hectares *(62,000,000 acres)*. Together, they are the **largest man-made lakes in the world**.

1968: The rights of Indians to share in maintaining law and order in their own communities was furthered tremendously in August when Corporal R.J. Anderson of Fort Good Hope, Northwest Territories, swore in two Indians, Edward Cook and Noel Kakfwi as the **1st Indian justices of the peace in Canada**. That October, the Department of Indian Affairs approved the Caughnawaga Indian Band Council in Quebec to form its own police department, the **1st Indian police department in Canada**.

1968: On April 28th at the age of 98, Walter Sitch became **Canada's 1st great-great-great-grandfather** when his great-great-granddaughter gave birth to a son in Halifax, Nova Scotia.

1968: The University of New Brunswick (UNB) was the **1st university in Canada to offer degree programmes in computer science**. Electronic commerce involves all aspects of business, such as marketing, accounting, process design, operations, strategy, human resources, and organizational change, as they relate to computer networked and online commerce. In 1997, UNB was the **1ˢᵗ university in Canada to offer a business major in electronic commerce**. Two years later, it hosted the **world's 1ˢᵗ Electronic Commerce International Case Competition for graduate students**.

_1969:_ Growing from a small group of students at the University of Toronto in Ontario to more than 25,000 supporters, Pollution Probe's mandate is to work toward preservation of the environment through research, education, and advocacy. It was **Canada's 1ˢᵗ environmental organization**.

_1969:_ The British Columbia outdoor closed speed skating championship held at Dawson Creek, British Columbia, in 1969 was the **coldest speed skating meet ever held in Canada**. The temperature was a cool −48.3°C _(-55°F)_!

_1969:_ The yo-yo was devised originally as a weapon by Native peoples of the Philippines. This year, twenty Ottawa, Ontario students broke some 500 strings in a more recreational manner in their 24-hour non-stop endeavour becoming **Canada's 1ˢᵗ marathon yo-yo champions**.

_1969:_ Surgeons in Toronto, Ontario, performed the **world's 1ˢᵗ plastic cornea implant in a human eye** on November 6ᵗʰ.

_1969:_ The **1ˢᵗ person in the world to win 10 International Log Rolling Championships** was Jubiel Wickheim of Shawnigan Lake, British Columbia, between 1956 and 1969. He also won the U.S. Open Championship, Canadian Championship, and Vancouver Island, British Columbia,

Championship several times. He is the **most winning log roller in Canadian history**. Jube was a founding member of the **1ˢᵗ Can-Log Hall of Fame**, also becoming its first member. He has since retired from log-rolling competition and lives on Vancouver Island.

_1969:_ The Canadian Broadcasting Corporation (CBC) voluntarily banned tobacco ads on its national network, a major change in broadcasting policy indeed. This was the **1ˢᵗ ban on tobacco advertising in Canada**. The province of British Columbia followed suit on September 1, 1972, becoming the **1ˢᵗ province to ban the advertising of tobacco on television, radio, or in any publication**.

_1969:_ September 9ᵗʰ saw the passing of the _Official Languages Act_. This was the **1ˢᵗ time that Canada became officially bilingual**. This _Act_ made French and English equal in all agencies under federal jurisdiction. The _Act_ also established "bilingual districts" where all federal services would be offered in either language to a minority group of either language comprising a minimum of ten percent of the population.

_1969:_ The **1ˢᵗ automated banking machine (ABM) in Canada** revolutionized how Canadians managed their bank accounts, providing the option to do so out of normal banking hours. The CIBC Instant Teller™ was first introduced as the "24-hour cash dispenser" on December 1ˢᵗ this year, dispensing packets of $30 at a time when activated by a key. Today's ABMs enable customers to do far more than just deposit and withdraw funds of much higher amounts from their account. They also lower bank overhead and enable tellers to provide faster service for other more complex banking transactions.

1970: The residents of St-Pierre-Jolys created a special new festival to celebrate Manitoba's Centennial this year. They even welcomed Her Majesty Queen Elizabeth II (b. 1926) of London, England, and HRH Prince Philip (b. 1921) of Corfu, Greece, Duke of Edinburgh, to launch the 1ˢᵗ **ever St-Pierre-Jolys Frog Follies in Canada**. Other participants included a wide range of entertainers including the Shawinigan Majorettes, the "Mutins de Longueuil", the "Petits Chanteurs de Montréal", the Winnipeg Judo and Karate School, Angèle Arsenault (b. 1943) of Abrams Village, Prince Edward Island, the St. Boniface Intrépides Choir, and Andy Desjarlais and his Early Settlers. Another exciting event at this festival was the 1ˢᵗ **Canadian National Frog Jumping Championship** which was judged by a number of regional mayors and politicians. The winning frog was Georges, belonging to Albert Driedger, the Reeve of Hanover Municipality, who jumped a remarkable 2.17 m *(7 ft. 1.25 in.)*. This entertaining festival expanded in 2009 by joining with the St-Pierre Agricultural Society's Agricultural Fair which together now welcome more than 2000 visitors every day of the festival.

1970: **Canada's largest collection of worms** belongs to Carl Klauck of Holland Landing, Ontario. He has more than 500 million Alabama red wigglers—which is pretty good considering he started with only 3,000. Actually Klauck is an inventor: he uses the little critters to purify soil. Carl knew that worm castings, the waste excreted after eating, made for very rich soil. He then discovered that decomposed organic garbage and sewage sludge were the best food for these worms—an ingenious method of recycling garbage. These hungry worms munch through 300 million metric tonnes *(330.7 million tons)* of garbage—a week!

1971: Herb Flewwelling was a former diver and Olympic diving coach for the Canadian diving team. Divers trying new and difficult dives for the first time can easily be injured. So, Herb invented the **1ˢᵗ swimming pool bubble machine in the world**, in Pointe-Claire, Quebec. Known as the Bubbler, the unit uses high pressure jets to mix air with water. This forms a mound of bubbles in the pool which softens the impact when a diver hits the water and thereby reduces injuries. Herb's invention was so successful that it quickly became a standard device used by divers around the world. Herb later moved on to become the head coach of the Edmonton Springboard and Platform Diving Club in Alberta.

1971: Educator, chemist, and inventor Dr. James Edwin Guillet (1927-2005) of Toronto, Ontario, was a professor of chemistry at the University of Toronto and inspiration behind **more than 100 inventions in plastics and chemicals**. He and his associate Dr. Harvey G. Troth, a British researcher, were given the gold medal and Canada's Patent No. 1,000,000 for their invention of the **1ˢᵗ biodegradable plastics in the world**. Their concept involves chemically bonding sensitized molecules into the plastic's molecular chain. They begin to decompose and turn to dust when they absorb ultraviolet light from direct sunlight. Unfortunately, the slightly higher cost of these plastics for such products as garbage bags has slowed the interest among manufacturers in using biodegradable plastics. Hopefully, this will change as we become increasingly sensitive environmentally.

1971: Two teams at Gloucester High School in Ottawa, Ontario, set the **1ˢᵗ Canadian record for playing non-stop basketball**. They played for 103 hours 14 minutes in a game whose final score was 3,426 to 2,411.

186

_1972_: Every July, the City of Boissevain, Manitoba, hosts the world turtle derby featuring two classes of racing events. In the Stone Race, the last turtle off the mark is the winner. In the Flat Race, the first turtle to reach the end of the course is declared the World Champion. More than a hundred hard-shelled competitors vie for this prestigious title in the city known as the "Land of Tommy Turtle." The **1ˢᵗ world turtle derby** was held in August of this year. It has become an international event with Canadian and American races. Although the Miss Turtle Derby Pageant is gone, the triathlon, a flea market, and related festivities continue to entertain.

_1972_: The Canadian National Exhibition (CNE) opened on August 16ᵗʰ in Toronto, Ontario, with a very unique presentation. It was the **1ˢᵗ display in the Western World by the People's Republic of China**.

_1972_: Most people have heard of homing pigeons. Well, Harry P. McKeever of Victoria, British Columbia, collected more than 100 canaries in two aviaries at his home. In the summer of 1972, Harry released his pets who were at liberty for five years although the first one returned home just two years after its release. This became the **1ˢᵗ colony of homing canaries in the world**!

_1972_: Roland Galarneau of Hull, Quebec, has been nearly blind since birth. Working in his basement workshop for six years, he transferred discarded materials, old wires, and telephone relays into a form of computer capable of translating French, English, and other languages into Braille at a rate of 100 words per minute. Roland typed the text onto perforated tape in a teletypewriter, then fed it into the computer which translated and printed the information in Braille. This was the **world's 1ˢᵗ computerised method**

of transferring printed texts to Braille. Roland was appointed a Member of the Order of Canada in 1976.

The North Pole is too far north even for the polar bear *(Ursus maritimus)* whose natural habitat is subarctic rather than Arctic. James Bay, at about 50°N, is the furthest south they live all year round. This, the **largest non-aquatic carnivore (meat-eating animal) on earth**, inhabits the coastlines of the Arctic Ocean in Canada. Subsisting on seals in the winter and on water-fowl, berries, even cub polar bears in the summer, the average adult males may weigh up to 650 kg *(1,433 lb.)*. Some individuals exceed 800 kg *(1,764 lb.)* while females weigh up to 350 kg *(772 lb.)*. A full-grown male polar bear may attain a height between 2 m and 3 m *(6.6 ft. and 9.8 ft.)*. Northern Ontario named Polar Bear Provincial Park after this large inhabitant which is also the **only member of the bear family which actively preys on people**! Although polar bears are usually solitary creatures, some 600 to 1,000 bears gather for a few weeks, from mid-October to early November, between the Nelson and Churchill Rivers along a 160.9-km *(100-mile)* stretch of the western coast of Hudson Bay. This forms the **largest concentration of polar bears anywhere in the world**. As soon as the ice refreezes, the bears disperse across the frozen bay to hunt for seals.

<u>1973</u>: Bonzo Bear was the name of a 73.5-kg *(162-lb.)* Newfoundland dog. In July, 1973, he pulled the **heaviest**

recorded load ever pulled by dog power in Canada, a weight of 1995.8 kg *(4,400 lb.)* which he dragged a total distance of 4.6 m *(15 ft.).*

1973: On October 31, 1973, The Oshawa Group opened the Hypermarché Laval, Quebec, the **1ˢᵗ food and general merchandise giant supermarket in North America**. With 49 electronic, computerised checkout terminals in a store the size of four football fields, it was the innovator in bulk handling at the retail level.

1973: Snowshoer Richard Lemay of Quebec registered an all-time record for the 1.6 km *(1 mi.)* of 6 minutes, 23.8 seconds in a 1973 competition in Manchester, New Hampshire, USA, officially becoming the **world's fastest snowshoer**.

1974: Ron Gould of the National Research Council developed a pneumatic cannon used to test airplane parts likely to be struck by high-flying birds. Although this was the **1ˢᵗ Flight Impact Simulator in the world**, it is more commonly known as the "Chicken Cannon"! The reason is because it uses chickens for ammunition—four-pound chickens for testing windshields, and eight-pounders for testing tail assemblies. The cannon fires these dead chickens at speeds up to 965.6 km/h *(600 mph)*. It is also used to test railroad engine windows and any other parts of moving vehicles which may possibly be struck by birds. The popular comedy television programme *The Royal Canadian Air Farce* even used the Chicken Cannon regularly, but always shooting things other than chickens, to the delight of viewers.

1974: Neil Harpham of Prince Edward Island invented the **1ˢᵗ safety paint in the world for automobiles**. Cars using this paint are visible at night for up to 0.8 km *(0.5 mi.)* under a car's high beams because of glass beads mixed into the paint. This allows for a maximum amount of reflection and a minimum amount of glare.

1975: Visionary educators this year developed one of the most creative, bilingual, non-partisan, youth education programmes in all of Canada. They incorporated the **1ˢᵗ Foundation for the Study of Processes of Government** to enable enthusiastic students to understand better the role and function of Canada's federal government. It launched this year the **1ˢᵗ Forum for Young Canadians** held four times annually in Ottawa, Ontario, our nation's capital. Young leaders of tomorrow aged 15-19 years from schools all across Canada gain an experience of a lifetime interacting daily on Parliament Hill with our country's political leaders. Public and private sector sponsors provide grant funding and bursaries to enable these ambitious students to interact not only with Canadian decision-makers but also with their student peers who often come from totally different backgrounds and environments, some never before having travelled outside their own home town. Many supportive volunteers and Forum alumni also contribute their time, knowledge, and valuable experience to help make the Forum so successful. The programme is intense yet so varied and informative that participants cannot help but enjoy likely the most challenging experience they have ever imagined at such a young age. As part of the Forum's Ambassador Programme, they return home not only spreading the word about Forum to recruit future participants but also later in life having an increased ability to offer so much more inspiration, experience, and value to their community, their schools, and their governments. In addition to bonding with many new, like-minded friends and meeting high-profile people throughout the week, Forum students take part in classroom debates, discussion groups, creative activities, and even their own recreation of parliament. They also have the opportunity to visit numerous venues of national importance including the Supreme Court, National Arts Centre, Rideau Hall (the governor general's residence), and possibly some national museums in addition to working on Parliament Hill, to name but a few. One cannot underestimate the value and impact of life experiences and personal memories gained though this programme by the more than 16,000 young Canadians who participated in the Forum by 2013. Partaking in the Forum for Young Canadians not only educates students in a very unique environment but also develops further their public speaking, communication, leadership, and social skills—valuable additions to their résumé when applying later for university and employment positions. In 1985, the Foundation extended this programme to include the **1ˢᵗ Forum Teachers Conference** held in conjunction with the Forum for Young Canadians. Participants include up to sixteen high school and Cégep teachers from throughout Canada. They work both with the students and in numerous activities organized specifically for teachers. This conference affords educators an opportunity to see firsthand new ways to incorporate their newfound knowledge of our democratic systems and political past into their history, politics, social studies, and public affairs teaching curriculum. It is one of the best professional development conferences in Canada focusing on the processes of government. The Foundation added an international aspect to the Forum whereby a few students from other countries also are invited to attend the Forum programme. It then created in 2000 its first international programme for students and teachers from eleven other countries. The 1ˢᵗ **Canada-U.S. Youth Forum** came in 2001. Partnering the Youth Forum with the University of Ottawa enables primarily university-aged students to attain academic credit for their participation in this new, one-week forum. The Forum for Young Canadians truly is a one-of-a-kind, life-changing programme helping build a network of Canadian leaders of tomorrow in government, business, industry, and education from coast to coast.

_1975:_ The windows of the Royal Bank Plaza in downtown Toronto, Ontario, are coated with 2,500 ounces of gold worth $325,000 when constructed. They are the **most expensive windows in Canada**.

_1975:_ Film director, producer, screenwriter, and actor David Paul Cronenberg (b. 1943) of Toronto, Ontario, first wrote and published eerie short stories at an early age, taking after his journalist father. He also followed his piano player mother's interest in music, playing classical guitar until he was 12. David then produced films, containing some rather revolting special effects, such as _Shivers_ (1975), _They Came From Within_ (1975), and _Rabid_ (1977). _Shivers_ was **Canada's 1ˢᵗ drama/horror/science fiction film**. It is also known as _The Parasite Murders_. David's debut film is the story of a parasite designed to help ailing human organs but instead goes out of control with rather sickening results. He went on to direct the telepathy-based _Scanners_ (1981) and became sort of a mass media "guru" with _Videodrome_ (1983). Continuing with his cult status of "horror meister", he directed _Dead Ringers_ (1988), _Fly_ (1986), and _Naked Lunch_ (1992). His provocative movie _Crash_ (1996) won the Jury Prize at the Cannes Film Festival in France. His virtual reality essay *eXistenZ* (1999) also fared well at Cannes and the Berlin Film Festival in Germany. David is no longer a mere genre moviemaker but a fully realized author of international acclaim.

1975: The Opaskwayak Cree Nation in Manitoba, a member of the Swampy Cree Tribal Council, has long been recognized as a model for self-government. The late Chief Gordon G. Lathlin was the driving force behind achieving this goal. A small staff of five began providing general administrative and gravel services from a small house on the reserve townsite in 1968. Before long, self-determination and self-sufficiency became a reality through the development of numerous commercial initiatives including the Timberland Trailer Court, The Pas IGA, the Chimo Building Centre, and the Gordon Mathlin Memorial Centre providing recreational cultural activities year-round. The $8 million, three-level Otineka shopping mall, home to 25 retail stores encompassing 20 903.2 m² *(225,000 ft.²)* opened in 1975. This was the **1ˢᵗ First Nations shopping mall in Canada**. The Opaskwayak became in 1984 the **1ˢᵗ reserve in Canada to negotiate a gaming licence with a province**, now the successful Aseneskak Casino. Yet another record came in 1994 when this community hosted the **1ˢᵗ ever Cree Nations Gathering** attended by Cree people from coast to coast.

1976: On September 11ᵗʰ, CTV reported that 42% of Canada's population, some 10,713,500 people, tuned in to view the Soviet Union-Team Canada hockey game on television. This was the **largest television sports audience in Canadian history**.

<u>*1976*</u>: "Buffalo" Bob Kelso and "Rose Petal" Cloughton were short-wave radio enthusiasts. During a 15-minute ceremony performed by Reverend "Bird Dog" Wyrick in 1976, they became the **1ˢᵗ Canadians to marry on the Citizen Band radio network**.

<u>*1976*</u>: Autism Spectrum Disorder (ASD) is a chronic brain disorder that usually appears within the first three years of life. It may result in difficulties with learning, speech, social interaction and withdrawal from contact with people, and repetitive interests and activities. Although severely intellectually impaired, some autistic individuals may excel at some kinds of mental manipulations like arithmetic or in music and drawing. A group of parents founded the **1ˢᵗ Autism Society Canada (ASC)** this year as a national, incorporated, not-for-profit, charitable organization. Its mandate is to provide public education, advocacy, information, referral, and support for its regional societies. ASC works across Canada to reduce the profound impact of this disease on individuals and their families. It also supports the implementation of improved surveillance, quality research, and universally accessible resources for all Canadians with ASD.

<u>*1976*</u>: Leave it to a young lady to prove that Canadians are among the happiest people in the world. Lisa Lester of Winnipeg. Manitoba, winning the Manitoba Dental Association's smilathon, set the **world record for smiling** by grinning continuously for 10 hours 5 minutes!

<u>*1977*</u>: A very interesting structure entertains tourists in the heritage Gastown district of Vancouver, British Columbia.

Local merchants, property owners, and private donors provided the $58,000 necessary to enlist the skills of Canadian Raymond Saunders in solving the problem of a steam grate in the sidewalk being misused. Ray created the **world's 1ˢᵗ full-size steam-powered clock**. The design is similar to that of small models of steam clocks built back in the 18ᵗʰ century. Steam from the city's distributed low pressure downtown steam-heating system powers a piston in a small steam engine in the base of this faux-heritage clock. The steam moves a chain lift which carries steel balls upward inside the clock which when released drive a conventional pendulum clock escarpment. This is turn moves the hands on the four faces of the clock. Sound is produced every quarter hour by the steam making whistles chime the Westminster Quarters like "Big Ben" in London, England, and whistling the time each hour. The clock was based on an 1875 design and was custom-built in England. In addition to the steam source, three small electric motors control the valves of the five steam whistles plus the two fans used to blow a cloud of steam out the top of this landmark clock. The large central whistle came from the Canadian Pacific Railway steam tugboat *Naramata*. This very ornately decorated clock stands 5.5 m *(18 ft.)* tall and operates throughout the year.

_1977_: In Montreal, Quebec, on October 31ˢᵗ, the government signed the James Bay Land Claims Agreement into law. This agreement with New Quebec Cree and Inuit transferred Aboriginal rights and lands in return for $224 million, hunting and fishing rights, and greater self-government. This was done in return for the impending flooding of ancestral land with the construction of the new James Bay Hydroelectric Project. It became **Canada's 1ˢᵗ modern First Nations treaty**.

_1977:_ Internationally renowned concert pianist and specialist in Canadian music, Dr. Elaine Keillor (b. 1939) of London, Ontario, is a Distinguished Research Professor Emerita at Carleton University in Ottawa, Ontario. She was only 10 years old when she completed all the theoretical requirements to become the **youngest ever recipient of the Associate diploma in piano from the Royal Conservatory of Music** in Toronto, Ontario. She is a prolific composer of music and has received numerous prestigious awards throughout her career. She also performed with orchestras and in recitals across North America and in Europe as a pianist and chamber musician. She appeared regularly on Canadian and American radio and television programmes. Elaine obtained a Ph.D. in musicology in 1976 from the University of Toronto (U of T) and has taught at the U of T and York University in Toronto; Queen's University in Kingston, Ontario; McMaster University in Hamilton, Ontario; and Carleton University. In 1977, Carleton hired Elaine as a specialist in Canadian music. She immediately developed and taught the **1ˢᵗ university course in Canada to explore First Peoples' musical expression**. Her 16 recordings have gleaned the highest of praise for their artistry and performance. She became the **1ˢᵗ recipient in the category of Arts and Culture of the Canadian Women's Mentor Awards** in 1999. The Canadian Musical Heritage Society is devoted to the research, editing, and publishing of Canadian music composed before 1950, Elaine being the principal investigator of the Society. Her many acknowledgements include the 2004 Helmut Kallmann Award of the Canadian Association of Music Libraries, Archives, and Documentation Centres.

_1977:_ Retired businessman and electrician Willie Adams (b. 1934) of Fort Chimo, Quebec, turned to politics this year. Prime Minister Pierre Elliott Trudeau (1919-2000) of Montreal, Quebec, appointed Willie senator for the Northwest Territories on April 5th. He then began representing Nunavut upon its creation in 1999. Willie was the 1st **Inuk to sit in the Canadian Senate** and when he retired in 2009 was the second longest serving member of the Canadian Senate.

_1977_: In May, golfer Phil Katsouris of Bois des Filion, Quebec, made his first hole-in-one a definite record breaker. On the 12th hole of the St. Francis Golf Course, he made **Canada's longest hole-in-one**, a shot travelling 300.8 m *(329 yd.)*.

_1977_: At the age of only 20, Jean Jawbone's heart stopped for 3 hours 40 minutes on January 8th. A team of 26 at the Health Sciences Centre in Winnipeg, Manitoba, used peritoneal dialysis to revive Jean successfully. This was the **longest recorded heart stoppage of any human being**.

_1977_: For what accomplishment in October this year did Canadian lawyer Harvey Pollock receive a 30.5 cm *(1-ft.)* high wooden whistle? He was the 1st **winner** of the **world's 1st International Whistle-Off** in which Harvey took top honours in the solo and foreign whistling categories.

_1978_: The Yukon Territorial Council was comprised of ten members acting as a non-partisan advisory body to the commissioner of Yukon from 1900 to 1978. This council was replaced in 1977 by the current Legislative Assembly. It was elected for the first time in 1978 and is the 1st **and only legislature in Canada's territories which is organized along political party lines**. The legislative assemblies in the Northwest Territories and Nunavut are elected on the model of a non-partisan consensus government whereby there are no political parties in the legislature. Both legislatures have a premier, cabinet, private members, a politically neutral Speaker, and procedures in the legislature which follow the British parliamentary model of responsible government. The government is still comprised of the premier and cabinet but they must function by winning total confidence of the House in all votes. Cabinet solidarity also is mandatory regardless of the personal feelings of any individual member. The premiers are elected by secret ballot of all Members of the Legislative Assembly (MLAs). There also is no official "opposition" as in other Canadian governments but all MLAs are permitted to vote and act independently on any issues not involving government policy directly. Most of the proceedings also take place in the Inuktitut language thereby reflecting the Inuit culture.

_1978:_ Canadian forensic scientists made the **1ˢᵗ discovery in the world that a laser beam can reveal fingerprints**. The new method reveals fingerprints up to 10 years old and which are invisible using ordinary forensic methods.

_1978:_ Neo-hippies often attend music and art festivals throughout North America. The bands that perform at these festivals usually are called "Jam Bands" because many of their songs contain long instrumentals reminiscent of the hippie bands of the 1960s. The **1ˢᵗ Jam Festival in Canada** was held on August 26, 1978, in Ontario. Some of the bands included the Commodores, Kansas, Dave Mason, the Atlanta Rhythm Section, and the Doobie Brothers.

_1979:_ A conference honouring Scotland's national poet was hosted by Canada in London, Ontario. It was the **1ˢᵗ time in 94 years that fans of Robbie Burns (1759-1796) of Alloway, Scotland, met outside Britain for the annual Burns Federation Conference**.

1980: The Global Positioning System (GPS) determines the precise position of a receiver by measuring the distance of the receiver from at least four passing satellites whose orbits are known precisely. This was the **1ˢᵗ time in Canada the Global Positioning System was used**.

R.A. Kipp was the founder of Kipp Kelly Limited in Winnipeg, Manitoba. The company developed the Kipp Kelly machines used in many metallurgical and raw materials handling companies to separate one material from another. The company specialized in manufacturing specific gravity separators, vibration tables, gravity tables, electrostatic separators, air flotation stoners, and air float separators. It also developed the **1ˢᵗ machine in the world to separate diamonds from clay**.

1980: On July 20ᵗʰ, some 4,000 thinkers from all over the world gathered in Toronto, Ontario. This 5-day congress sponsored by the World Future Society and the Canadian Futures Society was the **1ˢᵗ Global Conference on the Future ever held**.

1980: Two-thirds of Canada's electricity and fifteen percent of the world's hydroelectric power is generated by Canadian rivers. The $15-billion James Bay Hydroelectric Project in Quebec was completed in 1980. It is the site of the **largest single generating plant for hydroelectric power in the world**. It involves massive diversions of water from the Eastmain, Opinaca, and Caniapiscau (Koksoak) rivers to dammed reservoirs on La Grande Rivière. Known as LG II, this project increased the average flow of La Grande Rivière from 1700 m³/sec. to 3300 m³/sec. *(60,034.9 ft³/sec. to 116,538.4 ft³/sec.).* It includes 8 dams, 198 dikes, 5 reservoirs covering 11 900 km² *(4,594.6 mi²)*, and a tiered spillway three times the height of Niagara Falls. The total project generates more than 10,283 megawatts of electric power, selling most of it to customers in the United States. It also has the **world's largest underground powerhouse**.

1981: Harness racing driver Bill O'Donnell (b. 1948) of Springhill, Nova Scotia, became this year the **1ˢᵗ harness racing driver in the world to win over $4 million in total earnings**. He drove *Nihilator* in 1985 to a win in a record 1:49.2, the **1ˢᵗ ever sub-1:50 mile in harness racing in the world**. Bill also became the **1ˢᵗ harness driver in the world to earn over $1 million in one season**.

1981: John Kim Bell (b. 1953) was born a Mohawk on the Kahnawake Indian Reserve in Quebec of a father who was a professional wrestler, and an American musician and actress mother. He became a concert pianist and symphony orchestra conductor. In 1980-1981, he became the **1ˢᵗ North American Indian to conduct a symphony orchestra in North America** with his appointment as apprentice conductor of the Toronto Symphony Orchestra. His interest in creating an organization to increase native awareness of artistic opportunities and to assist native artists in becoming professionals resulted in his founding the **1ˢᵗ Canadian Native Arts Foundation in Canada**, in 1985.

1981: On January 25, 1981, at Terrebonne, Quebec, Yvon Jolin officially became the **1ˢᵗ man in the world to jump 8.97 m *(29 ft. 5 in.)* over 18 barrels wearing ice skates**. And on March 1, 1987, Marie-Josée Houle became the **1ˢᵗ woman in the world to jump 6.84 m (22 ft. 5.25 in.) over 11 barrels wearing ice skates**. Both world records still hold today.

_1982:_ Garbage recycling has become an increasingly major objective in Canada for more than two decades in an attempt to reduce the amount of garbage we deposit in landfill sites. The City of Kitchener, Ontario, introduced the **1ˢᵗ blue box recycling containers in Canada**, used to collect paper, glass, and cans for recycling. The programme has spread across our country and is now even expanding into the **1ˢᵗ green torpedo box recycling containers in Canada** in Toronto, Ontario. These tests have been extremely successful in recycling wet waste. The objective through the full recycling programme was to divert 60% of residential garbage from landfills by 2006 and 100% waste diversion by 2010.

_1982:_ When brewpubs first became legal in Canada, John Mitchell opened the Horseshoe Bay Brewery in British Columbia. It was attached to the Troller Pub in Vancouver, British Columbia, the **1ˢᵗ brewpub in North America**. It also brewed the **1ˢᵗ modern cask conditioned ale in North America**. John again visited England to explore the varieties of homebrews available there. On his return to Canada, he joined architect and partner Paul Hadfield in opening Spinnakers on Victoria, British Columbia's harbour waterfront on May 15, 1984. Raymond Ginnever, an accountant, soon became a third partner. When completed, Spinnakers became the **1ˢᵗ single purpose brewpub in Canada**, since the time of prohibition. Years of continued success and expansion resulted in today's Spinnakers Brewpub and Guesthouse including not only the brewpub but also two highly successful bed and breakfast guesthouses.

1982: In June, the House of Commons passed the **1ˢᵗ *Access to Information Act* in Canada**. It came into effect in July of 1983 and gives the general public greater access to government information. It entitles individuals to request information concerning the conduct of our federal government. We also are entitled to receive that information at a reasonable cost and within a reasonable timeframe.

1982: Coming to Ville-Marie, Quebec, in 1653 to teach French and Indian children how to read and write, and how to cook, spin, and sew, Marguerite Bourgeoys initiated the building of the first Notre Dame-de-Bon-Secours Chapel in 1657 and opened a school the following year. She continued to build new schools over the years and established an uncloistered order of teaching nuns, the Sisters of the Congregation de Notre Dame. This order spread throughout the continent. She also put extensive efforts into helping the poor and caring for the sick. On October 31, 1982, Marguerite was canonised by Pope John Paul II (1920-2005) of Wadowice, Poland, making her **Canada's 1ˢᵗ female saint**.

1982: Donald Starkell (1932-2012) of Winnipeg, Manitoba, and his son, Dana Starkell (b. 1962) really enjoy canoeing. They even prefer portaging their 6.1-m *(20-ft.)* canoe from one body of water to another under human power. They left Winnipeg on June 1, 1980, and completed the **longest journey in the world ever made in a canoe**. They paddled on rivers and oceans, arriving in Belém, Brazil, on May 1, 1982. Their total distance travelled was 19 603 km *(12,181 mi.)*.

1982: Dianna Gordon and George Mittleman of Toronto, Ontario, first met in an Ottawa, Ontario bridge tournament in 1970. They have been playing mixed bridge ever since. At the Biarritz World Bridge Olympiad in France in October, 1982, they defeated 450 couples from 60 countries becoming the **1ˢᵗ Canadians to win a world bridge title**.

1982: The art of structure demolition has evolved tremendously over the years with specialists now capable of dynamiting multi-storey complexes in the centre of major cities without damaging any nearby buildings. On June 13ᵗʰ, fifteen members of the Black Leopard Karate Club took a more unique approach to the art. They became the **1ˢᵗ in the world to demolish a seven-room wooden farmhouse by foot and unaided hand, in just 3 hours 18 minutes**. The house was located west of Elnora, Alberta. This record was surpassed on May 11, 1996, by 15 members of the Aurora Karata Dojo in Ontario who used only their bare hands to demolish a 10-room house in just 3 hrs. 6 min. 50 sec., the **fastest bare-handed house demolition in the world**.

1982: The Canadian Broadcasting Corporation (CBC) won an Oscar this year for its production of *Crac*, the **1ˢᵗ Oscar won by the CBC's French-language network**. At the 55ᵗʰ Academy Awards in 1983, the **1ˢᵗ Oscar won by the CBC's English-language network** was for *Just Another Missing Kid*, a documentary film made for the CBC's public affairs programme *The Fifth Estate*.

1982: The **largest crossword puzzle published in the world** was compiled by Robert Turcot of Quebec City, Quebec, in July. His puzzle comprised 82,951 squares containing 12,489 clues across, 13,125 down, and covered 3.56 m² *(38.28 ft.²)*.

1983: The Festival Juste pour rire/Just For Laughs Comedy Festival in Montreal, Quebec, began on July 14ᵗʰ as a four-day French comedy show. Over the years, it continued to expand into what is now a 12-day bilingual festival drawing 1.7 million spectators every summer. It is the **world's largest comedy event**. It is presented by over 2,400 artists from 9 countries presenting 2,000 shows in some 25 venues and along St. Denis Street. The Festival truly goes beyond the limits of imagination in provoking laughter with shows broadcast on television internationally to millions more viewers.

_1983:_ The Aboriginal Peoples Television Network (APTN) was created this year broadcasting to northern Canada by satellite from Winnipeg, Manitoba. Five years later, it expanded its network through approval of a Pan-Northern television distribution service known as Television Northern Canada (TVNC) which was launched in 1992. Then in 1999, the network spanned the country becoming the **1ˢᵗ national Aboriginal television network in the world**. It broadcasts today through cable, satellite, terrestrial feeds, and a national High Definition (HD) feed to some 10 million Canadian households and commercial establishments, the network's HD simulcast feed arriving in 2008. APTN offers a wide variety of Aboriginal programming in English (56%), French (16%), and Aboriginal languages (28%) including documentaries, news magazines, entertainment specials, movies, dramas, sports events, educational programmes, and various other formats.

_1983:_ Back in the 1970s, Richard Hunt began experimenting with drying surplus fruit on the roof of his house after putting it through a blender or meat grinder and spreading the resultant purée on Saran Wrap. Demand for this new product at local fairs was insatiable. In 1983, he turned over his initial business enterprise to Rod Harris of Kimberley, British

Columbia, Val Ritchie, and Fred Danenhower, to concentrate his energies on the two retail outlets in the Okanagan Valley of British Columbia. They formed EDG Foods Ltd. (Edible Dried Goods) and began marketing *Fruit Stix*, the **1ˢᵗ pure fruit snack bar in the world**. Sometimes referred to as fruit leather, these fruit bars were available in strawberry, grape, orange/pineapple, raspberry, apricot, and peach/pear flavours, and contained no food additives. They were made solely by gently drying pure fruit, an all natural food product still very popular today.

1983: At the age of 15, Diane Rakiecki (b. 1961) of Kelowna, British Columbia, was in a car hit by an impaired driver killing her father and leaving her in a wheelchair. She overcame her disability and turned to wheelchair sports with her eye on the Special Olympics. In 1983, she became the **1ˢᵗ woman in Canada to complete a wheelchair marathon**. She also entered the 2000 New York City Marathon in New York, USA, in which she was the second female handcycle finisher.

1983: In July of 1983, Alberta Government Telephones introduced the **1ˢᵗ commercially operating cellular mobile radio system in North America**. NovAtel Communications Ltd., now known as NovAtel Inc., of Calgary, Alberta, operated the system on the 400 MHz band. The national system was established in 1985 through the inauguration of a national franchise granted to the Cantel Cellular Radio Group in conjunction with each provincial telephone company. NovAtel also designs, markets, and supports a broad range of products using GPS (Global Positioning System) and INS (Inertial Measurement Unit) technology for determining precise geographic locations. This capability is particularly useful in surveying, aviation, automotive, marine, and machine control applications.

1984: Toronto, Ontario-based Shell Canada Limited, active in Canada since 1911, is an integrated energy resource company involved in natural gas and petroleum, petrochemicals and refined oil products, and alternative fuels research. It also is the **largest producer of sulphur** and the second-largest producer of natural gas in Canada. In 1984, Shell Canada became the **1st refinery in the world designed to process only synthetic crude oil**. As natural oil reserves become increasingly depleted worldwide, this new synthetic technology provides an environmentally friendly, totally biodegradable, renewable line of lubricating products having numerous benefits over traditional petroleum-based products.

1984: Four adjoining Rocky Mountain national parks were declared Canada's Rocky Mountain World Heritage Site, a UNESCO World Heritage site, this year. They include Banff National Park of Canada, covering 6641 km² *(2,564.1 mi.²)*; Jasper National Park of Canada, covering 10 878 km² *(4,200 mi.²)*; Kootenay National Park of Canada, covering 1406.4 km² *(543 mi.²)*; and Yoho National Park of Canada, covering 1313.1 km² *(506.2 mi.²)*. Three British Columbia provincial parks—Mount Robson Provincial Park, covering 2248.7 km² *(868.2 mi.²)*; Hamber Provincial Park, covering 24 km² *(9.3 mi.²)*, and Mount Assiniboine Provincial Park, covering 390.5 km² *(150.8 mi.²)*—were added in 1990. Together, these parks comprise 22 899.7 km² *(8,841.6 mi.²)*, the **largest tract of mountain parkland in the world**.

1984: Pierre Harvey (b. 1957) of Rimouski, Quebec, is a true Canadian sports legend. He was a member of the National Road Cycling team from 1976 to 1984. He finished 24th and was the **1st Canadian in the Montreal Olympic Games** in Quebec when just 19 years old. Pierre won three World Cup gold medals for cross-country skiing between 1981 and 1998. He was the **1ˢᵗ Canadian male athlete to participate in both the Summer and Winter Olympic Games in the same year**, doing so in 1984. He competed in the Summer Olympic Games road cycling in Los Angeles, California, USA, and in the Winter Olympic Games cross-country skiing in Sarajevo, Yugoslavia. Pierre was inducted into the Canadian Olympic Hall of Fame in 2006.

_1984:_ Canadian astronaut Marc Garneau (b. 1949) of Quebec City, Quebec, carried a hockey puck with him in honour of his homeland when orbiting the earth on board the U.S. space shuttle _Challenger_ in October. This was the **1ˢᵗ hockey puck in the world to travel at a height of 350 km _(210 mi.)_ above the earth**!

_1984:_ Dr. Daurene Elaine Lewis (1943-2013) of Annapolis Royal, Nova Scotia, was a seventh generation descendent of Black Loyalists who settled in Annapolis Royal, Nova Scotia, in 1783 and a relative of Rose Fortune (1744-1864) of Virginia, USA. She graduated from Dalhousie University with a Diploma in Teaching in Schools of Nursing. After earning an MBA from Saint Mary's University, she spent 30 years working in a wide range of positions all related to healthcare and business. Her list of volunteer experience and community involvement is impressively lengthy indeed. Daurene was elected Mayor of Annapolis Royal in 1984 for 4 years making her the **1ˢᵗ black female Mayor in North America**. Four years later, she entered provincial politics becoming the first black woman in Ontario to run in a provincial election. Of her many awards, Daureen was the recipient of an honorary degree from Mount Saint Vincent University (1993) where she had been the executive director of the Centre for Women in Business. Her name was added to the Black Cultural Centre's Wall of Honour in 1994. She received the Global Citizenship Award commemorating the United Nations 50th Anniversary (1995) plus the Progress Club's Woman of Excellence Award for Public Affairs and Communication (1998). Daureen continues to sit on a lengthy list of Boards and Committees. In 2002, she became a Member of the Order of Canada.

1984: Lynn Russell Williams (b. 1924) of Springfield, Ontario, became the **1st Canadian elected to head the giant United Steelworkers of America Trade Union**, based in Pittsburgh, Pennsylvania, USA. This Toronto, Ontario union leader was elected on March 29th.

Up to 10,000 ships are known to have been sunken in the Great Lakes, 58% of them lost by storms. This makes the Great Lakes the **world's largest graveyard for wrecked ships**.

1984: Padmanadi Vegetarian Restaurant in Jakarta, Indonesia, is a renowned vegetarian eatery serving mainly Chinese and Indonesian plus some Indian and Thai food. It is of Chinese-Buddhist design and offers more than 200 dishes on its menu. Padmanadi Vegetarian Restaurant in Edmonton, Alberta, is the **1st Canadian branch of the original Padmanadi Vegetarian Restaurant**. This medium-sized restaurant, with seating for over 50 patrons, serves a wide range of common and specialty dishes. This restaurant also makes certain to participate in World Vegetarian Restaurant Month serving an All You Can Eat Buffet on a date chosen each October. It also welcomes guests to celebrate World Vegetarian Day on October 1st.

1985: The Canadian Expo '86 Exhibition in Vancouver, British Columbia, became the home of the **tallest unsupported steel flagpole in the world** erected on August 22nd. It was constructed from 54 400 kg *(120,000 lb.)* of steel, stood 86 m *(282 ft.)* tall, and supported the **world's largest hockey stick and puck**. This 62.5-m *(205-ft.)* long hockey stick constructed of Douglas fir beams reinforced with steel became a permanent and popular exhibit after Expo 86 in front of the Cowichan Centre in Duncan, British Columbia, where it is recognized for its symbolic and artistic value. The hockey stick is forty times life size and weighs in at 28,188 kg *(62,143.9 lb.)*. It was transported to Vancouver Island, British Columbia, by barge and three flat-bed trucks on August 21, 1987. It was dedicated at its new home on May 21, 1988.

1985: This summer, British American Tobacco sponsored the **1st Symphony of Fire fireworks competition in the world**. It was known initially as the Benson & Hedges Symphony of Fire and involved a multi-day fireworks exhibition. Different countries from around the world participated in a friendly international competition of fireworks choreographed to music. On different nights during the summer, each participating country would showcase their talent, first at La Ronde in Montreal, Quebec, this year. In 1987, the event also began at the Lake Ontario waterfront of the Exhibition Grounds in Toronto, Ontario. The competition expanded to Vancouver, British Columbia, in 1990. When the Canadian government legislated tobacco advertising restrictions in 2000, the company still sponsored the occasion but changed the name to Symphony of Fire. The Vancouver competition is known as the HSBC Celebration of Light, sponsored by HSBC Canada. The one in Toronto has since been renamed the Canada Dry Festival of Fire. The Symphony of Fire is the **largest annual fireworks competition in the world**.

_1986:_ Munmohan Singh "Moe" Sihota (b. 1955) of Duncan, British Columbia, first joined the British Columbia legislature in 1986. A feisty, tenacious, and controversial politician, Moe practiced law and worked as a social worker before entering the political arena. He served as a member of the New Democratic Party. He became the **1ˢᵗ Sikh Indo-Canadian to be elected to any federal or provincial riding**. Moe later became the **1ˢᵗ Sikh Indo-Canadian cabinet minister**.

_1986:_ Vancouver, British Columbia, has one of North America's largest Chinese communities. Modern cultures of the day tend to believe that life is enhanced through the acquisition of increased wealth, possessions, status, and influence, amongst other things. Taoist principles suggest that less is more, that experience can be heightened by reducing one's possessions. Governments of the People's Republic of China and Canada collaborated this year in creating the Dr. Sun Yat-Sen Classical Chinese Garden here. Dr. Sun Yat-Sen (1866-1925) of Xiangshan, Guangdong, China, was the first major figure in Chinese history who travelled extensively and brought back Western ideals to his homeland. The garden is designed in accordance with the private gardens developed in Suzhou during the Ming Dynasty. It is a refuge for inspiration and contemplation, and is the **1ˢᵗ full-scale Classical Chinese Garden built outside China**. It took more than 50 artisans from Suzhou a full year to construct the garden. And they did so in the traditional Chinese way— using no nails or power tools. This enabled them to create a garden almost identical to those in China centuries ago.

1986: On May 2ⁿᵈ, Dr. Wilbert Keon (b. 1935) of Sheenboro, Quebec, fitted a Jarvik 7-70 artificial heart in 42-year-old patient Noelle Leclair. He performed this operation at the Ottawa Civic Hospital in Ontario enabling Noella to live until a human heart was found several days later. This was **Canada's 1ˢᵗ artificial heart transplant.**

1986: Dr. Imants Lauks invented the **1ˢᵗ silicon chip blood analyzer in the world.**

1987: The Canadian Bank Note Company printed the last paper $1 bills on April 20, 1989. They were replaced by a unique brass coin which is less expensive to make and outlasts the paper bills by twenty years. The **1ˢᵗ $1 "loonie" coin** made its debut in circulation on June 30, 1987. The coin attained its nickname because of the loon pictured on its rear side. It is made of nickel, copper, and recycled tin.

1987: Paul Holc (b. 1987) of Vancouver, British Columbia, born to Alice Holc six weeks premature and weighing in at 2.89 kg *(6 lb. 6 oz.)* on October 16ᵗʰ, became the **youngest heart transplant recipient in the world.** He underwent a heart transplant at Loma Linda Hospital in California, USA. Paul was just 2 hours and 34 minutes old at the time of his operation.

1987: A tagged female monarch butterfly *(Danaus plexippus)* established a world record after migrating the **longest distance flown by a monarch butterfly ever recorded.** Donald Davis released this butterfly at Presqu'ile Provincial Park near Brighton, Ontario, on September 6, 1986. It was recaptured on a mountain near Angangueo, Mexico, in 1987 having flown a direct distance of 3432.7 km *(2,133 mi.).* In reality, though, the actual distance travelled could well be twice that figure. Millions of these butterflies travel from southern Canada to central Mexico every fall in the **longest and largest insect migration in North America**, some 8000 km *(4,971 mi.)*, and some even return in the spring.

_1988:_ An historic marriage was held on January 9th in Leith, Scotland, in a private ceremony. Canadian Sylvana Tomaselli (b. 1957) of Placentia, Newfoundland, married Earl George Philip Nicholas Windsor (b. 1962) of St. Andrews, England. She became the **1st Canadian to marry into the British royal family**. George is the oldest son of the Duke and Duchess of Kent.

_1988:_ The Macdonald Railway Tunnel through the Rogers Pass in the Canadian Rockies is the **longest railway tunnel in the Western Hemisphere**. It was built over a period of five years at a cost of $500 million. It was completed this year extending a total of 14.6 km *(9.1 mi.)*. It duplicated the Connaught Tunnel and was designed to reduce the grades for trains travelling from east to west to 0.7 per cent. It was the **1st tunnel in North America using a concrete "Pact-Track" floor system**. This eliminated the need for crushed rock ballast and wooden railway ties. The result was greatly reduced maintenance costs. The first revenue train passed through the Macdonald Railway Tunnel at noon on December 12th.

_1989:_ Researchers at the National Research Council (NRC) invented the **1st optical security device in the world**. It is an ultrathin, gold-coloured patch made from layers of ceramic material. When viewed at an angle, this patch turns green. A major security advantage is that it cannot be printed, photocopied, or photographed. It makes counterfeiting considerably more difficult when the patch is added to banknotes.

1990s: Residents Ken and Linda Parker of Six Nations of the Grand River in southern Ontario began landscaping their yard at this time, initially planting just 12 species of native plants which they sold from pallets on their driveway. It wasn't long before their venture grew into a nursery where they now sell more than 350 species. Sweet Grass Gardens is the 1ˢᵗ **Native-owned and operated native plant nursery in North America**. These special plants have great significance to the First Nations culture and are used for food, dyes, medicines, and ceremonial applications.

1990: After her own daughter was born, obstetrician and gynaecologist Dr. Beverly Brodie of Charlottetown, Prince Edward Island, realized the need for the 1ˢᵗ **Baby Safe product in the world** which she and two friends invented and patented in 1990. It consists of two water-resistant bags of rice connected to a removable, washable, flannel pad. It holds a sleeping baby secure on any flat surface. It ensures a safe and comfortable sleep for infants giving firm support to the baby's back and stomach. It also enables a baby to sleep on their side without rolling over.

1990: University of Saskatchewan student Lance Connell threw a fresh Grade A egg to his classmate Everett Tromblay. The egg remained intact after travelling 68.1 m *(223 ft. 4 in.)* through the air and set a **Canadian egg-tossing record**.

1990: Professional hockey player Brett Hull (b. 1964) of Belleville, Ontario, shot a 50-goal season for the first time on February 6ᵗʰ following in his father's footsteps. Bobby Hull (b. 1939) of Point Anne, Ontario, recorded his first 50-goal season 28 years earlier. Thus, Bobby and Brett became the 1ˢᵗ **father-and-son 50-goal scorers in National Hockey League history**.

1990: "The Word On The Street Canada" is an annual festival held on the last Sunday in September. Its primary objective is to bring together the writing, publishing, library, book and magazine retail, and literacy groups to improve and promote literacy skills. This is **Canada's largest annual book and magazine festival**. It began in Toronto, Ontario, this year but spread to Halifax, Nova Scotia and Vancouver, British Columbia in 1995, to Calgary, Alberta in 1998, and to Kitchener, Ontario in 2002. More than 375,000 visitors enjoy this festival. Each festival team showcases its most relevant authors, artists, presenters, and representatives in its own format while maintaining the global goals of the festival. The organization partnered with local literacy programmes in 2007 to develop workshops designed to assist adults in improving their functional literacy skills. This truly is a remarkable festival which hopefully will spread to more and more cities across Canada in the years to come.

1990: A floating device designed to convert the energy contained in the rise and fall of ocean waves to produce electricity or hydrogen fuel was invented in 1990 by geologist Alan Vowles of Flin Flon, Manitoba, and his school teacher brother Gerald Vowles of Belleville, Ontario. They successfully harnessed the world's largest known source of clean, renewable energy, the action of waves on the ocean. They named their creation the Wavemill, the **1ˢᵗ system in the world to use wave energy as a source of power generation**. They realised that wave energy is constant and more concentrated than either wind or solar energy. This totally non-polluting and comparatively inexpensive system has been patented in the United States, Canada, and several western European countries. Alan and Gerald established the Wavemill Energy Corporation to develop and market their products which serve to do more than generate power. The Wavemill is ideally located in saltwater locations. It is also an exceptionally efficient floating desalination plant saving almost half the current costs for the desalination of seawater. The brothers inaugurated their business with sales of electricity to Caribbean island countries.

1991: Dennis Mraz, working in Saskatoon, Saskatchewan, received the Ernest C. Manning Award of Distinction for developing the **world's 1ˢᵗ direction changer for horizontal conveyor belts**. It now is used in major mines throughout North America.

1991: Three-time world champion figure skater Elvis Stojko (b. 1972) of Richmond Hill, Ontario, was also a martial arts and dirt bike enthusiast. In spite of suffering with a pulled groin, he still won an Olympic silver medal at the 1988 Winter Games in Nagano, Japan. At the World Championships in Munich, Germany, in 1991, Elvis performed the **1ˢᵗ quadruple combination toe-loop/double toe loop jump in competition in the world**. At the Champions Series Final at Hamilton, Ontario, he landed the **world's 1ˢᵗ quadruple combination toe-loop/triple toe loop jump in competition**. Elvis also skated the performance of his life in the free skate overcoming poor judging at the 1997 World Championships in Lausanne, Switzerland, to bring home the gold medal. He was awarded the Lionel Conacher Award in 1994 by the Canadian Press for Athlete of the Year.

1991: Lieutenant Anne Reiffenstein (née Anne Proctor), Lieutenant Holly Brown, and Captain Linda Shrum graduated from artillery training this year. They were the **1ˢᵗ Canadian female officers in combat arms**. Promoted to major, Anne became the **1ˢᵗ woman to command a**

Canadian combat arms sub-unit when she became battery commander at 1ˢᵗ Regiment Royal Canadian Horse Artillery at CFB Shilo east of Brandon, Manitoba, in 2003.

1991: When a large tree in Memorial Park in Hope, British Columbia, was diagnosed with a bad case of root rot, local artist Peter Ryan convinced Hope authorities to cut down the tree from a high point on the trunk leaving a 3.7-m *(12-ft.)* high stump. This unique artist then used his chainsaws to carve this trunk into a remarkable piece of art of a bald eagle with a salmon in its talons. The resultant sculpture was so incredible that it began attracting tourists and residents alike. Before long, Hope became the **1ˢᵗ Chainsaw Carving Capital of the world**. Since Peter carved that first tree trunk, local businesses and not-for-profit organizations have engaged his services to carve more than two dozen of these unique carvings throughout Hope adding yet another fascinating tourist attraction to the city.

1991: The Toronto, Ontario branch of the Royal Scottish Country Dance Society organized a 512-person reel on August 17ᵗʰ, the **largest genuine Scottish country dance in the world**. It took 15 months to plan. Rehearsals began in June although the full space at the Canadian National Exhibition required for this event was unavailable until the actual day. Sales of books, T-shirts, and videos, combined with supporters like the St. Andrew's Society, helped make the affair a total success. The majority of dancers from Canada were joined by a few from England, New Zealand, and the USA. They all celebrated the success of the dance with an appropriate ceilidh.

1992: At the 1992 Summer Olympic Games in Barcelona, Spain, the Canadian rowing crew clocked the full rowing course in just 9 minutes 29.53 seconds, the **fastest average speed ever achieved by a men's eight rowing team over the full course**. This was an average pace of 21.85 km/h *(13.58 mph)*.

1992: One evening at Expo '92 in Seville, Spain, Scott Killon began at the Canadian pavilion, then visited a number of other areas of the exhibition in the course of the evening. In the process, he established the **world handshaking record** after shaking hands with 25,289 different visitors in a period of just eight hours.

1992: The Arctic expedition in search of the Northwest Passage by the Royal Navy Ships *HMS Erebus* and *HMS Terror* from Greenhithe, England, in 1845 ended in tragedy. Rear-Admiral Sir John Franklin (1786-1847) of Spilsby, England, commanded a complement of 134 officers and men on this venture intended also to conduct various zoological, botanical, magnetic, and geological surveys across the Canadian Arctic. The entire expedition disappeared and little was known of its fate until 1859 when Royal Navy Lieutenant William Robert Hobson (1831-1880) of Nassau, Bahamas, from the steam yacht *Fox*, uncovered a message left in a cairn while exploring Victory Point near Cape Felix at the northern end of King William Island. Apparently, both ships had been trapped in ice for some year and a half beginning in late 1845. John died on June 11, 1847, while all remaining crew members also perished soon thereafter. Inuit legends even tell of cannibalism amongst the desperate crew. The exact location of the missing wrecks was never known but in 1992, the Government of Canada declared them to be a national historic site, highly important in the development of Canada as a nation. This is the 1st **and only undiscovered national historic site in Canada**. Since 2008, four separate expeditions have been initiated in an attempt to locate the wrecks but as yet have been unsuccessful in their quest.

_1992:_ Scientists at Environment Canada developed the **1st method in the world to predict the strength of the sun's ultraviolet (UV) rays based on changes in the ozone layer from day to day.** This method measures the sun's UV rays on a UV Index based on a scale from 0 to 10. A typical midday value in the summer is 10 in the tropics. This is where UV is the highest on earth. They then began adding UV Index information for Canadian and holiday destinations to daily weather forecasts on radio, TV, and in newspapers. This made Canada the **1st country in the world to issue nationwide daily forecasts of the following day's anticipated levels of UV radiation.**

_1993:_ The rare blue phase of black bear is called a glacier bear. The Tatshenshini and Alsek watersheds in the extreme northwest corner of British Columbia were preserved as parkland in 1993. They are part of a 97 000 km² _(37,452 mi.²)_ international wilderness corridor protected as a UNESCO World Heritage Site. This is the **only home in Canada of the glacier bear.**

_1993:_ The **1st and only potato museum in the world** is the Prince Edward Island Potato Museum in O'Leary which opened this year for the first time. Visitors from around the world come to view a Potato History Exhibit, Machinery Gallery, The Amazing Potato Exhibit and Community Museum, and the Potato Hall of Fame. The site also includes numerous heritage buildings, a large collection of farm implements and machinery used in the potato industry, and a gift shop. This museum contains the **largest exhibit of potato**

artifacts in the world. In 1999, the Potato Hall of Fame was added to the building now covering more than 650.3 m² *(7,000 ft.²)* of display space.

<u>1993</u>: Representatives from all of Saskatchewan's five First Nations—Nakota (Assiniboine), Dakota, Lakota, Cree, Saulteaux, and Dene—designed and constructed the **1ˢᵗ First Nations Gallery in Canada**, in Regina, Saskatchewan. Guarding the entrance is the "Trickster", a life-size alabaster and bronze sculpture. This is the principal character in First Nations creation stories. The Gallery is a part of Regina's Royal Saskatchewan Museum. It displays 10,000 years of history, art, and culture of Saskatchewan's Aboriginal peoples.

<u>1993</u>: The **largest bowl of strawberries in the world** had a net weight of 2.39 metric tonnes *(5,266 lb.)*. The berries were picked at Joe Moss Farms near Embro, Ontario. They filled the bowl at the Kitchener-Waterloo Hospital in Ontario on June 29ᵗʰ. This fund-raising event was organized by the Hospital Auxiliary. Joe Moss, who donated the strawberries, raised almost ten thousand dollars for the hospital.

<u>1994</u>: Eleven artists participated in carving the **world's tallest totem pole** known as *The Spirit of Lekwammen* or "Land of the Winds" this year. Lekwammen is the name of the traditional longhouse of the Songhees Band. It took approximately three and a half months to carve the single red cedar pole from the Nimpkish Valley of Vancouver, British Columbia; a single tree more than 500 years old. It was erected on the northwest shore of Victoria, British Columbia's Inner Harbour prior to the Victoria Commonwealth Games rising to a height of 54.94 m *(180.3 ft.)*. Its carving was a Spirit of Nations project co-ordinated by Island carver Richard

Krentz (b. 1945) of Pender Harbour, British Columbia. The pole symbolizes the welcome and respect by the Songhees people for all the nations participating in the Games. It honours the 80 Songhees men lost at sea in 1884 while attempting to assist Japanese fishermen. For safety reasons, the pole was lowered in sections on August 26, 1997. There was the possibility of it being an air traffic hazard as the Inner Harbour also is an airport landing strip for seaplanes. The 15-m *(49.2-ft.)* base remained at the site while the other three sections were taken to the Songhees Indian Village. Two sections were re-erected there. The final piece was re-carved by Richard, then returned to the original site in the Inner Harbour beside the remaining 17-m. *(55.8-ft.)* section of the pole.

> The 1st **and only local legal tender currency in Canada on par with the national dollar** are Salt Spring dollars on Salt Spring Island in British Columbia.

1994: As much as many tropical forests and more than good farmland, wetlands sustain more life than any other ecosystem. They play a major role in maintaining the stability of the world's environment, occupying 6% of the earth's land and freshwater area. A wide variety of wildlife use wetlands as their breeding and rearing habitat. Wetlands nurture hundreds of different species of animals and are constantly suffering from intrusion by agricultural, urban, and industrial land development. Approximately 14% of the planet's wetlands exist in Canada with the largest area of wetlands located in Ontario, Manitoba, and the Northwest Territories. Eighty-five percent of

Canada's wetland losses result from agricultural expansion which has taken over more than 20 million hectares *(49,421,076.3 acres)* since the first European settlement in our country. Although 80% of the wetlands near major urban centres have been converted to urban expansion or agricultural applications, less than 0.2% of Canada's entire wetlands lie within 40 km *(24.9 mi.)* of 23 of our largest major urban centres which contain 55% of Canada's population. Fortunately, major programmes are now in place to promote the conservation of our country's wetlands. Our federal government is the **1ˢᵗ national government in the world to bring forward a federal wetland policy**. Parallel wetland initiatives are also being implemented by our provincial governments covering 70% of our total wetland resources. Canada is also a member of the North American Waterfowl Management Plan along with the United States and Mexico. Hopefully, these initiatives will better educate people on the critical importance of wetlands to the survival of our planet and reverse the reckless onslaught mankind has made on these areas for centuries.

1994: The British Columbia government in June 1993 established Tatshenshini-Alsek Wilderness Park. The following year, it combined this new park with Yukon's Kluane National Park, and Alaska's Wrangell-St. Elias National Park and Glacier Bay National Park. This produced a contiguous tract of parkland totalling nearly 90 000 km² *(34,749.2 mi.²)* in area, the **largest internationally protected wilderness in the world**. The United Nations made it a UNESCO World Heritage Site.

1994: Lollapalooza is an American music festival first organized in 1991 by Perry Farrell (b. 1959) of Queens, New York, USA. It features alternative rock, rap, and punk rock bands, dance and comedy performances, and craft booths. The 1ˢᵗ **Lollapalooza festival in Canada** was held in Barrie, Ontario, on July 28, 1994, in Molson Park. A crowd of 35,000 music lovers enjoyed the Smashing Pumpkins, the Beastie Boys, and George Clinton (b. 1941) of Kannapolis, North Carolina, USA, amongst many other performers, in spite of the rain which turned the park into a sea of mud.

_1995:_ La Sûreté du Québec (Quebec Provincial Police) swore in the 1ˢᵗ **six Inuit constables in Canada** on August 31ˢᵗ.

_1995:_ M&M Meat Shops, selling more than 350 different restaurant-quality meat products, is **Canada's largest retail chain of speciality frozen food**. Its founders are Mac Voisin, previously an owner of a construction business, and Mark Nowak, Mac's brother-in-law. On April 28-29, M&M Meat Shops partnered with J.M. Schneider in Kitchener, Ontario, to turn pork, water, milk ingredients, salt, toasted wheat crumbs, modified starch, spice, sodium, and sodium nitrite into the **longest continuous sausage in the world**. The result was one continuous link of 315,000 sausages extending a total length of 46.3 km _(28.77 mi.)_. Ultimately, the record sausage was cut, boxed, and sold. M&M Meat Shops then donated 50 cents per box to support the Crohn's and Colitis Foundation of Canada.

_1996:_ A gopher is a small, short-tailed, burrowing rodent native to North and Central America. The tiny town of Torrington, Alberta, (pop. 192) is home to the 1ˢᵗ **Gopher Hole Museum in the world**. This small museum contains 44 exhibits with 71 stuffed gophers (already dead and not killed for this purpose) dressed in all sorts of elaborate costumes and set in elaborately painted backdrops. Unfortunately, gophers cause damage to crops, fields, and cattle. Horses and cattle often break legs after stepping into a gopher hole. Badgers also take over abandoned gopher holes enlarging them and intensifying the problem. The museum displays some of the hundreds of letters and newspaper articles written about it. The original intent behind the museum was to encourage tourism. It succeeded in bringing over 26,000 visitors from around the world just in its first four years—a lot of notoriety for such a small museum.

_1996:_ Vincent Thériault, a resident of Grande Anse, New Brunswick, designed the **world's 1st egg-shaped, totally enclosed lifeboat made from reinforced fibreglass**. For his invention, Vincent was given the Ernest C. Manning Innovation Award.

_1996:_ Westport is a picturesque little town at the head of the Rideau Waterway in eastern Ontario. It is located in the upper waters of the Rideau River and Rideau Lake system. It currently produces up to 125 000 m³ _(163,493.8 yd.³)_ of waste water annually. To treat it properly, Delta Engineering of Ottawa, Ontario, developed a unique new technology which made Westport the **1st community in Canada to turn the town's sewage into snow**. The new Snowfluent environmental waste process sprays liquid sewage in a fine mist from a tower converting the effluent into white snow crystals during very cold nights in the wintertime. In so doing, it destroys many of the inherent bacteria producing instant snow with higher purification than the existing treated water in the town. The remaining residue is used as fertilizer for the reed canary grass and is also harvested as mulch. When the snow melts in the springtime and filters through a grass bed, it also destroys some of the other harmful chemicals which have built up in the ground. Another major advantage of this system is that it produces zero discharge into the Rideau River. Hopefully, this unique system will be installed elsewhere in Canada in the near future. Mind you, doesn't it make one wonder what they do during the summer months!

_1996:_ Until 1996, Canada used a two-dollar paper note in its currency. The one-dollar paper note had already been replaced earlier with excellent success. Then, on February 19th, the two-dollar note also was removed from circulation and replaced with the **1st bi-metallic Canadian coin in full circulation**. It consists of an outer ring made of nickel and an inner core made of aluminum-bronze. More commonly referred to as our "Toonie", this new **1st $2 Canadian coin** will save the federal government more than $250 million over the next twenty years.

_1996:_ An incredible discovery occurred during construction of the Duke Point Road extension to the Duke Point Ferry Terminal in Nanaimo, British Columbia, in August. Exquisitely preserved specimens of the Upper Cretaceous Period (98 million BC to 65 million BC) were discovered in some of the rock. Included were dawn redwood, numerous angiosperms, and several species of fern. There also was a 72-million-year-old palm tree fossil, the **largest fossil leaf ever discovered in Canada**.

_1997:_ The spectacular Confederation Bridge spans Northumberland Straight over a distance of 12.9 km _(8 mi.)_ joining Borden-Carleton, Prince Edward Island, to Cape Jourimain, New Brunswick. It opened on May 31st and cost $1 billion to construct. It has the distinction of being the **longest bridge in the world over ice-covered waters** as well as being the **world's longest bridge spanning seawater**. It takes 12 minutes to drive over the S-shaped bridge but that is a major improvement over the 3-hour ferry voyage it replaced. Call boxes equipped with telephones, fire extinguishers, and an external alarm button are located at 750-m *(820.2-ft.)* intervals across the entire bridge to assist motorists in safe passage in the event of an emergency. The Confederation Bridge definitely makes exploring the scenery and peoples of the area much easier.

1998: The IVI Checkmate Corp. offers a variety of wireless terminals. Its Elite 780 has a built-in modem and thermal printer, is lightweight, and is ideally suited to purchase scenarios whereby the sale terminal is brought directly to the customer for point-of-sale (POS) transactions. The Royal Bank of Canada this year joined forces with IVI Checkmate introducing **Canada's 1ˢᵗ hand-held portable wireless terminal for debit and credit transactions**. The target market for this new product is primarily service and hospitality companies including home repair businesses, delivery services, transportation companies like taxi cabs and limousines, restaurants, full-service gas stations, and portable sales kiosks. This system is much more reliable because it utilizes a dedicated data network rather than having to compete with voice transmissions on the same network, a major step forward for e-commerce in our country.

1998: Clay Stacey co-ordinated his second major project with Saskatchewan seniors in 1998. The work of members from 150 Saskatchewan seniors' clubs, the tablecloth project again expressed the co-operative spirit so prevalent throughout the province. They created 183 individual tablecloths, then sewed them together to form a single tablecloth measuring 515 m *(1,689 ft. 8 in.)* in length. The **world's longest tablecloth** was unveiled on September 12ᵗʰ in Regina, Saskatchewan, before a large crowd of spectators. Once again, Saskatchewan seniors outdid themselves and made our country proud. Unfortunately, *The Guinness Book of Records* did not accept this accomplishment as a new world record primarily because "it does not appear to be attached to a table". Could this be the next major project for Saskatchewan seniors? Nonetheless, some 60,000 names were woven into the tablecloth plus the following words which best exemplify no doubt the feelings of Canadians from coast to coast—"Our seniors make a world of difference."

1998: Former federal cabinet minister and chief of the Blood Tribe, Roy Fox also was president and CEO of the Indian Resource Council of Canada (IRC). He was instrumental in launching the **1ˢᵗ First Nations Employment and Training Centre (FNET) in Canada** as the training and employment division of the IRC. This has given First Nations self-management and much greater influence on giving Aboriginals access to the half million jobs generated by the Canadian energy industry. FNET developed the **1ˢᵗ training programmes in Canada in drilling rigs and contracting designed specifically for Aboriginal peoples**. Thanks to Roy, First Nations and not the federal government determine future development of oil and gas resources on **Canada's largest First Nation** land in British Columbia, Alberta, Saskatchewan, Manitoba, Ontario, the Atlantic Provinces, Yukon, and the Northwest Territories. For his many contributions over the years, Roy received the National Aboriginal Achievement Award in 2002.

1999: The **longest running play in the history of Canadian theatre** was the *Phantom of the Opera*. It ran 4,226 times between September 20, 1989, and October 1, 1999.

July 1st: Each year, the Canadian Society in Taiwan, established in 1983, holds a very unique celebration on Canada's birthday to celebrate its members' love of Canada. The famous Canada D'Eh Beach Party is a massive, all-day beach party held in Taipei, Taiwan, attracting upwards of three thousand party goers each year. It is the **largest Canadian beach party outside of Canada**. Fun-filled activities for young and old include beach volleyball, beach soccer, face painting, kids games, tug o'war, plenty of food, Aboriginal dancing, belly dancers, lots of live entertainment, wonderful gifts and prizes, and of course a big Canada D'eh cake, all culminating with a magnificent 30-minute fireworks display. The event has had many sponsors over the years including Manulife Asset Management Lion Travel, the Canadian Trade Office in Taipei, Ford, McCain's, NOYU Teas, KOH Coconut, Air Canada, Bombardier, Costco, Crown World-Wide Movers, HOLA stores, Jason's Supermarket, the Luxy Club, the Taipei County Government, Taiwan Beer, The Tavern-Premier, Smirnoff Ice, Capone's, Forumosa.com, New Taipei City, JIIC Jia Dah Immigration Consultants, ICRT Radio, and Cargocare. A portion of the event's proceeds are donated to a different worthy cause each year. It truly is a party not to be missed!

2000: Captain Maryse Carmichael (b. 1971) of Quebec City, Quebec, had the enviable job of VIP (Very Important Person) pilot. She flew the prime minister or the Governor General of Canada whenever requested. This year, she became the **1st female pilot to fly with the Canadian Force's**

national aerobatic team, the *Snowbirds*. Maryse was promoted to the rank of major in 2001.

2000: When he was 14 years old, Waterdown, Ontario native Gary Duschl (b. 1951) learned from a fellow high school student how to make chains from gum wrappers. As of March 11, 2013, his gum wrapper chain measured 22 621 m *(74,216 ft.)* comprised of links from 1,762,233 gum wrappers, and only Wrigley wrappers! It weighs in at approximately 599 kg *1,102.3 lb.).* It is the **longest gum wrapper chain in the world**, a record Gary has held since 1995. He adds an average of .6 m *(2 ft.)* per day and has it measured by a land surveyer every March 11th. His ultimate goal is to have his gum wrapper chain grow to 41.8 km *(26 mi.)*!

> The Peace River drains about one-seventh of British Columbia and is a major tributary to the Mackenzie River, which flows to the Arctic Ocean. The Peace River is the **only river in North America to flow across the Rocky Mountains from west to east**.

2000: Smooth jazz is one of the world's fastest growing music formats. Until now, many people could hear, enjoy, and buy smooth jazz albums but were unable to hear them on the radio. There also lacked a permanent forum for Canadian smooth jazz artists in particular including Carol Welsman (b. 1960) of Toronto, Ontario; Diana Krall (b. 1966) of Nanaimo, British Columbia; and Brian Hughes (b. 1955) of Edmonton, Alberta. Fortunately for us, CIWV-FM, WAVE

94.7 FM officially went on the air on September 1ˢᵗ becoming **Canada's 1ˢᵗ smooth jazz radio station**. It broadcasts from Hamilton, Ontario, and is enjoyed by smooth jazz enthusiasts throughout the Southwestern Ontario region. Listeners can also tune in from anywhere else in the world through Internet access on their computer. The station began broadcasting solely on the Internet after August 1, 2011, allocating its frequency to broadcast a relaxing adult music format on its "sister station" CHKX-FM.

_2000:_ Adelle Richards, director of community relations for Radio Sarnia Lambton, co-ordinated a very special fundraising event in celebration of Valentines Day. The Montreal-based group _See Spot Run_ and other groups provided live music, and participants brought over 2 metric tonnes _(2.2 tons)_ of donations for the area's local food banks. There also were vendors selling flowers, chocolates, and other theme gifts. The event was called "The Big Kiss". It set a world record when 1,588 couples kissed at the Sarnia Sports and Entertainment Centre on February 13ᵗʰ, the **most couples in the world kissing simultaneously**. Sarnia, Ontario, now considers itself the Kissing Capital of the world!

_2000:_ On April 10, 1965, local grocer Herbert Ainsworth (1909-1965) founded the annual Elmira Maple Syrup Festival, now the **largest maple syrup festival in the world**. Although he died just six days before the first festival, it has turned into a highly successful event raising more than $850,000 to date for communities throughout the Elmira, Ontario, region. It instills community spirit in its local residents through the planning and operation of this annual festival. The estimated 2,500 visitors turned into a crowd of 10,000 that first year. The 36ᵗʰ annual festival this year set a world record attracting 66,529 visitors who participated in pancake flipping contests, exhibitions of local arts and crafts, and the discovery of local history in the heritage tent and on the heritage tour. They also ate 15,000 portions of pancakes smothered with 820 litres *(180.4 Imperial gallons)* of pure maple syrup! This year, Rapid Duct Supply participated by bringing the **world's largest maple syrup bucket** to the festival, able to hold 605 litres *(133.1 Imperial gallons)* of this golden nectar.

> The annual Metro Toronto Home Show in Ontario features some 350 exhibitors whose displays are divided into five categories: Renovation; Home Décor; Kitchen and Bath; Garden and Artistry; and Artisans. Held in January, it is the **largest home show in North America**.

2000: The Festival International de Jazz de Montréal, initiated in 1979, stages some 400 concerts over a period of 11 days each July. An average of 1.6 million jazz enthusiasts spend some $3 million to enjoy both star names and home-grown artists at this, the **world's largest jazz festival**.

2000: More than a billion people in China and throughout the world employ Traditional Chinese Medicine which has been practised for thousands of years. This encompasses a wide range of therapies including Chinese herbal medicine, acupuncture, manipulative therapy, rehabilitation exercises, energy control therapy, and shadow boxing. The province of British Columbia became the **1st place in Canada to regulate Traditional Chinese Medicine (TCM)**. By doing so, the provincial government committed to providing a health care system incorporating the best of both old and new health care practices, recognizing TCM as an important and valued health option to Canadians. Regulation is provided through the mandate of the restructured College of Acupuncturists of British Columbia known now as the College of Traditional Chinese Medicine and Acupuncture Practitioners of British Columbia.

2001: The Department of Education, Culture and Employment in the Northwest Territories developed Occupational Standards this year for the diamond industry. These were the 1ˢᵗ **standards in the world in the diamond cutting and polishing industry**. They established the level of knowledge and skills required to be considered competent in a given occupation in this industry. All trainees in factories in the Northwest Territories work under these strict standards and rigorous certification testing in the process of becoming competent professional diamond cutters.

2001: Lance Matthews, working in Mansfield, Ontario, **invented a new medical crutch that frees both hands of people suffering from lower leg injuries or disabilities**. He calls it the iWALKFree and is helping thousands of amputees and others around the world with this unique device. He received the Ernest C. Manning Innovation Award for his work.

2001: The City of Aylmer, Quebec, developed a comprehensive web site on the Internet this year enabling users to make online reservations of community centres, arenas, and sports equipment. They also can register in municipal courses and activities, pay permits, invoices, subscriptions, and purchase products and services. It also was the 1ˢᵗ **municipal web**

site in Canada to enable payment of taxes and tickets in real time on the Internet.

_2001:_ The Calgary Scope Society organized the first annual "Picture This Film Festival", **Canada's 1ˢᵗ Disability Film Festival** celebrating disability culture. This five-day film and video festival by and about persons with disabilities attracted entries from around the world. The two categories for entries include "Disability culture films about people with disabilities or disability organizations", and "films or videos on any topic which has been directed, produced, or written by people with disabilities". The Festival enables the disability community to connect better on a national and international scale. It also helps Calgary, Alberta, strengthen its leadership role in the disability movement.

_2002:_ A common problem in the egg industry is identifying why eggs become cracked or broken during processing. Wayde McNally, president and CEO of Sensor Wireless, a technology firm on Prince Edward Island, addressed this challenge by developing the **world's 1ˢᵗ Crackless Egg**. This inedible egg is built to the exact weight and size of a Grade A egg but contains special sensors which identify problems with grading and production lines. When placed in a production line, the Crackless Egg reports unusual pressure on it to a Palm Pilot or handheld computer. The usual source of damaging pressure comes from eggs rolling into other eggs or bumping, particularly at the entrance and exit of vertical lift elevators in production lines. This unique invention can save at least $37,000 annually for a producer generating 85,000 eggs per day if it reduces the number of cracks by just one percent. In 2005, Wayde won the Manning Award of Distinction for his invention.

_2002:_ After more than a year in development, the **1ˢᵗ successful plastic beer bottle in the world** was unveiled by Brick Brewing of Waterloo, Ontario. There are numerous advantages to this new, light-weight bottle: it chills quickly; the beer stays cold longer than in glass bottles or cans; the bottles are re-sealable; they are unbreakable; and environmentally, they are recyclable. European breweries had little success in the past in their attempts to develop a plastic beer bottle, facing problems later overcome by Brick Brewing. After years of development and testing of this innovative and unique wide-mouth plastic beer bottle, it is now up to the consumer to accept its many advantages. Currently, 70% of domestic beer sales in Canada are in glass bottles with the remainder sold in cans or on tap. Another record for Brick Brewing was its being the **1ˢᵗ brewery in Canada to bring back the stubby beer bottle**!

_2003:_ On November 11ᵗʰ, Canadian Peacekeepers serving in Afghanistan received 2,200 medium-size pizzas from Canada. Being more than 10 000 km _(6,213.7 mi.)_ away, this was the **largest and longest distance pizza delivery in the world**.

_2003:_ Back in 1942, U.S. Army G.I, Carl K. Lindley of Danville, Illinois, USA, Company D, 341ˢᵗ Engineers, was homesick while working on the Alaska Highway. So, he erected a sign at Watson Lake, Yukon, stating the distance and pointing the way to his hometown. Tourists have followed suit ever since, hammering their signs onto 16-foot poles and "planting" them in the Sign Post Forest. Today, there are more than 50,000 signs in the Forest making it the **largest collection of signposts in the world**! Watson Lake, considered the gateway to Yukon, is the primary transportation, communication, and distribution centre for mining and logging in the southern Yukon and northern British Columbia.

2003: Dr. James Andrew Smith (b. 1975) of Quebec City, Quebec, completed his B.Sc. and M.Sc. degrees in Electrical Engineering at the University of Alberta (U of A) specializing in the fascinating and rapidly expanding field of robotics. He completed his thesis with cohorts working on a 400 kg *(881.8 lb.)* outdoor mobile robot named "Polar Bear", the title of his paper being "A Tracking System for a Seismic Surveying Mobile Robot". This was a hydraulically actuated system used to follow people outdoors. The Polar Bear is the **undefeated tug-of-war champion** having competed for a number of years at the Intelligent Ground Vehicle Competition. James went on to earn his Ph.D. in Mechanical Engineering at McGill University in Montreal, Quebec. A critical element in his dream of building a very unique new robot was his research in the ambulatory robotics lab and mechatronic locomotion lab at McGill. This centered primarily around galloping and bounding on fixed-toe and hybrid wheeled-leg robots. The net result was his inventing "Scout II", the **world's 1ˢᵗ galloping robot**, a dynamically stable four-legged robot. It seems that attaining these complex robotic movements had been a major stumbling block for robotics developers until now. James also worked on PAW robots which have four legs with wheels at the ends. The results of his achievements were presented at the AMAM 2003 Conference in Kyoto, Japan. James conducted post-doctoral research in Sports Science on legged systems from 2006 to 2008 at the University of Jena's lauflabor locomotion laboratory in Jena, Germany. From there, he became a professor in electrical engineering at Ryerson University in Toronto, Ontario, specializing in biomedical engineering. He now wants to apply his success to date to orthosis design, analysis and correction of pathological gaits, and legged robots thereby using his knowledge and experience to develop practical medical applications using robots. In addition to his world record, James also received teaching awards at U of A and was a co-recipient of four Institute of Electrical and Electronics Engineers (IEEE) Real World Engineering Projects awards since 2007. What's next for this brilliant young professor? Well, "Jena Walker II" is on the drawing board—a bipedal robot!

_2004:_ Many electronic products like televisions and computers contain hazardous materials including lead and mercury. It is essential to recycle these products and related peripherals like printers and electronic notebooks wherever possible to avoid contaminating soil and groundwater when they are disposed of in landfills. This year, residents in Alberta alone discarded more than 190,000 televisions and 90,000 desktop computers. That is why the province launched **Canada's 1st e-recycling programme** to manage properly the recycling of metals, glass, and plastics used in these products. The not-for-profit Alberta Recycling Management Authority (ARMA) manages this important programme.

_2004:_ Soccer players on **Canada's 1st international homeless football team,** calling themselves the _Canucks_, practice on pavement in four-member squads. This is the style of the Homeless World Cup. Members train in the parking lot of St. Leonard's House, a community support complex in Brampton, Ontario's east end. They first competed for this international trophy in Gothenberg, Sweden, on July 25th as one of 28 participant countries. With similar efforts on the part of other social workers across Canada, this new sport hopefully will be seen expanding nationally in the years to come.

<u>2004</u>: Joan Orr (b. 1961) of Edinburgh, Scotland, and Teresa Lewin (b. 1961) of Woodstock, New Brunswick, formed the company Doggone Crazy. They produced the **1ˢᵗ clicker training DVD in the world** in which all the training is done by children. It is designed to help people of all ages learn how to apply this highly successful technique easily and even have fun doing it. Clicker training is a proven method for building a strong, loving, and respectful relationship between children and their dog. Doggone Crazy! (www.doggonecrazy.ca) also produced the **1ˢᵗ board game in the world designed to teach kids and families how to read dog body language** and to act safely around dogs.

<u>2005</u>: Created in 1970, Athabasca University (AU) in Athabasca, Alberta, is Canada's leading distance-education and online university. By 2008, it served some 32,000 students annually and has had 260,000 registered students since its founding. In 2005, AU became the **1ˢᵗ Canadian university to become accredited in the USA**. This resulted from a three-year assessment by the Middle States Commission on Higher Education (MSCHE).

<u>2005</u>: Research scientists at the University of Alberta in Edmonton, Alberta, have created the **1ˢᵗ device in the world able to re-grow teeth and bones**. Jie Chen is an engineering professor and nano-circuit design expert. He helped create this unique machine along with Ying Tsui, another engineering professor, and Tarek El-Bialy of Egypt from the university's dentistry faculty. The tool is based on low-intensity pulsed ultrasound tooth regeneration technology. The wireless device, smaller than a pea, is

inserted into a person's mouth, mounted either on braces or a removable plastic crown. It must be activated for 20 minutes each day over a period of four months to stimulate growth by gently massaging gums. It stimulates tooth growth from the root. This unit also can stimulate jawbone growth in order to fix a person's crooked smile. They plan to use it to repair fractured or diseased teeth.

_2007:_ The 550 residents of Leaf Rapids, Manitoba, came within weeks of setting a North American record ahead of San Francisco, California, USA. This April, it still became the 1st **town in Canada to ban plastic bags officially**. The town's new bylaw prohibits all retailers from selling or distributing single-use plastic bags. To help enforcement, the town officials gave each resident cloth shopping bags. Tofino, British Columbia, passed a similar resolution in May 2007 but did not entrench it in a bylaw, relying instead on voluntarily compliance by local residents and merchants. Then in January 2008, Huntingdon, Quebec, became the first municipality in the province to follow this lead, and they did pass a bylaw. Even advertisers there cannot deliver fliers in plastic bags and residents are not supposed to use green plastic bags to line their garbage bins.

_2008:_ Calgary, Alberta, began construction of the first leg of its C-Train in 1978 with service commencing in 1981. Expansion continued through to 2007 and no doubt will be an ongoing process as the city maintains a healthy growth rate. This light rapid transit system has served hundreds of thousands of commuters annually since its inception, operating on electricity generated from main line power sources. By September of 2008, it became the **world's 1st wind-powered public transit system**. The Ride the Wind!™ programme provides electricity to the C-Train generated by 37 commercial-scale wind turbines installed south of the city, producing 1.3 million kilowatt-hours of electricity annually. This results in a reduction of 21,000 tonnes *(23,148.5 tons)* of greenhouse gases and other air pollution produced by fossil fuel power generating systems used previously. The programme provides a 100% emission-free C-Train. This is equivalent to taking 4,000 cars off the road for a year.

2009: The Wood Buffalo Regional Emergency Services in the Regional Municipality of Wood Buffalo, Alberta, began using **Canada's 1st Mobile Firefighting Training Unit (MTU)** this year as a portable simulator moved from community to community to train firefighters. The simulator includes various rooms of a standard house including a mock kitchen, living room, and second story room. Moveable wall panels enable users to design various different training scenarios. The advantages of using MTU include portability and the ability to provide realistic fire fighting training opportunities in both rural and urban centres. This first MTU was purchased for use in Fort McMurray, Alberta, and all its surrounding hamlets giving its firefighters tools and techniques to do their job more safely.

2009: St. George's Golf and Country Club in Toronto, Ontario, hosted a very special event from November 24th to 29th, sponsored by the Dominion of Canada General Insurance Company. It was **Canada's 1st national championship for club curlers**. Competing teams included championship men's and women's teams from all ten provinces and three territories including separate entries from Northern and Southern Ontario. World champion curler Glenn Howard (b. 1962) of Midland, Ontario, spoke at the opening banquet to start off the event while Toronto Mayor David Miller

(b. 1958) of San Francisco, California, USA, and celebrity curling skip Sherry L. Middaugh (b. 1966) of Rosetown, Saskatchewan, were on hand to congratulate the winners at the closing banquet. The Chatham Granite Club from Ontario beat the men's team from British Columbia 7 to 4 while the ladies' team from Ontario squeaked by with a victory over Manitoba 6 to 5. The Canadian Paraplegic Association and developmental curling initiatives across Canada will benefit from the profits generated from this new championship event each year. This competition was an exciting experience indeed for many of those amateur curlers who travelled for the first time outside their home province or territory to compete in what has become known affectionately as "The Dominion".

2009: Senator Paul Yuzyk (1913-1986) of Fort Garry, Manitoba, was an author, editor, professor of history and associate professor of Slavic studies at the University of Manitoba in Winnipeg, professor of Russian and Soviet history at the University of Ottawa in Ontario, and history teacher. He filled his political role in the Canadian Senate from 1963 until his death sitting as a member of the Progressive Conservative Party caucus. His many books included *For a Better Canada*, *The Ukrainians in Manitoba: A Social History*, and *Ukrainian Canadians: Their Place and Role in Canadian Life*. As far back as 1964, Paul advocated the concept of multiculturalism rather than just biculturalism in our country as a fundamental characteristic of Canadian identity, for which he became known affectionately as the "**Father of Multiculturalism**" in Canada. The Government of Canada in 2009 created the Paul Yuzyk Award for Multiculturalism. This award recognizes the exceptional contributions of individuals and groups to our country's multiculturalism and diversity. A certificate of honour is given to the award recipient who then is asked to choose a suitable, non-profit, Canadian organization to receive the award's grant of $20,000. John Yaremko (1918-2010) of Welland, Ontario, was the 1ˢᵗ **recipient of the Paul Yuzyk Award for Multiculturalism**. He served for 25 years filling numerous positions in the Ontario legislature. This generous philanthropist was very active in the Ukrainian Canadian community and a strong advocate for human rights, education, and multiculturalism.

_2009:_ Vancouver, British Columbia, saw the expansion of art and culture with a unique new happening, **Canada's 1ˢᵗ and only annual city-wide festival of drawing**. This multi-venue event hosted by the city's art galleries and museums begins in historic Gastown offering an exciting collaboration by more than 80 artists of free lectures, tours of 13 private galleries and 3 museums, artist presentations, public performances, 17 exhibitions, panel discussions, and so much more. It showcases a range of contemporary and historical works for a full three weeks each July and August. The contemporary art world increasingly recognizes drawing as an important art form unto itself becoming the principal medium chosen by many artists today. The historical aspect of this festival is augmented by a number of works by Dutch masters, all coming together effectively adding a whole new light on summers in Vancouver.

_2009:_ Dr. Larry Widrow, a professor of physics, engineering physics, and astronomy at Queen's University in Kingston, Ontario, and John Dubinsky of the University of Toronto in Ontario were part of an international team of astronomers led by Dr. Alan McConnachie of the Herzberg Institute of Astrophysics in Victoria, British Columbia, working on the

Pan-Andromeda Archeological Survey (PAndAS). They used the Canada-France-Hawaii telescope to create the **largest map in the world of the Andromeda and Triangulum galaxies**. Their objective was to explore the structure and content of these two galaxies which are closest to our own. Galaxies are large collections of stars. The team uncovered evidence of a nearby cosmic encounter indicating that these two galaxies actually collided some two to three billion years ago. This map enables scientists to test their hypothesis that galaxies cannibalize other galaxies in order to grow larger themselves. They also observed that Andromeda appears to be ripping the Triangulum Galaxy apart.

_2009:_ Governments in Canada and the USA have a responsibility to test all new products intended for human use and to force companies to prove the safety of their products before the government permits them to be sold. Of particular concern are chemicals used in personal care products including lipstick. Isoprene and epichlorophydrin are both considered to be human carcinogens and therefore are of definite concern. They are used as emollients to soften the skin but better alternatives are available. Canada became the **1ˢᵗ country in the world to ban chemicals in personal care products** when it declared these chemicals to be environmentally toxic. A new series of assessments will be necessary on many such chemicals before companies will be permitted to use them in such products in the future.

_2012:_ Talon International Development, Inc. built the Trump International Hotel & Tower Toronto® in Ontario, the **1ˢᵗ residential building in Canada to reach 65 stories in height**. This opulent stone, steel, and glass structure exhibits the ultimate in sophisticated comfort for its guests rising over 274.3 m *(900 ft.)* above street level and providing a dramatic view of the city's skyline and Lake Ontario. Exhibiting the attention to detail always paid by Donald Trump (b. 1946) of Queens, New York, USA, in all his projects, Trump Toronto® provides 261 luxurious rooms and suites; Executive Suites; the 371.6-m² *(4,000-ft.²)* Presidential Suite with two full bedrooms, soundproof media room, and private dining room with chef-prepared gourmet meals; STOCK™ Restaurant and destination lounge; a 1393.6-m² *(15,000-ft.²)* world-class Quartz Crystal Spa, the city's most exclusive spa and wellness facility; 24-hour concierge service; 24-hour in-room dining; wired and wireless high-speed Internet access; the latest in business and entertainment conveniences; a heated indoor pool, steam baths and saunas; a fully equipped fitness facility and exercise studios; valet indoor parking; and Trump Attaché™ personalized service which records each guest's preferences for reference on future visits. It also is the **1ˢᵗ in Canada to provide flat-screen LCD IP televisions throughout the entire building**. Its ideal location in the heart of downtown Toronto is perfect for guests to attend their business meetings plus a wide range of exciting local entertainment venues. Trump Toronto® provides uncompromising standards for the most sophisticated traveler plus lavish accommodations for weddings, conventions, private parties, and romantic gourmet dining. This truly is a a unique venue well worth exploring.

2012: Of British Columbia's several ice-free ports, Vancouver handled 123.9 million tonnes *(136.6 million tons)* of bulk, general, and container cargo in 2012. It is the **largest dry cargo port on the Pacific Coast of North America**. There were 3,081 foreign vessel calls plus 191 cruise ships.

THANK YOU!

So, did you enjoy learning so many exciting and new things about Canada? If so, by all means, please review the coloured inserts in the centre of this book. You can increase this informative and educational experience more than **TWELVE-FOLD** by ordering the complete **6-volume** *Uniquely Canadian* hardcover set today. This collection contains many more lengthy, detailed, and informative stories in all **28 categories**. The remarkably **extensive** *Index* and **coloured icons** make it easy to find what you need in an instant. Each volume also contains a convenient silk bookmark making it easy for you to resume reading where you last left off. You can see the beautiful cover designs and other elements in this hardcover version in the centre pages of this pocketbook.

Don't forget, this is the best educational gift you could give your children or grandchildren. These stories may not answer all their questions on a particular subject, but they will help tremendously and they certainly will stimulate people's imagination and encourage them to do further research on their own. *Uniquely Canadian* is the perfect resource tool to give students new ideas and information on subjects for their various school assignments. At the same time, it makes a wonderful read for anyone just relaxing on a hot summer day or curled up in front of the fire on a cold winter night.

I hope that you, like me, now appreciate Canada all that much more after having read these stories. I know that I certainly have a greater respect, love, and pride in my motherland and its people than ever before. Thank you for your interest in our remarkable country!

Donald